Fundamentals of PURCHASING & SUPPLY MANAGEMENT

Edited by

P.M. Price, Ph.D.

N.J. Harrison, M.Ed.

Copyright © 2014 by Access Education

All rights reserved.

No part of this book may be reproduced in any form or by any electronic or mechanical means including information storage and retrieval systems, without permission in writing from the author. The only exception is by a reviewer, who may quote short excerpts in a review.

Printed in the United States of America

First Printing: August 2014

First edition

ISBN 978-1-934231-03-6

Library of Congress Control Number: 2001012345

Table of Contents

Chapter 1: The Wonderful World of Purchasing — 1
By Dr. Philip M. Price and Natalie J. Harrison, M.Ed.

- Purchasing: What Is It and Why Do It — 3
- The Place of Purchasing in the Supply Chain — 4
- The Rest of the Book — 8
- Review Questions — 9
- Case Exercise: The Purchasing Fairy Tale of the Three Little Pigs — 11

Chapter 2: A Closer Look at the Purchasing & Procurement Process — 13
By Dr. Philip M. Price and Natalie J. Harrison, M.Ed.

- The Language of Purchasing and Supply Management — 14
- The Five Ws of Purchasing — 16
- The Purchasing Process — 21
- A Quick Nod to Purchasing Policies — 30
- Review Questions — 32
- Case Exercise: The Case of Jo-Jo's Jams — 33

Chapter 3: Purchasing the Right Quantity — 35
By Dr. Morgan Henrie and Dr. Philip M. Price

- Introducing Quantity and the EOQ — 36
- Quantity Decisions & Inventory Management — 38
- Ordering & Holding Costs — 41
- Workings of the EOQ Model — 43
- Orders per Year, Reorder Point, and Safety Stock — 49
- A Final Look at Quantity Considerations — 56
- Review Questions — 59
- Case Exercise: EOQ with Discounts at Myers of Michigan — 60

Chapter 4: The Right Quality in Purchasing — 61
By Dr. Morgan Henrie

    Strategic View: Quality and the Purchasing Process — 62

    Defining Quality and Specifications — 63

    Quality Supplier Identification — 66

    The Costs of Poor Quality — 67

    Measuring Quality: Statistical Quality Control — 68

    Quality for the Purchasing Professional — 72

    Review Questions — 74

    Case Exercise: Joe Jones and the ISO 9000 — 75

Chapter 5: Looking at Time and Place — 77
By Dr. Philip M. Price

    Time and Place in Manufacturing — 78

    Just in Time (and at the Right Place, too!) — 83

    Holding Inventory: Considering Time and Place — 84

    Transportation: Considering Time and Place — 86

    Review Questions — 92

    Case Exercise: Time for a Repeat Purchase of Luxury Lamps — 93

Chapter 6: Understanding the Right Price — 95
By Dr. Morgan Henrie and Dr. Philip M. Price

    Getting Started with Getting the Right Price — 95

    Competitive Structures in the Supply Market — 97

    Getting a Fair Price — 99

    Understanding Cost in an Enforceable Contract — 108

    Total Cost of Ownership Theory — 108

    Legal Considerations — 110

    Review Questions — 112

    Case Exercise: Centralized Purchasing and the No-Tipsy Bar Stool — 113

Chapter 7: Supplier Selection — 115
By Dr. Morgan Henrie and Dr. Philip M. Price

Defining the *Right Supplier*	115
Finding the Right Supplier	120
Purchasing Relationships	125
Evaluating the Current Supplier	126
Review Questions	130
Case Exercise: QuickBuilt Limited, KPIs, and Supplier Selection	131

Chapter 8: Understanding Negotiation in the Purchasing Process — 133
By Dr. Francis Jeffries and Dr. Philip M. Price

The Basics of Negotiation	134
Approaches to Negotiation	136
Phases in a Negotiation	139
Ethics in a Negotiation	145
Becoming a Skilled Negotiator	147
Review Questions	149
Case Exercise: Planning for Negotiations	150

Chapter 9: Purchasing, Contracts, and the Law — 153
By Dr. Philip M. Price

What is a Contract?	154
The Law of Contracts	156
Binding Contracts	159
Breach of Contract	167
Warranties	170
Review Questions	172
Case Exercise: Defenses for Faulting on a Contract	173

Chapter 10: Purchasing on the Global Stage — 175
By Dr. Philip M. Price and Natalie J. Harrison, M.Ed.

Globalization and Market Entry Strategies	176
Purchasing and Global Sourcing	178
Selecting Global Suppliers	181
Global Business Considerations	183
A Look at International Documentation	188
Review Questions	193
Case Exercise: Global Purchasing at Luxury Lamps Ltd.	194
Case Exercise: INCOTERMS and the Dunbar Company	195

Chapter 11: The People Side of Purchasing — 197
By Natalie J. Harrison, M.Ed.

Purchasing and Interpersonal Relationships	198
Relationships Through Emotional Intelligence	200
Personality in the Purchasing Process	202
Developing Communication Skills for Purchasing	206
Review Questions	209
Case Exercise: Rating Your Emotional Intelligence	210

Chapter 12: Business Strategy and Purchasing — 213
By Dr. George Geistauts

Competition and Conflict	214
The Nature of Strategy	215
Strategic Analysis and Planning	217
Environmental Scanning	218
Strategic Industry Analysis	223
Fundamental Competitive Strategy	227
Strategic Relationships and Values	231
Strategic Evaluation of Purchasing	232

Review Questions 235
Case Exercise: Business Strategy, Purchasing, & Rogers Design 236

Index **241**

About the Authors **247**

Chapter 1

The Wonderful World of Purchasing

Dr. Philip M. Price & Natalie J. Harrison, M.Ed.

Welcome to the wonderful world of purchasing! Most of us have explored this world many times before. Every time we walk into the grocery store to buy the fixings for our evening's meal, we are immersed in the world of purchasing. We must consider a variety of supply options (or *products*) and the cost, convenience, and quality of each before making a final decision. For example, if we have a carb craving for a big plate of spaghetti, we must consider first if we prefer the convenience of a frozen microwaveable spaghetti Bolognese or if we prefer the quality of a freshly made meal. If we then choose quality over convenience, we must consider a range of 20 to 100 different pasta options, from spaghetti to linguini to rigatoni to tortellini, depending on your own grocery store's propensity for purchasing pastas. As we look at the plethora of packages of pasta, we consider the cost, size, brand, quality, and packaging of each. After we have selected our pasta of choice, we must next consider a wide variety of red and white sauces of different brands, prices, levels of meat or cheese content, and degrees of flavor and spiciness. Finally, we must consider if we want any meats, vegetables, or garnishes to accompany our spaghetti meal, perhaps heading off to the deli counter to find freshly grated Parmesan cheese or off to the vegetable aisle to get the ingredients for a fresh Caesar salad.

While this entire process took a long-winded paragraph of text, it may take us only seconds in the store. Because most of us have spent many years shopping at grocery stores, we have become skilled and adept grocery store purchasers. Over the past ten years, we have honed our purchasing prowess even more with the explosive growth of internet sales. We now have a variety of online stores, eBay, and Craigslist all at our fingertips as we search for the best deals. Therefore, as we delve deeper into the world of purchasing throughout this book, much of it may just seem like plain old common sense. Using and refining these common sense skills are critical in the business environment, however, because of both the OPM factor and the scale of purchases.

When we shop on behalf of someone else, especially on behalf of a big business with much deeper pockets than our own, our mindset changes and we tend to shop a little differently. The OPM (or "Other People's Money") factor kicks in, messes with our minds, and influences our decision-making process. When purchasing pasta for ourselves, we can easily decide if we want to spend $5 more to get high quality, Italian-made specialty pasta. We are usually comfortable with our decision because we have considered cost, quality, and whether or not this meal was for a special occasion. When purchasing for our workplace, however, we start to behave a little differently because we are spending "other people's money" and our natural tendency is to lean toward one of two extremes. For example, if we are buying pens for our supply cabinets at work, some of us may opt for the pens that are $2 more per pen than the standard order because they are fancier, better quality, and, hey, our company can afford them. Others of us may feel that the company's eyes are upon us and that we want to impress our bosses and bosses' bosses with our money-saving selection. We scour all online sources for cheaper options, finally selecting pens that are $2 less per pen than the standard order but just happen to be of a far inferior quality.

No matter which extreme is our natural inclination in the working environment, both can be detrimental to the company. Buying the pricier pen may make your coworkers happier, but you may be wasting thousands of much-needed dollars, especially if a large number of pens is ordered. For example, if you are ordering 10,000 pens, you are dipping into your company's pockets for an extra $20,000 just to have fancier pens. At the other extreme, if you order the inferior quality pens that are $2 cheaper, you may think you are saving the company $20,000. However, you may actually be wasting the entire order of 10,000 pens when the pens break and leak after less than a week of use.

Understanding purchasing in the business environment is important not only to counteract the OPM factor but also because of the impact of the scale of purchases. What may mean $10 savings for a personal, individual purchase could translate to $1,000,000 savings on a business scales as tens of thousands of items are purchased. Furthermore, what may appear to be a $1,000,000 savings on an airline engine part may actually result in future costly repairs and safety recalls.

Not only is the scale of purchases larger in the business environment as many companies order thousands upon thousands of a single item, the scale is also broader. Manufacturers and retailers order many different items, often from many different suppliers. For example, a computer manufacturer may order keyboards, screens, processors, memory cards, graphics cards, built-in speakers, USB ports, DVD drives, and software from different suppliers for each of its ten different laptop models.

Although we are accomplished purchasers on an individual level, purchasing becomes more complicated at the business level. There are often so many moving parts that it's hard to keep track of them all. Throughout this book, we will explore many of these moving parts as we guide you through the wonderful world of purchasing!

PURCHASING: WHAT IS IT & WHY DO IT?

When we think of the word *purchasing* at its most basic form, we can associate it with two words: buying stuff. In the business world, its definition becomes a bit more sophisticated. **Purchasing** is a function of an organization that ensures its materials and services are met by acquiring goods and services in the right quantity of the right quality, delivered to the right place at the right time, while maximizing the service provided and minimizing the total cost to the organization. Not only is purchasing concerned with the actual buying (or purchasing) of goods, but it also covers receiving purchase requests from sales and manufacturing departments, coordinating with inventory control to know what stock items need to be purchased, researching and planning for the purchase, setting criteria for a successful purchase, and returning incorrect orders or faulty products. Purchasing also covers researching and buying services needed by an organization.

As we will learn in Chapter 2, purchasing is known by many other names, including *procurement* and *acquisition*. Later in this chapter, we will also learn that there is a strategic, long-term approach to purchasing called *supply management*.

No matter what we call it, purchasing is a vital part of every commercial, non-profit, and government organization. As most of us know from personal experience, diligent research can help us find the lowest cost and highest quality goods and services when making a large purchase. We comparison-shop in our local grocery stores to see who has the lowest price for frequently purchased items. We consult the Kelly Blue Book online to find what we should be paying for our next new or used car. We check with Travelocity, Expedia, Priceline, and Kayak to find the best rates on vacation hotel rooms. We may even check the Better Business Bureau online to make sure a home improvement contractor we are about to hire doesn't have any customer complaints on file. As part of a consumer- and information-based culture, we have an intrinsic understanding of the power of purchasing to leverage lower costs and higher quality.

In the world of business, purchasing can also help organizations to reduce costs, not only by finding lower prices for specific products, but also by streamlining inventory. **Inventory** is the collection of goods, materials, and physical resources held by an organization. Back in 2005, Walmart found that it just had too much of this inventory. The retail giant found that its stores and distribution centers were cluttered with multiple brands of the same items. At the same time, the stock value of Walmart Stores, Inc. had decreased by 5% over the previous twelve months. To reduce purchasing and storage costs and decrease store clutter, Walmart decided to streamline its inventory by carrying only the most popular brands and styles of many items. Although many customers were initially disappointed with the reduced selection of brands and goods, Walmart kept customers coming in the doors by using the initial money saved from inventory streamlining to improve and redesign store interiors.

Purchasing also allows organizations to gain better terms and service from their suppliers. The multinational computer manufacturer Dell, Inc. has been known for many years for its build-to-order production strategy, i.e., you tell Dell what specifications you want for a computer and Dell builds it for you. Because of this build-to-order strategy, Dell knew it might get stuck with excess inventory of unpopular computer components as customers' needs and desires changed. Therefore, Dell makes all major purchasing decisions from its corporate headquarters. The company uses this consolidated buying power to search the global market for the most flexible suppliers. Using this strategy, Dell finds suppliers that offer terms that best suit the company's needs, including supplier production and storage facilities close to Dell's manufacturing plants and suppliers willing to keep trucks at Dell's facilities, from which supplies are taken and purchased only on an as-needed basis.

Finally, purchasing provides companies with the opportunity to live up to specific corporate missions and to manufacture higher quality products. For example, Ben & Jerry's **Homemade Holdings, Inc.** is a U.S.-based ice cream manufacturer known for its social mission of improving the quality of all life locally, nationally, and internationally. The company used purchasing research and strategy to help fulfill this mission. Since 1985, all of the company's milk and cream had been supplied by St. Albans Cooperative Creamery, a cooperative owned jointly by local dairy farmers. In the late 1980s and 1990s, Ben & Jerry's decided that, to meet its social mission, it would not use milk from cows that had been treated with rBGH, a genetically engineered growth hormone used by most dairies across the U.S. to increase milk production. After researching the dairy market, Ben & Jerry's made the purchasing decision to supply the cooperative with $600,000 so that it could reconfigure operations to provide rBGH-free dairy products.

Although Ben & Jerry's was sold to the Anglo-Dutch multinational food company Unilever in 2000, the ice cream manufacturer remained dedicated to its social mission. Most recently, the ice cream manufacturer pledged to make their products GMO-free (or free of genetically modified organisms), dropping iconic chocolate manufacturer The Hershey Company as a supplier in 2014 because Hershey is not committed to producing foods that are GMO-free. As a result, one of Ben & Jerry's long-standing favorite flavors, Coffee Heath Bar Crunch, has been renamed "Coffee Toffee Bar Crunch" because it no longer contains Hershey's Heath bars.

Because purchasing is far more complex than simply finding the lowest priced or highest quality item, developing a deeper understanding of purchasing is of vital importance in the business world. Purchasers, suppliers, marketing and sales departments, manufacturing managers, Chief Operating Officers (COOs), Chief Executive Officers (CEOs), and just about anyone working in the business world would benefit from an understanding of both *purchasing* and its strategic partner, *supply management*.

THE PLACE OF PURCHASING IN THE SUPPLY CHAIN

Now that we understand why purchasing is important, let's consider how it fits into the business environment. In most business settings, the function of *purchasing*, which may also be operating under the guise of *procurement* or *acquisitions*, resides within the realm of *logistics* at the individual company level or *supply chain management* at the cross-company strategic level. Before we get ahead of ourselves, let's examine what these terms mean.

Logistics is the function within an organization that handles the flow of goods and information into, within, and out from that organization. ***Supply chain management*** is the business discipline and function within an organization that focuses on the flow of goods, information, and related finance across multiple organizations, often as goods move and transform from a raw materials or unfinished stage to a finished product received by an end user. Although these terms are different, they are often used interchangeably by some organizations to signify anything that has to do with the movement of goods.

As goods come into and depart from an organization, they follow a supply chain. This flow of goods and corresponding information, or **supply chain**, might have a *logistics focus* by concentrating more on the internal perspective of one organization or it might have a *supply chain management focus* with a broader, multi-organizational perspective. Figure 1.1 shows a simple supply chain, in which a supplier provides goods to a manufacturer, who in turn supplies manufactured finished goods to a retailer, who, at the end of it all, provides these finished goods to customers or end users. In this simple supply chain, purchasing takes place in four areas: at the supplier level, which may itself purchase the goods it is selling; in the manufacturer's headquarters, where goods are purchased from the supplier; at the retailer's purchasing office, where goods are bought from the manufacturer to stocks its stores shelves; and at the end user level, in which individual customers buy the finished goods they have plucked from the retailer's shelves. At all four levels, we have different people engaged in purchasing.

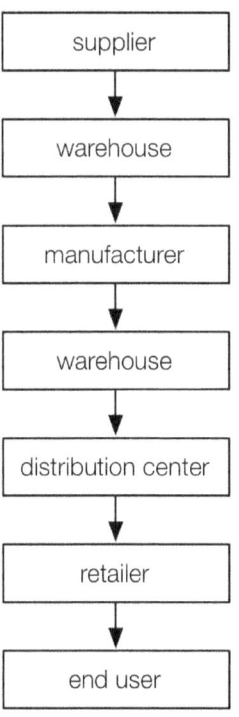

Figure 1.1 - The Simple Supply Chain

Most supply chains today are not that simple, however. Manufacturers purchase multiple goods from multiple suppliers. Retailers purchase thousands of goods from a variety of suppliers. Actual supply chains may look less like the simple supply chain of Figure 1.1 and more like the global supply chain in Figure 1.2 below, in which the purchasing function can be found in *all* of the suppliers', manufacturers', and retailers' locations.

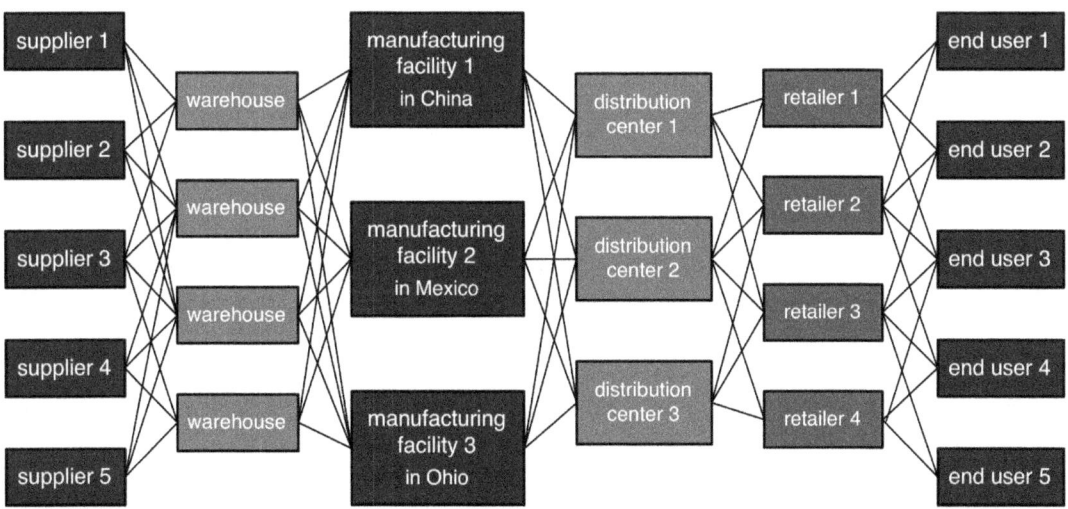

Figure 1.2 - Example of a Complex Global Supply Chain

As you may have guessed from the corporate examples mentioned earlier in this chapter, purchasing plays a strategic role in the realm of logistics and supply chain management. In Price and Harrison's model of logistics management from *Looking at Logistics*, purchasing and supply management play a key role in **inbound logistics**, defined as those logistics activities that take place at the beginning of the supply chain until goods are received from the supplier. As a corporate function, purchasing plays a key role in the coordination of inbound logistics systems and process. This coordination is called **materials management**. As shown in Figure 1.3 below, purchasing and supply management are *inbound processes* that fall under the larger function of *materials management*.

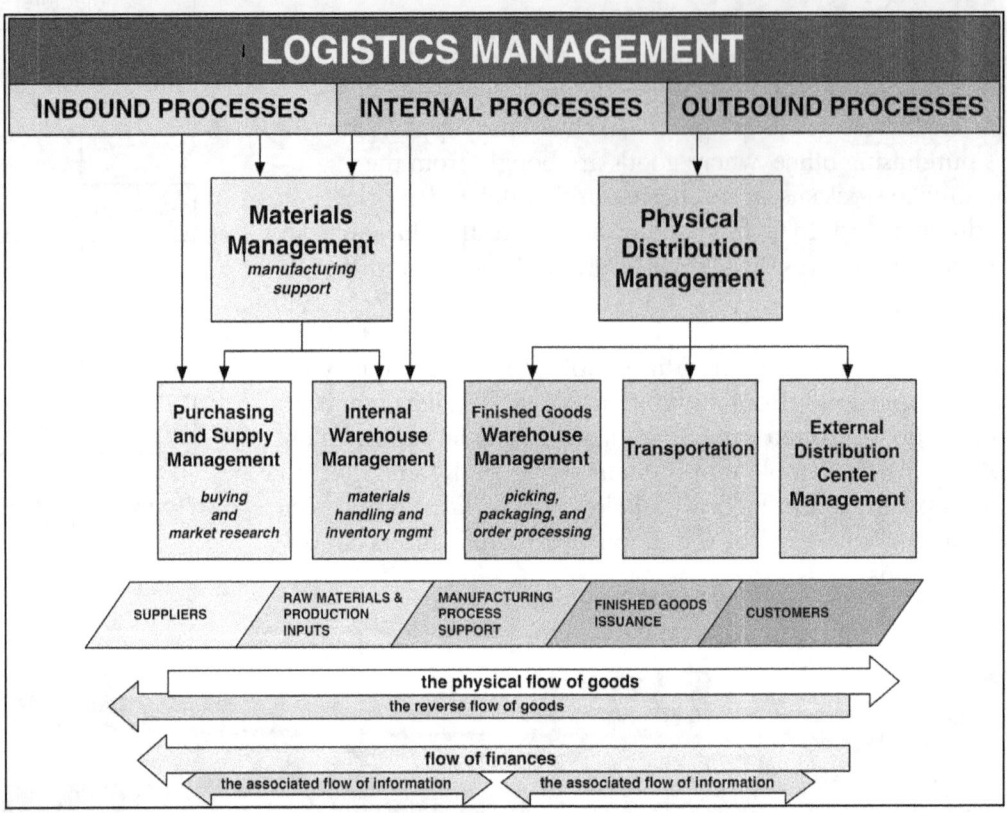

Figure 1.3 - Price & Harrison's Model of Logistics Management

In most of today's organizations with highly effective and efficient supply chains, purchasing and supply management professionals are part of the *logistics* or *supply chain management team*.

As mentioned earlier, some organizations use the terms *purchasing* and *supply management* interchangeably, but they are actually two different pieces in the same puzzle. **Purchasing** is a function of an organization that ensures its material needs and service needs are met by acquiring goods and services in the right quantity of the right quality, delivered to the right place at the right time, while maximizing the service and minimizing the total cost to the organization. The short-term goal of initial inbound logistics management is the immediate acquisition of goods or services, which falls under the umbrella of *purchasing*. The longer-term goal of inbound logistics is a strategic one: working closely with suppliers of needed goods and services to ensure their long-term availability. For example, what good is only 5000 gallons of Racing Red paint to Wobbly Wheels, Inc. for their new line of Turbo-Charged Wheel Barrows if the paint manufacturer will be ceasing production of Racing Red paint in six months due to the rising cost of one of its ingredients. This longer term strategic approach to purchasing and supplier relations is called ***supply management***.

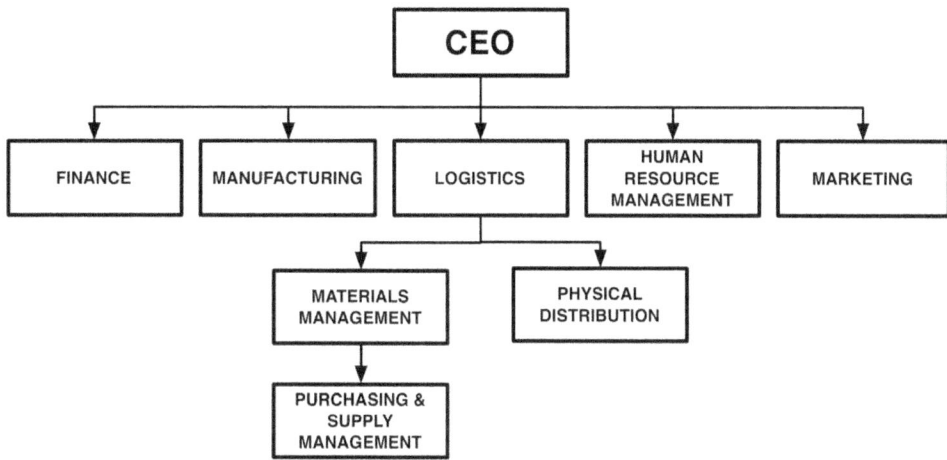

Figure 1.4 - Place of Purchasing & Supply Management in the Organization

As shrewd consumers in today's highly competitive marketplace, we want to make wise purchasing decisions by buying a quality product while saving ourselves money. Therefore, as individual consumers, we often view our suppliers and their salespeople through world-weary eyes as competitors and adversaries, trying to get our business while increasing their own profits. With the *supply management approach*, however, suppliers are not viewed as competitors or adversaries. They are instead viewed by today's purchasing professionals and their organizations as important counterparts in their products' supply chains. Organizations work with their suppliers to develop long-term relationships, not only to ensure long-term supply availability, but also to streamline the product or service acquisition process to make for faster and more effective inbound logistics management processes.

Using the supply management approach, an organization's purchasing department works together with its suppliers and also with its peers in production, engineering, finance, marketing, and quality assurance in a cross- functional team. This supply management team engages in many strategic, long-term activities related to purchasing or acquiring goods, including:

- *internal analysis*, in which organizations look inward and examine their own spending or purchasing processes in order to make them more efficient. In our earlier example, Walmart found that they were buying too many of the same item across different brands. After using internal analysis, the company decided to streamline its inventory.

- *supply market research*, in which organizations look not only at customer demand forecasts, but also at the long-term supply availability and cost increases in order to make long-term production decisions. In our recent example, Wobbly Wheels Inc. conducted supply market research and found that Racing Red paint would soon be discontinued.

- *strategic sourcing*, in which an organization works to identify, develop, and manage key suppliers to build supply chain relationships that outperform those of its competitors. In a previous example in this chapter, Dell used strategic sourcing to find suppliers that offered terms that best suited their needs, including suppliers with facilities located close to their manufacturing plants and suppliers willing to keeps trucks at Dell's facilities.

- *negotiating contracts*, in which an organization works with suppliers to agree on long-term supply contracts. As mentioned in our earlier example, Ben & Jerry's negotiated a contract with St. Albans Cooperative Creamery to reconfigure their operations to provide rBGH-free dairy products.

THE REST OF THIS BOOK

Now that you have been briefly introduced to purchasing and its relationship to organizations, get ready to delve much deeper into the wonderful world of purchasing and supply management.

Chapter 2, "A Closer Look at the Purchasing Process," explores the who, what, where, when, and why of purchasing. Chapters 3 through 6 examine the 5Rs of purchasing and supply management: the right quantity (Chapter 3), the right quality (Chapter 4), the right time and place (Chapter 5), and the right price (Chapter 6).

Chapters 7 through 9 introduce many of the practical, nitty-gritty details of purchasing and supply management practices. Chapter 7 considers the issue of "Supplier Selection." Chapter 8 guides us through the tricky world of "Negotiation and Ethics" in today's challenging business environment. Chapter 9 examines "The Legal Side of Purchasing and Supply Management" with input from a practicing attorney.

The last section of the book, Chapters 10 through 12, guides us through the some of the "big picture" issues of purchasing and supply management. Chapter 10, "Global Purchasing and Supply Management," examines the practices and principles of purchasing and supply management in the international context. Chapter 11, "The People Side of Purchasing," explores the impact of the human element on purchasing and supply management. Finally, Chapter 12 tackles the challenging supply management issue of "Supply Strategy."

All twelve chapters of this book have been written by well-respected authors from both academia and industry, with each sharing the most contemporary practices and their own real-world experiences. Sit back, relax, and enjoy as we take you on this breathtaking journey through the wonderful world of purchasing and supply management!

CHAPTER 1 REVIEW QUESTIONS

1. In the introductory section of this chapter, we introduced the OPM factor. How might people behave differently when spending their own money compared to spending *other people's money*?

2. What role does *purchasing* play in an organization? List four companies or organizations from different industries that are likely to have a *purchasing* function.

3. In addition to reducing item costs, how can purchasing help an organization to achieve increased profits and/or customer service?

4. What is the social mission of Ben & Jerry's? How did the company use *purchasing* to address this mission?

5. What is *supply chain management*? How is it related to *purchasing*?

6. Using the example of a small scale, locally based scented candle manufacturer with a simple supply chain, where might purchasing take place within the organization?

7. Where might you find the purchasing and supply management function within a larger, global organization?

8. As individual purchasers for own own personal goods, we sometimes see suppliers as adversaries, trying to score the best deal and cheapest prices for ourselves. How is this similar to or difference from the *supply management approach* of companies today?

9. In addition to Dell, what other companies might use *strategic sourcing*? Provide an explanation for your answer.

10. After reading the "Rest of the Book" section in this chapter, which upcoming chapter are you most interested in reading? Why?

CHAPTER 1 CASE EXERCISE

Once upon a time...

The Purchasing Fairy Tale of the Three Little Pigs

Once upon a time, there were three little business piggies who, much to their dismay, learned that the big bad wolf, called Competition, was on her way. It was a well known fact that Competition's intention towards our three Piggies was not of a kind, caring, and generous nature. Instead, she rather fancied pork for her supper! The three little business piggies decided it was important to build some kind of protection to prevent the wolf from being able to get to them. "Let's build a house," they all delightedly squealed in unison. Fortunately, our little business piggies had three weeks before the wolf would arrive. Unfortunately, they could not agree on the best type of house, so they decided to each build their own house independently. The piggies each called their own purchasing officer and instructed them to immediately purchase the materials necessary to build them a safe house.

Our three independent little business piggies had quite different business strategies. Our first little business piggy was extremely cost conscious and wanted every thing to be at the lowest cost. His brothers often joked that he should have been a born a little chick since he was so "cheep cheep" and always worried about his bill! Our first piggy told his purchasing officer to find the best deal on the cheapest construction material available, straw. The piggy's purchasing officer worked with a straw supplier to get a great deal on just the right quantity of mid-grade straw, which arrived exactly when and where the piggy needed to construct his house. Our story's villain, the big bad wolf called Competition, arrived just as our first piggy had constructed his house and locked himself inside. Competition was really craving our piggy's pork, so she huffed and puffed and blew the straw house down! Our poor little business piggy escaped out a back window and ran to the second piggy.

Meanwhile, our second little business piggy was far less cost conscious than his first brother and was known for being a bit of a show boat. He always had the finest and fanciest pen and, dated only the most attractive sows, and ate only the most expensive gourmet slop. He told his purchasing officer to find the most expensive, most attractive, and highest quality housing material in the world. His purchasing officer found a supplier of beautiful pink ivory wood in Mozambique, knowing his piggy boss would be impressed because this wood was from the royal tree of the Zulu warriors. Not just any piggy can have a house made of royal Zulu wood! The wood supplier told him that he could guarantee that half of the wood could ship from Africa on time to arrive when and where the piggy needed it, but he couldn't guarantee the timeliness of the second half of the shipment because of current scarcity of supply. The supplier was hopeful, however, that the second half of the shipment would arrive on time. The piggy's purchasing officer knew that his boss would settle for no lesser product, so he decided to order the pink ivory wood and accept the risk of not getting the entire shipment on time. Naturally, the first half of the shipment arrived when and where our second business piggy needed it, but the second half of the shipment was still in transit. The business piggy began construction and was able to construct half of his house on schedule, but waited and waited for the rest of his beautiful pink ivory wood. Just as the second half of the wood shipment arrived, the big bad wolf called Competition arrived, too! This time, she didn't need to huff and puff. She simply walked right through a wall not-yet-built to get her highly desired pork prize. Our poor little business piggy, along with the first little business piggy who had sought shelter with his brother, escaped out a beautifully carved ornate rear door and ran to the house of the third piggy.

Meanwhile, our third little business piggy was quite the practical and logical creature. He always took in all the data and analyzed all the possible solutions to find the one with the best outcome. His brothers jokingly referred to him as "Spork" (a combination of Star Trek's Spock and pork), not knowing that sporks were also the most inventive eating utensil of the nineteenth century. Our third little business piggy instructed his purchasing officer to find the most durable building material available for a reasonable cost and with a guaranteed on-time shipment. The piggy's purchasing officer did her research and found a highly rated brick supplier located only 200 miles away. Not only was the purchasing officer able to procure enough builder-grade bricks guaranteed in the right quality, but the supplier could deliver them two days early, allowing our piggy to begin construction on this time-sensitive project even earlier than dreamed! When the bricks arrived where and when promised, our third little business piggy immediately began construction on his house... and finished it two days ahead of schedule! When he finished, he stood back and admired his sturdy little brick house. It wasn't as cheap as his brother's straw house or as luxurious as his other brother's half completed pink ivory wood house, but it was a fine house and he knew it would protect him. Right on schedule, the big bad wolf called Competition arrived. Our third little business piggy and his two very scared piggy brothers were locked safely in this solid little house, enjoying a nice cup of tea, while outside, Competition huffed and puffed, and huffed and puffed, and huffed and puffed some more. Our piggies simply turned up the volume on the television and relaxed while the Competition huffed and puffed herself into an asthma attack and decided to look elsewhere for low hanging pork.

And they all lived happily ever after.

The end.

INSTRUCTIONS:

In our story, how well did each of our piggies and their purchasing officers do from a business standpoint?

In this situation, if you were one of the piggy's purchasing officers, which of the following would be the most important to you: the best price, the best quality, the appropriate quantity, on-time delivery, delivery to the right location? Explain your answer.

Chapter 2

A Closer Look at the Purchasing and Procurement Process

Dr. Philip M. Price & Natalie J. Harrison, M.Ed.

Purchasing touches almost every aspect of our daily work and home lives. If you take a look around you right now, you'll see that almost all of the items you see were purchased by someone. Unless you are naked and outside in the middle of a field or a forest or a flowing stream, the concrete, carpet, or lavishly expensive wood flooring beneath your feet was once purchased. With pervasiveness of purchasing in our lives, we are all experienced and savvy purchasers. We take the activity of purchasing seriously because wise purchases leave us with more expendable cash for even more purchases!

While we all have an almost inherent understanding of purchasing and its role in our lives, the corporate world takes purchasing to a higher level of sophistication and complexity. Not only are purchases on a larger scale, but they also span the globe and must adhere to standard procedures, corporate policies, and international laws.

In this chapter, we will take our initial steps into this complex world of the corporate consumer. First, we will look at the many words used to describe the act of "buying stuff" and the strategic activities of supply management. We will then delve into the Five Ws – who, what, where, when, and why – of purchasing. Next, we will examine the stages of the purchasing process and see that we already engage in these stages on a regular basis. You may even be in the middle of one right now! Finally, we will introduce the nature of policies, procedures, and manuals in the corporate and government purchasing processes.

THE LANGUAGE OF PURCHASING & SUPPLY MANAGEMENT

Just as there are many words for "snow" among people of the far north, there are multiple monikers for "buying stuff" in the business environment. As we discussed in Chapter 1, in the business world, the term *purchasing* refers to both a functional activity and a department within an organization. As an activity, ***purchasing*** is the short- to medium-term acquisition of goods and services in the right quantity of the right quality, ensuring that they are delivered to the right place at the right time, while maximizing the service and minimizing the total cost to the organization. In an organization, a ***purchasing department*** is concerned not only with actually buying (or purchasing) goods, but it also handles receiving purchase orders from sales and manufacturing departments, coordinating with inventory control to know what stock items need to be purchased, research and planning for the purchase, setting criteria for a successful purchase, and returning incorrect orders or faulty products.

Another word commonly heard in purchasing circles is ***procurement***. Although there is much inconclusive debate concerning the difference between purchasing and procurement in the blogosphere, both words share the same meaning and both are used to signify the same functional activity. For example, the leading research and educational association for purchasing professionals, the Institute of Supply Management (ISM), awards a Certified Purchasing Manager (C.P.M.) designation but uses the word procurement to refer to purchasing activities throughout its certifying exam.

In most organizations, the functional department that handles purchasing activities will likely be called either the *Purchasing Department* or the *Procurement Department*, depending on the organization's history, preference, and culture. Some executives prefer to say that they work in "procurement," perhaps because it sounds more corporate or more mysterious. I have even heard a few professionals that fancy themselves a bit too much say that "purchasing" sounds "gauche."

While we will use the words procurement and purchasing interchangeably in this text, we will defer more frequently to purchasing because its core meaning is understood on a deeper human level. It reminds us that we are not involved in some abstract, theoretical practice, but that we are indeed spending money. Unfortunately, this is something we tend to forget when the OPM factor (other people's money) is involved.

Another commonly heard synonym for purchasing is ***acquisition***. Often used by federal and state government offices, *acquisition* shares the same meaning as *purchasing* and *procurement*. All three words are used to signify the same functional activity and department within an organization. Some less reliable anecdotal sources on the internet may incorrectly tell you that the words "acquisition" and "procurement" signify a greater focus on efficiency and effectiveness than "purchasing," perhaps because they work for Acquisition or Procurement departments and are trying to elevate their own status in the dog-eat-dog world of international commerce. All three words – purchasing, procurement, and acquisition – are concerned with efficiency and effectiveness in buying goods and services in the right quantity of the right quality delivered to the right place at the right time while maximizing the service and minimizing the total cost to the organization.

As we mentioned in Chapter 1, *purchasing* (and its synonyms) refers to the immediate or short-term to mid-term acquiring of goods and services. The long-term strategic approach to purchasing and supplier relations is called *supply management*. We also mentioned that some of the core activities of supply management were: internal analysis, market research, strategic sourcing, and negotiating contracts. Some additional activities within an organization that are related to supply management include: contract development and administration, physical distribution and warehousing, inventory control and management, product development, manufacturing, relationship management, supplier evaluation, economic forecasting, and materials management.

In a large company, several thousand employees may be working on a variety of supply management activities. In smaller companies, perhaps only one or two people may be handling all corporate supply management activities. No matter many people handle supply management, its role remains of strategic importance to the organization. In addition, the goals of supply management for companies both big and small include:

- improve the corporate bottom line, i.e., make the company more profitable;

- provide information for planning and forecasting;

- increase corporate efficiency and productivity;

- improve customer satisfaction levels, often with lower prices, higher quality, or enhanced service; and

- be mindful of the company's image and social responsibility.

Supply management must ensure that the products or services a company needs will remain steadily available for a long time into the future at a stable cost. To complete this vital mission, supply management professionals must develop relationships with current, past, and potential suppliers to try to glean as much information as possible about product long-term availability and future prices. Because they play a key role in gathering market intelligence, organizations benefit most when their supply management professionals are part of its senior management team. This allows the supply management manager to be knowledgeable of and understand all parts of the business, allowing them to develop supply management and purchasing strategies consistent with the company's goals and business practices.

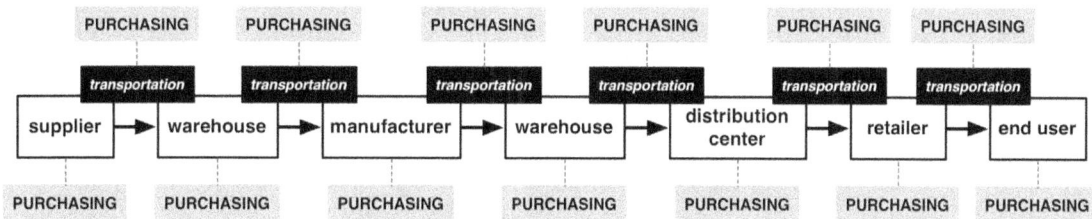

Figure 2.1 - Where Purchasing Happens in the Simple Supply Chain

The Five Ws of Purchasing

As we plunge ahead into the wild and exciting world of purchasing, let's begin by asking and answering the five Ws - the *who, what, where, when,* and *why* questions that burn in the heart of every aspiring purchasing professional.

First, *who* does the purchasing? Most organizations have someone who is responsible for directly acquiring or approving the acquisition of purchases from suppliers. This person could have one of many titles, including Purchasing Manager, Purchasing Officer, Procurement Manager, or Director of Acquisitions.

In larger companies, the Purchasing Manager (or its equivalent of another name) may also oversee a range of Buyers or Purchasing Agents, who investigate suppliers, negotiate contracts, complete the hands-on purchasing activities, and plan for product deliveries with the Warehouse Manager. In smaller companies, however, the Purchasing Manager may be the organization's sole Buyer or Purchasing Agent and conduct all purchasing-related activities by themselves.

Second, *what* is purchased? We mentioned earlier that, in purchasing, "goods and services" are acquired, but what exactly does this mean? Whatever an organization may need to function but does not produce itself are the *goods and services* to be purchased. **Goods** purchased may include raw materials, semi-finished goods, and finished goods used to produce the organization's final product.

  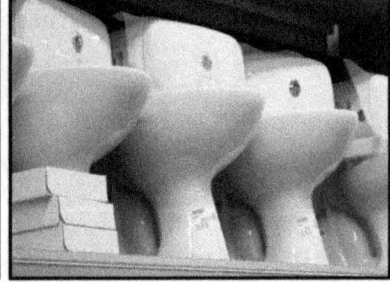

Figure 2.2 - Examples of Raw Materials (cut logs for wood floors), Semi-Finished Goods (processed and cleaned cotton for fabric manufacture), and Finished Goods (finished toilets in a warehouse)

Raw materials are items in their most basic, unfinished, or minimally finished form used to produce or assemble a finished product. Examples of raw materials include rubber for a tire manufacturer, wood for a paper manufacturer, and oranges for an orange juice processor. ***Semi-finished goods***, also called ***work-in-process***, are items that have been partially assembled or semi-finished that will be used to produce or assemble a finished product. Examples of semi-finished goods include processed rubber sheeting for a tire manufacturer, reams of paper for a book publisher, and orange juice concentrate for an orange juice processor. ***Finished goods*** are products that have been fully assembled and are ready to be delivered to the customer. Examples of finished goods include all season radial tires, paperback books, and cartons of orange juice.

Goods purchased also include *maintenance, repair, and operating (MRO) supplies* and *capital goods*. **MRO supplies** are the goods not used to become part of a finished product but are instead essential to the operation of an organization. For example, the cleaning supplies, light bulbs, copier paper, and machine oil in a manufacturing plant are all MRO supplies to be purchased. **Capital goods** are manufactured, finished products used directly and repeatedly to produce other goods. Examples of capital goods include tools, machinery, and buildings.

Figure 2.3 - Examples of MRO Supplies (cleaning supplies for a small office) and Capital Goods (machinery and equipment for a medium sized manufacturer)

Unlike goods, **services** purchased are not tangible products but are instead any action or activity that an organization needs but cannot or has decided not to complete itself. For example, a manufacturer may purchase a wide range of third-party services, from office janitorial services to transport rate negotiation assistance on international freight shipments.

Third, *where* is purchasing done? Much to the dismay of the neat-freak portion of the logistics management population, purchasing is not completed in a neat, orderly, predictable environment. It is instead conducted within the growing, messy, chaotic world of the global market. This messy, massive global market, however, makes for an environment of perfect competition.

When there are only a few suppliers or buyers for a product, imperfect market conditions result, allowing for one side to have more power and control over the market price of the goods. For example, if just one supplier were to have a monopoly on the soap market, it might cruelly and impersonally determine the maximum amount consumers would be willing and able to pay for this much-needed product. The end result might be $50 per bar for cleanliness and good personal hygiene instead of today's $3 bar to get you clean as a whistle.

Large numbers of buyers and suppliers, however, make for a more ideal purchasing environment. When the buyers and suppliers of an item exist in large numbers, there is more open sharing of information on prices and product availability. It is also much easier for buyers and suppliers to both enter and exit the market. Thus, when efficient and cost effective supply chains are desired, organizations seek these to purchase goods and services within these more competitive market conditions.

Because buying is done in a competitive global market, companies must also decide where purchasing is to be done within the organization. Within large organizations, the activity of purchasing may be either *centralized* or *decentralized*. When purchasing decisions and activities are controlled from one central location within an organization, it is called *centralized purchasing* or purchasing within a *centralized organization*. When purchasing decisions and activities are controlled from different locations or divisional levels within an organization, it is called *decentralized purchasing* or purchasing within a *decentralized organization*.

With **centralized purchasing**, larger volumes are purchased from a single supplier, who can offer lower prices, volume discounts, and better payment terms. Within the organization, purchasing is consolidated, efficiencies are increased, and purchasing's operational costs are lowered because the procurement of a specific product for the organization is done through one office in the company, often from the Purchasing Department at the company's global headquarters. Remember our example of Dell Computers in Chapter 1? In order to use its consolidated buying power to get lower costs and more leverage and flexibility from its suppliers, Dell decided to use centralized purchasing and make all major purchasing decisions from its corporate headquarters.

The down side of centralized purchasing is the lack of control it offers divisional and local managers within an organization. With **decentralized purchasing**, the procurement of a specific product for the organization is done through multiple offices in the company, often from each Purchasing Department in each of the company's regional offices. Divisional and local managers have greater control over those elements of the purchasing process that directly impact their departments and they feel a greater sense of ownership of the process. They can also plan for product deliveries that best suit their own time and place needs, instead of those of the organization as a whole.

For example, Ben & Jerry's has its headquarters and original manufacturing facility in Vermont in the United States. When the company expanded to global operations, it constructed an additional manufacturing facility in the Netherlands for its European sales. Because of the exorbitant cost of transporting refrigerated milk, Ben & Jerry's purchases its dairy products from local suppliers near its manufacturing facilities in each Vermont and the Netherlands instead of centrally purchasing all of its milk needed for worldwide operations from one company or location.

Most organizations engage in both centralized and decentralized buying strategies, in which products and services are purchased either centrally or locally, depending on amounts to be purchased, the organization's overall strategy, and purchasing timeframes. When companies like Dell or Ben & Jerry's decide to use centralized or decentralized purchasing for particular products, they are not limited to using this sourcing strategy for all of their products. For example, while Dell uses centralized purchasing for the majority of its computer components, the company may use decentralized purchasing for regionally-based advertising services or local packaging.

Fourth, *when* are purchasing activities conducted? As we will see when we explore the purchasing process later in this chapter, purchasing is an ongoing activity and is typically a continuous cycle of evaluating needs, evaluating potential suppliers, issuing purchase orders, evaluating supplier performance, and, again evaluating new needs. When examining how a company orders individual products from individual suppliers, however, purchase orders can be placed with varying degrees of frequency. For example, **one-off purchase** is a one-time purchase for a specific project that will not be repeated, such as your hot tub purchase for Dad or the U.S. government's acquisition for a replacement for the President's plane, Air Force One.

Another type of frequency-defined purchase is ***automatic inventory replacement*** which is the technique of automatically ordering goods when inventory reaches a specific level. The goal of automatic inventory replacement is to maintain predetermined levels of stock within an organization so that inventory will not run out, causing costly manufacturing delays. For example, a manufacturer would have an automatic inventory replacement agreement with all of its critical parts suppliers to ensure that it can continue its manufacturing operations without a Purchasing Manager having to take the time to determine a need and then place an order with the supplier.

A final frequency-defined type of purchase is ***forward buying***, the practice of purchasing goods in advance of requirements. This practice is used to avoid supply shortages and ensure a constant supply of goods for production and other operations. When storage space is available, forward buying is also used to acquire goods at a lower fixed price when it is anticipated that prices will soon rise. A computer manufacturer might use forward buying with a processor chip supplier to compensate for both potential Customs delays as products arrive from overseas and anticipated cost increases in component parts.

Fifth and finally, *why* is purchasing important?

In Chapter 1, we covered some of the more obvious reasons regarding *why* the function of purchasing is important to an organization. Let's now crunch some numbers and see why purchasing is important in practice.

Obviously, in order for companies to function, they need goods and services. In today's competitive global environment, it is neither cost effective nor efficient for a company to produce all of the goods and services it might need. Imagine automobile manufacturers creating every single part of each car manufactured themselves, from the rubber in the tires to the entire satellite radio system! Even the smallest cottage industries rely on purchasing some amount of raw materials and packaging. For example, a brand new (and imaginary) local Alaskan vintner, Wasilla Winter Wines, will not need to purchase as many goods and services as an automobile manufacturer, but it will need to purchase gardening and distillery equipment, glass bottles and printed labels for finished wine, and advertising services to come up with a catchy Wasilla Winter Wines jingle for a local radio ad.

In addition to being a necessary corporate function, effective and efficient purchasing can be used to save money and have a significant impact on a company's bottom line. Consider the impact a new Purchasing Manager had on Wasilla Winter Wines' bottom line...

As a new small business, Wasilla Winter Wines did not need department managers. The company owner and various members of her family did whatever company functions were necessary when they were necessary. For example, the company purchased its bottles and labels from one packaging provider in small quantities as they were needed. As the company grew, it placed larger orders for bottles and labels but continued to pay the original rates. After five years of steady growth, the Wasilla Winter Wines owner and CEO decided that it was time to hire a Purchasing Manager because she was spending at least 60% of her time in purchasing-related activities. On his first day of work, the new Purchasing Manager looked at Wasilla Winter Wines' purchasing records and gasped in horror. He immediately got bulk purchase bids from three different bottle and label producers, including their current provider. The Purchasing Manager then negotiated a two-year contract with the company providing the best offer for Wasilla Winter Wines, which, interestingly, happened to be the same company they had been using! Under the new contract, however, Wasilla Winter Wines was given a 15% discount on all orders over $1000. So what effect would this have on Wasilla Winter Wines' bottom line in the first year of this new purchasing contract?

As shown in Figure 2.4 below, from simply renegotiating a packaging contract, Wasilla Winter Wines is now $60,000 richer each year! This simple act of good purchasing, which took the Purchasing Manager only two days to complete, resulted in a 30% increase in the company's profits! Wasilla Winter Wines' Purchasing Manager won't stop here, however. He can continue to look for ways to improve the efficiency and cost of all corporate purchasing, from negotiating better purchasing contracts with distillery equipment providers to finding discount office supply wholesalers that offer free delivery.

	Before Discount	After 15% Discount
Production Labor Cost per Bottle of Wine	$3.00	$3.00
Packaging Cost per Bottle	$4.00	$3.40
Corporate Overhead Allocation per Bottle	$1.00	$1.00
Total Cost of Bottle Produced	$8.00	$7.40
Selling Price per Bottle	$10.00	$10.00
Profit per Bottle	$2.00	$2.60
Profit per 100,000 Bottles (annual production)	$200,000.00	$260,000.00
Total Extra Profit After 15% Discount		$60,000.00

Figure 2.4 - Annual Profit for Wasilla Winter Wines after Negotiated 15% Supplier Discount

The rewards reaped from efficient and effective purchasing practices can allow companies like Wasilla Winter Wines to have extra resources to: provide increased customer service; invest in marketing to attract new customers; construct new production and distribution facilities to expand the product's geographic reach; reinvest in product research and development to improve products and develop new product lines; attract and retain top quality employees; and provide greater returns to shareholders.

THE PURCHASING PROCESS

After companies have negotiated great savings or found world-class suppliers at affordable rates, they do not rest on their past glorious achievements of great savings. Instead, they strive for continuous improvement in their purchasing practices. No matter how great a new contract with a supplier may appear, it is of little use if the desired products are delivered at the wrong time or in incorrect quantities. Purchasing Managers monitor and manage the entire process of purchasing a good or service, from the moment the company expresses a need for a particular product to the moment the product is received and the purchasing order is closed out. This section of the chapter will introduce the seven stages of this very important ***purchasing process***, as shown in Figure 2.5 below.

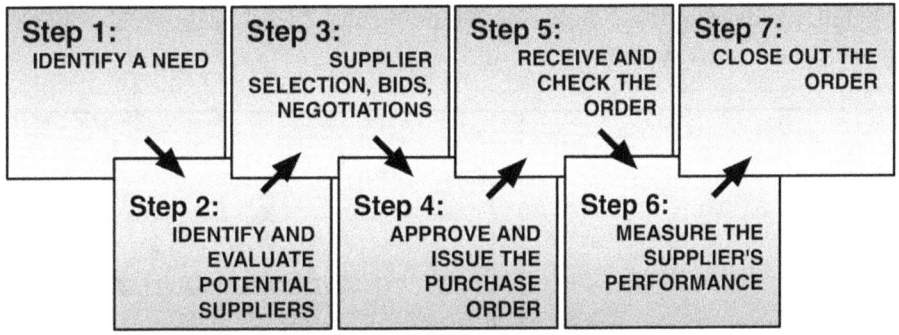

Figure 2.5 - The Seven-Step Purchasing Process

To help us as we explore the seven stages of the purchasing process, let's use a scenario that may be familiar to many of us. Your father is retiring after working for McBlahBlah's Boring Business Machines for 50 long years. His retirement party is only a few weeks away. Everyone in the family has decided to pool their resources to buy Dad one magnificent, expensive, extravagant gift: a backyard hot tub with super-powered jests and a built-in television. Because you are studying purchasing, you have been elected as the family's Purchasing Officer. (Lucky you!) Let's consider how your own purchasing process is similar to that of Purchasing Managers from large and small companies alike.

STEP 1 - Identify a Need

Before Dad's retirement party, the family held a meeting to determine what he needed most for his amazingly, awesome birthday present. When the family decided what was needed (i.e., a hot tub with super-powered jets and a built-in television), they informed you, the family Purchasing Officer, so that you could, in the words of Aunt Tillie, "Take care of it."

In most mid- to large-size companies, when an individual or a department within an organization experiences or anticipates a need for a good or service, they typically do not go out and acquire it themselves. If they did, like Wasilla Winter Wines did in its early days, they would not achieve economies of scale and reduced prices for larger orders. Instead, they let the Purchasing Manager or department know what is needed, in what quantity, at what quality, and at what time and place.

In most mid- to large-size organizations, when a need for a good or service is determined, the Purchasing Manager is informed. Typically, the individual or department needing specific goods sends a ***purchase requisition*** to the Purchasing Manager. This purchase requisition is not an actual order for the goods; it is a request for the Purchasing Manager to purchase these goods.

Although purchase requisition forms differ from organization to organization, they most commonly contain: the specific details of the items requested (also known as ***specifications***); the preferred vendors or suppliers; the quantity of items needed; the date of the requisition; the desired date of receipt; the estimated unit cost of each item; the internal department or account to be charged; and the signature or details of a company official authorizing the purchase. While purchase requisitions have traditionally been paper-based forms filled out by the requestor and hand delivered, mailed, or faxed to the Purchasing Manager, they are increasing becoming computerized for instant information transmission.

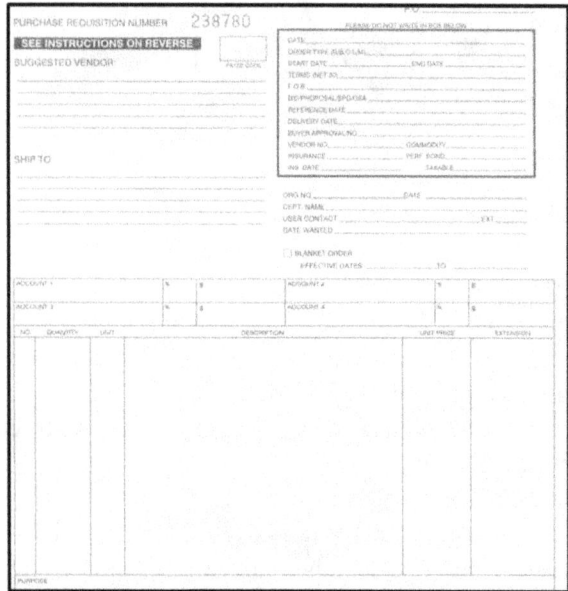 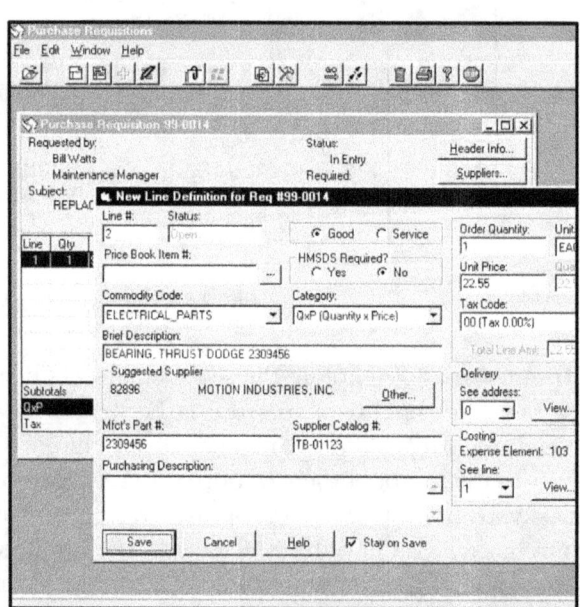

Figure 2.6 - Example of a Purchase Requisition Form (left) and an Electronic Purchase Requisition Form from 4Site's Asset Management Software System (right)

We know now that when goods are requested, a purchase requisition form is used. When services are requested, however, a ***statement of work (SOW)*** is used. The SOW describes the services needed, where and when they are needed, and the type of supplier needed. It may also include specific personnel requirement, performance, and assessment details and the terms and conditions of payment.

The Purchasing Manager then uses the SOW in soliciting bids from potential suppliers. After a supplier has been selected and a contract has been awarded, the statement of work becomes part of the contractual agreement. It is used as a basis for evaluating whether or not the supplier has provided the needed service when, where, and how needed.

Before we move on through the rest of the purchasing process, we must consider whether an organization has existing contracts or other relationships with **_preferred suppliers_** for the goods or services requested. This situation occurs when suppliers and their products have been tried and tested. The organization feels comfortable with a specific supplier for a specific product or range of products. When this occurs, an organization does not need to complete Steps 2 and 3 of the purchasing process: selecting potential suppliers, obtaining bids, and negotiating contracts. For example, after Wasilla Winter Wines negotiated a new two-year contract with their existing bottle and label supplier, Palmer Packaging, the Production Department could then send a purchasing requisition for needed bottles to the Purchasing Manager (Step 1), who would then send a purchase order directly to Palmer Packaging (Step 4), completely bypassing the supplier identification, selection, and negotiation processes (Steps 2 and 3).

Similar to preferred supplier considerations, a company must also consider whether or not it has an agreement of reciprocity with another company. **_Reciprocity_** is a mutually beneficial practice between two companies in which they agree to buy each other's products or services. For example, Wasilla Winter Wines may have an agreement of reciprocity with Doug's Distillery DooDads, in which both companies agree that Wasilla Winter Wines will purchase machine parts exclusively from Doug's Distillery DooDads, who, in turn, agrees to purchase multiple cases of Wasilla Winter Wines' finest vintage for its extravagant holiday parties state-wide.

After Step 1, when a purchase requisition has been received for new goods or services, some companies also consider a **_make or buy decision_**. At this point, companies consider whether it would be more efficient and cost effective to buy the goods or services from suppliers or to make the goods (or complete the services) themselves. A company may elect to **_make_** its own product or service if:

- *it has the equipment and resources to produce the product or perform the service;*
- *it can be accomplished at a significantly lower cost than buying it;*
- *a skilled supplier cannot be found who meets the necessary product quantity, quality, and delivery time and place criteria; or*
- *staff and equipment are readily available in-house that might go unused otherwise.*

When Ben & Jerry's Ice Cream was planning to introduce a new flavor, Phish Food, they could not find a marshmallow supplier with marshmallows of the right consistency for the flavorful new ice cream. The company opted for the "make" decision, realizing that they would have a better product and it would be more cost-effective if they manufactured the marshmallows themselves in house.

Sometimes a company may already manufacture a product that it can use for its own operations. Known commonly as **_insourcing_**, this practice occurs when a department, branch, or subsidiary within a large organization decides to acquire a desired good or service from a location within the company itself. For example, the American television network NBC was owned by General Electric (GE) in 2011. NBC may have decided to insource all of its network's small electronics needs, such as office televisions and microwaves, through its parent company, GE.

Conversely, companies may elect to buy goods from outside suppliers or outsource desired services to a third party if they don't have the equipment or staff necessary. Even when companies have the needed equipment and resources, they may still make a **buy decision** if:

- *it is not cost effective to make the goods or perform the services;*
- *the quality of the supplier's goods or services cannot be matched internally;*
- *suppliers hold a patent or trademark that doesn't allow other companies to produce the goods; or*
- *the organization wishes to have suppliers available as part of a global multi-sourcing strategy.*

Companies that decide to buy goods may purchase them as-is from the supplier without customization, also known as **off-the-shelf**, or they may ask the supplier to make modifications to the products that are specific to their unique needs.

In today's competitive global marketplace, many organizations are finding that it is far more cost effective to outsource a large portion of desired goods and services. For example, a maker of exclusive, expensive fountain pens may find that it is more cost effective to buy the pens its corporate headquarters needs for everyday use from a less exclusive, less expensive supplier.

When companies decide to *buy*, the Purchasing Manager typically deals with only a small number of suppliers for each good or service - sometimes only one! When companies decide to *make* required goods, the Purchasing Manager's job becomes considerably more complex. For each good made, the Purchasing Manager will have to select suppliers and negotiate purchasing contracts for each part of the item to be produced, which might include a variety of raw materials, partially finished goods, and completed parts. As a result, for a single requisitioned item to be produced, the Purchasing Manager may need to deal with as many as fifty suppliers!

STEP 2 - Identify and Evaluate Potential Suppliers

Thinking back to Dad and his souped-up hot tub, would you, as your family's trusted Purchasing Officer, simply walk into a store and purchase the first hot tub you see? Unless you want the wrath of Mom, Aunt Tillie, or Uncle Bingo plagued upon you, you are likely to want to spend the family's money wisely. Therefore, you will probably investigate different hot tubs, their prices, and their service agreements at a variety of local and online hot tub suppliers.

Similarly, when Purchasing Managers receive a purchasing requisition for a new good or service, they do not pounce on the first supplier who glances in their direction. They instead search for and compare multiple suppliers that could provide the needed product. The Purchasing Manager first sends an **RFI (request for information)** to a wide range of potential suppliers, asking them to provide information about the desired product, the organization itself, its locations, and its capabilities. Based on the information obtained from suppliers responding to the RFI, the Purchasing Manager then issues an **RFP (request for proposal)** or an **RFQ (request for quotation)** to potential suppliers as an invitation to submit a bid for a contract to provide the needed goods or services. The RFP or RFQ sent would outline the quantity, quality, time, and place goods or services are needed. It would also contain a deadline for suppliers' proposal or quotation submissions and ask suppliers to outline the overall cost for the proposed purchase. Finally, it might contain information about the expectations of the selected supplier, their performance, and the product. When the organization receives proposals and quotations form potential suppliers, it is ready to move on to Step 3, the bidding, selection, and negotiation process.

The amount of energy and time a Purchasing Manager invests in preparing RFIs, RFPs, and RFQs in Step 2 depends on the importance and size of the completed product for which the requested good or service is needed. The intensity of the Purchasing Manager's search for a supplier will also be influenced by relationships with existing suppliers. A few types of purchasing situations, in order of increasing intensity in supplier relationships and strategic importance of products purchased, are:

- ***straight repurchase***, in which there is a contract for the good or service with an existing supplier at a set price. In this situation, no RFIs, RFPs, or RFQs would not be needed and Step 2 would be skipped entirely. For example, Wasilla Winter Wines would have a straight repurchase of its honey jars and labels after signing a contract with its supplier, Palmer Packaging.

- ***straight purchase***, in which a new good or service of little strategic importance is desired. Because the product is less important, the time and energy needed to write RFIs, RFPs, or RFQs to purchase goods cannot be justified. When Wasilla Winter Wines purchases toilet paper for its production facility restrooms, for example, it does not take the time to send out an RFI to purchase products for its two bathrooms serving twenty employees. Instead, the Purchasing Manager makes bulk purchases from a local warehouse-style wholesaler.

- ***modified purchase***, in which there is an existing supplier under contract but also a change in the need, such as a larger number or different type of product. In this situation, the organization may ask the existing supplier to outline how it will meet the new or changing requirement. It may also solicit information from a few additional suppliers to compare against their existing supplier. For example, if Wasilla Winter Wines, Inc. bought out three other vintners in neighboring states, it would triple its output of 100,000 bottles of wine per year to 300,000 bottles. The Purchasing Manager would need to ascertain Palmer Packaging's ability to triple its production of bottles and labels. If this packaging supplier could not meet the anticipated demand in the desired timeframe, Wasilla Winter Wines would then have to submit an RFI to additional potential suppliers.

- ***new competitive purchase***, in which a new good or service is required and the finished item is of high strategic importance and/or will be produced in very large quantities. In this situation, the Purchasing Manager will complete all or most of the activities covered throughout Step 2. For example, because of its threefold growth, Wasilla Winter Wines needs to explore faster bottling machinery. The bottling machinery and corresponding conveyor mechanisms are costly items and are critical to the company's operations. Therefore, the Purchasing Manager will send an RFI to as many bottling machinery manufacturers as he can find. He will then spend many hours analyzing them before issuing a highly detailed RFP.

STEP 3 - The Dirty Work: Supplier Selection, Bids, and Negotiations

Selecting the right supplier is often the most important decision a Purchasing Manager can make. When purchasing Dad's extreme hot tub, you are likely to study all of the possible hot tubs' specifications and retailers' prices with great intensity. You are spending your family's hard-earned money, after all! You may even try to negotiate a lower price by playing one retailer against another. ("Well, AquaWorld is offering the same hot tub for $1000 less. Maybe I should go there...") In the end, thanks to your diligent work at this stage of the purchasing process, you may spend $1000 less than budgeted, allowing everyone to throw a big retirement bash for Dad and his friends at a local bowling alley.

When selecting a supplier, a Purchasing Manager can use one of two techniques: *competitive bidding* or *negotiation*. After sending out an RFP or an RFQ for a specific product, an organization receives bids (i.e., proposals or quotes) from potential suppliers. The Purchasing Manager then examines all of the bids to find a qualified supplier who best meets the organization's needs, such as low cost and high levels of service. This technique of **competitive bidding**, which pits potential suppliers against each another for the organization's business, is typically used:

- *in competitive markets with multiple suppliers offering the same item;*
- *when a large volume of the good or service is needed;*
- *if the organization does not yet have a preferred supplier for the product; and*
- *when there is enough time for the time-consuming competitive bidding process.*

If, after sending out an RFI, the Purchasing Manager finds that there are very few suppliers of the needed good or service, the timeframe does not allow for competitive bidding, immediate supplier involvement is needed, or the item requested must be manufactured and its complexity does not allow for accurate cost estimates, he/she may instead engage in the purchasing technique of negotiation with one potential supplier. **Negotiation** occurs when a buyer and one potential supplier engage in an open discussion in an attempt to reach a mutually beneficial purchasing agreement. The negotiation process may be as simple as a single telephone call or e-mail or as complex as a series of meetings, interviews, and site visits over the course of a year. It can also help to develop strong initial buyer-supplier relationships because both parties have openly discussed their abilities and expectations. Good negotiation takes great finesse and is more of an art than a science. If a Purchasing Manager is new to, uncomfortable with, or simply seeking support for an important upcoming negotiation, he/she may elect to seek the services of a third-party broker or negotiation service provider. We will explore the nebulous world of negotiations later in Chapter 8 of this text.

Throughout the process of both competitive bidding and negotiation, the Purchasing Manager uses set evaluation criteria when considering potential suppliers. These criteria might include factors such as:

- *Does the supplier have the ability, experience, physical resources, and adequately trained workforce to provide the goods or services of the right quantity and quality at the right time and place?*

- *Is the supplier financially sound? What do their current customers and employees think of them?*

- *How is their distribution handled? What is their track record for on-time deliveries?*

- *Is the supplier committed to this relationship? Are they ready to work with us now?*

During supplier selection, an organization must also consider whether its needs would be best met by selecting a single supplier or multiple sources of supply for the desired good or service. At first glance, it may seem most obvious to select a single supplier. A single supplier can offer the best volume discounts and higher levels of service, such as Just-in-Time service; it may be willing to offer an organization more information; and it provides a platform for a solid, long-lasting buyer-supplier relationship. An effective Purchasing Manager must also consider the advantages of selecting multiple sources of supply, such as: suppliers do not become complacent in the quality of their products and service because they are in constant competition with one another; costs can be lower when the market is extremely competitive; and, if one of the suppliers experiences labor problems or equipment failure, the flow of supply to the organization is still guaranteed.

Whether a single supplier or multiple sources of supply are selected, we cannot move on to purchase orders and Step 4 of the purchasing process until we mention a growing trend in the world of corporate purchasing - auctions! An auction is the sale of goods or services by a supplier in which potential buyers bid against one another for the desired items.

When an organization must purchase a large quantity of a basic item or service and is not concerned with using a preferred supplier, it may consider holding a reverse auction to select a supplier. In a ***reverse auction***, an organization announces the goods or services it needs to purchase. In-person, telephone, or online potential suppliers may then bid their cost for the goods or services against other potential buyers. The cost bids go lower and lower (as opposed to traditional auctions with rising bids) until one supplier is left offering the lowest bid. Overall, auctions offer a much quicker purchasing process and sometimes a more cost effective result than competitive bidding or negotiations but can bring greater risks with unvetted suppliers.

STEP 4 - Get the Purchase Approved and Purchase Order Issued

When the supplier has been selected, the terms of the purchase arrangement are then established between the buyer and the supplier. These written arrangements are contained in a legally binding document called a ***purchase order*** or a ***purchase agreement***. This document, signed by authorized officials representing both the buyer and the supplier, contains details outlining the purchase, such as: a description and specifications of the goods or services; the quantity to be delivered; the exact place, time, and method of delivery; the price of the overall purchase; descriptions of the quality required of the goods and related services; and the purchase order number and purchase due date.

When setting the price of the overall purchase within the purchase order or other similar contract between the buyer and supplier, both parties work toward agreeing on a fair and reasonable price.

These costs set may be either *fixed* or *variable*. For situations in which the supplier is producing a new, complex item, the costs in the purchase order may be stated as **variable**. For most situations, buyers and suppliers have a reasonable feel for what the cost of the desired items or services will be. In these situations, their purchase order may be a **fixed price contract**, in which the prices for goods delivered are set at a fixed level. Also quoted may be a **landed price**, in which the price cited by the supplier to the buyer includes all transportation and customs duties costs.

For many years, purchase orders in large organizations had been entirely paper-based, with copies of copies of copies of purchase orders sent to multiple departments across an organization for much needed information sharing. Each department would have their file drawers full of old purchase orders at the end of each fiscal year. Today, most large organizations forward electronic copies of purchase orders to other departments or, better yet, their purchase orders are part of a larger EDI (electronic data interchange) system, with real-time information sharing.

When a good or service or range of related goods or services are to be ordered multiple times from the same supplier, an organization may issue a blanket purchase order. A **blanket purchase order (BPO)** is an open order for goods or services from a specific supplier within a specific timeframe, such as a year. When goods or services covered under a BPO are needed, a routine order release is issued and the requested goods or services are delivered to the buyer. Blanket purchase orders are a common, efficient means of doing business for most large organizations, especially for regularly needed production and maintenance goods and services.

After an organization has sent a purchase order or a routine order release (under a BPO agreement) to a supplier, it is ready to move on to Step 5 of the purchasing process and receive the goods and check the order.

STEP 5 - Receive and Check the Order

Thinking back to Dad and his retirement surprise, you have selected the perfect hot tub with super-powered jets and a built-in television at an amazingly low price. You have placed your order with a local hot tub distributor, Hot Tubs by Harry, who will be delivering it to Dad's house while he is out of town at a scrapbooking convention in Hoboken. When Hot Tubs by Harry arrives, do you simply let them install it on the back deck themselves and drive off because you are just too comfortable in Dad's shiatsu massage chair to get up? If you are the responsible Purchasing Officer that your family believes you are, you instead greet the Hot Tubs by Harry delivery people at the door, receive the order from them, check the order after it has been installed (i.e., make sure the water heats up and the super-powered jets and television both work), and sign that you have received the order.

When suppliers make a delivery to an organization, the Purchasing Department is not as directly involved in receiving the ordered goods as you were when receiving Dad's hot tub. Instead, the Purchasing Manager relies on the Warehouse and Quality Control Departments to receive and check the order.

The Purchasing Department does, however, monitor the entire order receipt process remotely. When the order is received and checked, the Purchasing Department is informed. This information is transmitted automatically in real time if the organization has a computerized inventory management system linked in to automatic identification technology. For example, the Purchasing Manager at Wasilla Winter Wines (WWW) immediately knows when and how many bottles ordered are received into the WWW warehouse because the crates of bottles are scanned using a bar code reader and entered into the WWW inventory management software program. A short time later, after the Warehouse Manager has checked the order and entered additional information into the inventory management program, the Purchasing Manager knows the condition of the order received.

Throughout the order receipt and checking process, it is critical that the Purchasing Manager stay informed. Ensuring that the order has been received in the right quantity, of the right quality, and at the right time and place is a true measure of the success of the purchase.

STEP 6 - Measure the Supplier's Performance

From the end of Step 4 through to the end of Step 5 of the purchasing process, the Purchasing Manager must vigilantly monitor the supplier's actual performance. While it is great to find a supplier who offers amazingly low prices, it is absolutely critical that the supplier deliver what it is ordered in the right quantity, of the right quality, at the right time, and to the right place. It is also important that the supplier: (1) be responsive to buyer's request, even if it just a request for additional information; (2) be reliable, responsible, and respectful; and (3) be flexible to changes that may arise in the buyer's needs and schedule. Supplier flexibility is especially important for *expediting*. Goods are typically purchased according to a predetermined schedule. In some cases, the buyer may need to goods or services sooner than agreed. A supplier is viewed favorably if it can **expedite** the order, i.e., deliver goods or services more swiftly and efficiently than planned.

It is important for the Purchasing Manager to evaluate supplier performance to enhance future purchasing operations and supply chain efficiency. When the Purchasing Manager finds that a supplier does not meet the performance criteria stated in the purchase order or other contractual agreement, he/she can contact the supplier to allow them the opportunity to improve. Often, because the supplier wants to keep the buyer's business, being informed of poor performance can results in subsequent higher-than-expected levels of supplier service. If the supplier's level of performance does not improve, the buyer may cancel the purchase order and know to avoid that supplier in the future.

Although it is important to know when a supplier's performance is substandard, it is equally important for a Purchasing Manager to know when a supplier's performance exceeds expectations. Exceptional suppliers can become an organization's **preferred suppliers**, suppliers who have proven themselves as reliable suppliers who consistently offer higher levels of service or lower prices. Many medium- to large-size organizations keep a list or database of preferred suppliers to which they refer when sourcing for a needed product or service. Having a preferred supplier database allows for a more streamlined supplier selection process, in which a buyer may solicit competitive bids from only a few preferred suppliers (instead of the many suppliers available) or even go straight to the negotiation process with one preferred supplier.

STEP 7 - Close Out the Order

After the goods or service have been received and the supplier's performance has been evaluated, the Purchasing Manager is ready to close out the order. At this stage, the Purchasing and

Accounting Departments validate that what was ordered was received and that the terms and conditions of the purchase agreement or contract were met. This is also called a three-way-match because the purchase order, receipt documents, and supplier invoice are compared. If all three match up, the supplier's invoice is approved for payment and the purchase order is closed out, marked as completed, and filed.

A Quick Nod to Purchasing Policies

In the global business environment, purchasing can become a far more complex process than buying a souped-up hot tub for your dad's retirement party. You are likely dealing with a multitude of products and past present, and potential suppliers. If you are the Purchasing Manager of a medium- to large-sized organization, you are likely to have a variety of Buyers and other purchasing employees working for you. You will likely have to share information and coordinate your purchasing efforts with the managers from multiple departments across the organization, such as the Manufacturing, Marketing, Warehousing, Quality Control, Finance, and Logistics Departments. You are also likely to hit speed bumps along the way, such as shipping delays, product discontinuations, and rising transportation costs and prices. Finally, you must do all of this while obtaining goods and services in the right quantity of the right quality, ensuring that they are delivered to the right place at the right time, while maximizing the service and minimizing the total cost to the organization. Whew!

Because the task of purchasing is so complex and because it has a vital impact on the fiscal bottom line, many companies establish and follow purchasing policies. A ***policy*** is a set of guidelines, rules, or principles that guide an organization in its corporate activities. A policy can provide consistency and a predictable reliability in an organization's actions from employee to employee across both small and large companies.

Policies can be either formal, written ones or informal, unwritten ones, often understood by the entire organization and based on years of common practice. A Purchasing department must be cautious of unwritten policies because they can lead to unguided and unpredictable purchasing actions. When new employees are hired, they might not have been fully briefed in or have had time to practice the organization's unwritten purchasing policies, leading to purchasing chaos. A Purchasing department must also be cautious of adhering too closely to its written policies. When always followed to the letter, formal, written purchasing policies can sometimes limit the development of new ideas and hinder the organization's flexibility.

Despite the cautionary words, purchasing policies are important to the success of an organization's procurement activities. The U.S. government follows a voluminous set of purchasing policies known as the ***FAR***, an acronym for ***Federal Acquisition Regulations***. FAR was established in 1974 under the Office of Federal Procurement Policy (OFPP) Act, but it is updated regularly to reflect current needs and trends. Similar to the FAR, the U.S. Department of Defense has its own set of purchasing policies known as the ***DFAR***, or ***Defense Federal Acquisitions Regulations***.

Although most purchasing policies will not fill nearly as many pages as the FAR or DFAR, all purchasing policies can accomplish the following four goals. First, purchasing policies can outline operational aspects of the organization's purchasing process, such as which items are purchased externally and which are made internally, or ***insourced***, which purchasing activities are centralized and which are decentralized, which products are purchased under reciprocity agreements, and how hazardous materials are handled when purchased. Organizations may also have formal, written ***purchasing procedures***, which would provide more detailed step-by-step operational instructions to which employees would adhere when engaged in any purchasing activities.

Second, purchasing policies can define the roles of the Purchasing department and those within it, especially in their relations with suppliers. They can outline the responsibilities of managers and purchasers and clarify issues of decision- making hierarchy in the organization. They can also address how supplier relations should be handled, including who contacts suppliers and when, who meets with them or travels to their location, and who handles complaints about suppliers' products.

Third, purchasing policies can outline how specific purchasing activities or approaches can help a company carry out its corporate or social mission. For example, a purchasing policy for Ben & Jerry's Ice Cream is likely to be that they will not purchase dairy products produced from cows treated with growth hormones, keeping purchasing in line with the organization's social mission.

Fourth and finally, purchasing policies can define the ethics and conduct guidelines for those engaged in the purchasing process. Purchasing, after all, is all about money. Suppliers want to make money by getting the Purchasing Manager to buy their product. Organizations want their Purchasing Manager to get them the best deal in terms of cost and service. Without these guidelines, naive or unethical Purchasing Managers might accept money or gifts from suppliers and, in turn, buy their product, even though it might not be the best one for the organization. Not only those in purchasing, but, at the time of this publication, all employees of the U.S. government are not permitted to accept gifts from a federal contractor totaling more than $50 per year.

As we explore purchasing throughout this book, we will further uncover the need for policies in the complex and wonderful world of purchasing.

CHAPTER 2 REVIEW QUESTIONS

1. What is the difference between *purchasing* and *acquisition*?

2. What is *supply management*? What does it ensure for a company?

3. What is the difference between *centralized* and *decentralized purchasing*? Describe examples of two companies not mentioned in Chapter 2 that might each use centralized and decentralized purchasing respectively.

4. Describe two different situations in which the same company might a.) make a *one-off purchase* and b.) utilize *automatic inventory replacement*.

5. Look back at Figure 2.4, the Annual Profit for Wasilla Winter Wines after Negotiated 15% Supplier Discount. How much extra profit would Wasilla Winter Wines gain if the supplier discount was 30% instead of 15%?

6. When does a Purchasing Manager issue each an *RFI* and an *RFP*?

7. Provide an example of a company that might issue a *blanket purchase order* to a supplier. What items are likely to be included in this BPO? What advantages would having a BPO provide to both the purchaser and supplier in your example?

8. Why is it necessary for a company to measure its suppliers' performance?

9. Why are *purchasing policies* important to an organization? What might happen if a company didn't have any standard purchasing policies?

10. In the world of government acquisitions, what is the FAR? Do a bit of online exploration and find the government website for the FAR. What is its URL? Next, download a copy of the FAR and list the titles of Parts 5, 6, 7, 8, and 9 of the FAR.

Chapter 2 Case Exercise

The Case of Jo-Jo's Jams

Jo-Jo's Jams is a small music production company that produces both digital music and CDs. Jo-Jo's sold 200,000 music CDs in 2014. Although its digital sales are growing, the company anticipates its annual CD sales to hold steady at 200,000 for the next few years. The company's purchasing manager is trying to find a way to help the company increase profits without an increase in sales. The production cost for each CD is $3 and the corporate overhead is $1 per CD. These are both fixed costs that the company cannot change. The retail price for each Jo-Jo's CD is $10 and the company has no plans to raise the price of its CDs for the next few years.

Jo-Jo's Jams currently buys its blank CDs and cases from So-So CDs for $1 each. Jo-Jo's purchasing manager has successfully negotiated a new purchase agreement with Sili-Valley, Inc. to purchase 200,000 blank CDs and cases for $0.90 each.

Following the example in Figure 2.4 (Annual Profit for Wasilla Winter Wines after Negotiated 15% Supplier Discount), fill in the table below and answer the following questions:

A. How much profit did Jo-Jo's Jams make per CD both before and after the supplier switch from So-So CDs to Sili-Valley, Inc.?

B. What was Jo-Jo's Jams' annual profit when So-So CDs was its supplier?

C. What will Jo-Jo's annual profit be after the switch to Sili-Valley, Inc. as the CD and case supplier?

D. By how much will its annual profits increase? Was it a good idea for Jo-Jo's purchasing manager to negotiate the contract with the new supplier?

	Supplier: So-So CDs	Supplier: Sili-Valley, Inc.
Production Labor Cost per CD		
Cost per Blank CD and Case		
Corporate Overhead Allocation per CD		
Total Cost of CD Produced		
Selling Price per CD		
Profit per CD		
Profit per 200,000 CDs (annual production)		
Total Extra Profit After Switching to Sili-Valley, Inc.		

Chapter 3
Purchasing the Right Quantity

Dr. Morgan Henrie & Dr. Philip M. Price

Throughout their careers, purchasing professionals are regularly faced with the challenge of buying the right quantity. Buy too much and, although you get a better discount, the costs of holding inventory can eat away at savings. Buy too little and you have your operating and marketing departments very unhappy when you run out of required inventory.

Throughout life, we all encounter quantity decisions. Whether it is in business or on a personal level, we face the need to decide what quantities to purchase that will maximize our hard earned cash spent. If you are raising teenage boys, buying groceries is a major challenge because you never have enough on hand of what they will eat and way too much on hand of what they will not touch. Of course when you sign up for that cable TV subscription, should you order the basic 23-channel package or the super deluxe 129-channel package?

In the world of purchasing, managers, supervisors, purchasing professionals, and contracting personnel face exactly the same questions: the need to know exactly what must be ordered, the quantity to be ordered, and when the order should be placed to have it arrive at the required time and at the required place. In the manufacturing industry, quantity-based purchasing decisions are concerned with getting the right quantity of input goods needed to meet the production department's manufacturing schedules so they can produce the finished goods necessary to meet the marketing department's sales needs.

In the world of service, quantity decisions are associated with how many spare parts should be stored in the warehouse, when spare parts should be reordered, if a larger quantity should be ordered to obtain a quantity discount, or if the order should be just what the project or maintenance schedule requires now. Essential to these is the purchasing specialist's ability to answer these questions:

- *What should be ordered?* (This is usually based on the user's needs.)

- *How much of each item should be ordered?* (This is usually based on the quantities needed to complete one unit multiplied by the number of finished items needed.)

- *When should the order be placed so that it arrives at the right time?*

- *Where is the item required?*

Being able to answer these questions logically, while balancing the costs of ordering and holding the items, is critical to the company's long-term success. This chapter presents methods that allow purchasing professionals to answer these questions.

INTRODUCING QUANTITY AND THE EOQ

Developing answers to the questions of what to order, how much to order, and when to order has been an important business question as far back as the Roman era. As the Romans extended their geographic dominance and had to feed their armies, their leaders had to understand and decide: what quantity of food to order or pillage, where to pillage the food of the desired quality, and how to get it to the soldiers at the right time and place. During the agricultural era, stores selling staple goods, such as flour and salt, had to plan months in advance for what to order due to long lead times and delays. These lead times and delays were associated with the slow modes of transportation for delivery at the time, with most deliveries coming by either ship or wagon. Modern day management doesn't normally face the same weeks and months of transportation problems of bygone eras, but they do face a new set of procurement challenges in getting the right quantity to the right place at the right time.

Modern day managers now face the new challenges of global competition, funding limitations, and increasing levels of customer sophistication and expectations. To be competitive today, the 21st century purchasing manager must balance the "need for speed" with the cost of maintaining an inventory and deciding where to procure the best product at the best price. Balancing these competing needs is one factor in deciding what quantities to order and when to order them.

Identifying what, how much, and when to order can be based on many factors. For example, purchasing personnel may receive procurement requests from:

- *Service operations personnel requiring new or replacement parts, such as replacement oil filters;*

- *Manufacturing maintenance personnel requiring scheduled or replacement parts, such as a replacement belt for a factory conveyor;*

- *Warehouse personnel issuing a restocking request, such as restock of florescent light bulbs;*

- *Information technology personnel requesting new company-wide management software, such as material requirements planning computer programs;*

- *Project personnel requiring materials for their projects, such as concrete, bricks, or wood for a new building; and*

- *Manufacturing personnel for all of their finished products' inputs.*

Many of these requests provide specific requirements as to what, how many, and when the materials will be required. For example, the maintenance manager will state specifically that her department needs a case of 3-foot long florescent lights, where the case contains 12 light bulbs. The purchasing person will find the best available price and method to procure this specific quantity requirement. At other times, the purchasing person will be faced with the need to decide how many of a specific component should be procured to satisfy a recurring stocking need. Deciding how many items should be ordered and how frequently orders should be placed is often developed mathematically.

Developing mathematical answers to the questions of how much to order and when to order it is traced back to the early 1900s. In 1913, Ford Whitman Harris developed what is now the oldest known standard quantity-ordering model, commonly called the **economic order quantity model**, also known as the **EOQ model**. Ford Whitman Harris was, among many other things, an engineer, patent lawyer, and management scientist. In 1913, he published "How Many Parts to Make at Once" in *Factory, The Magazine of Management*, presenting the now familiar Economic Order Quantity (EOQ) model. In this article, Harris looked at the inventory's balancing function regarding the cost of ordering and the related cost of holding an inventory. Based on this analysis, Harris developed a now commonly accepted square-root formula that provides management a simple and straightforward method to derive the most economic quantity of an item to order under a specific set of assumptions. The concept of EOQ will be discussed in greater detail later in this chapter.

EOQ and other order quantity models are used to support decision-making in inventory management and purchasing management. Specific data needed, or **inputs**, for the EOQ model come from many sources, such as historical usage, costs, and forecasted future needs. If you were to look at one company, Frank's Dairy, an example of some of the EOQ inputs would be:

INPUTS FOR FRANK'S DAIRY

1. Frank's annual milk carton usage = (D) = 57,000
2. Franks cost of each carton = $0.80
3. Milk carton ordering cost = (S) = $35 per order
4. Milk carton holding cost = (H) = 30% of a single carton's cost = $0.80 x 30% = $0.80 x 0.3 = $0.24
5. Annual working days = 260

As will be discussed later in the chapter, these historical values will provide Frank's Dairy with critical information needed to determine the optimum order quantity.

QUANTITY DECISIONS & INVENTORY MANAGEMENT

According to the online glossary of the Council for Supply Chain Management Professionals, ***inventory management*** is *the process of ensuring the availability of products through inventory administration*. This definition can be broken down into three critical components: *a process*, *availability of products*, and *inventory*. First and foremost, inventory management is a process - and very frequently a complex process. This complex process involves interconnected tasks, such as determining what needs to be stocked, developing a forecast of required stocking levels, identifying minimum stock levels, and developing reorder or new order stock quantities. Each of these various activities impacts or is impacted by the other tasks. For example, if the ***order quantity*** (the number of items ordered) is larger than ***demand*** (the number of items needed), too many units will be received for the ***consumption rate*** (how fast the items will be used). In the grocery store business, if the manager orders more milk than can be sold by the sell-by date, the milk will spoil and will have to be thrown out. Conversely, if the grocery store manager doesn't order sufficient quantities of milk, some consumers may find that the store has run out of milk. The store not only suffers the immediate loss of a sale of a gallon of milk, but it could end up losing a customer as well, who will go to another store for his future milk needs. Think about the last time you found the store was out of the commodity you were after. How many times would you return to that store if they were always out of the product you were shopping for?

INVENTORY IN THE SUPPLY CHAIN

To avoid out-of-stock issues, companies hold various types of goods in inventory, such as raw materials, work-in-process, and finished goods. Each of these types of inventory is intended to *decouple*, or separate, one step of the process from the next. By holding inventory of a product at various stages of completion, ***decoupling*** the process allows the supply chain to continue, even if there is a temporary halt in the overall chain of events, such as production slowdowns caused by machine failure.

For example, let's consider inventory and decoupling in the wool supply chain. ***Raw material inventory*** is the wool taken from the sheep, which is stored in a temporary facility waiting to be processed at the factory. At the factory, there are several steps involved in turning the raw wool into a finished piece of wool cloth. Along the factory process line, the partially finished product is temporarily stored until the next process occurs. This is ***work-in-process*** (or partially finished) ***inventory***. Finally, the completed wool cloth is stored pending transfer to the distribution system and on to the consumer. This manufactured cloth is ***finished goods inventory***. In each inventory case, the various processes are decoupled from each other. This becomes more complex when the entire supply chain is considered because, as shown in Figure 3.1 below, inventory is found everywhere along the supply chain.

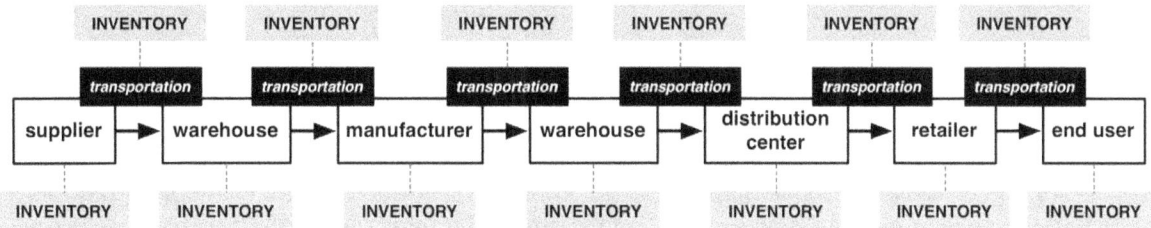

Figure 3.1 - Inventory in the Simple Supply Chain

When discussing inventory management, there is a spectrum of views on how much inventory firms should maintain. Within the various inventory level options, there are competing attitudes and ideas. One attitude is that inventory is something that hides inefficiency, because, if you always have more inventory in stock than you need, it may be possible that an inefficient purchasing department could operate without its inefficiencies affecting production. Another similar attitude is that having more inventory than is needed costs a company a lot of extra holding costs. A competing attitude is that holding inventory is an essential tool that ensures organizational capabilities to meet customers' needs. Inventory, in fact, can be described by all of these attitudes. Organizations must examine their inventory inefficiencies and holding costs while using inventory to provide operational continuity and maximize levels of service.

Maintaining a valid level of inventory is a balancing act. Figure 3.2 demonstrates an overview of the inventory management is trying to balance. The purchasing professional needs to minimize costs associated with buying and holding inventory. It also shows that the purchasing professional must ensure that

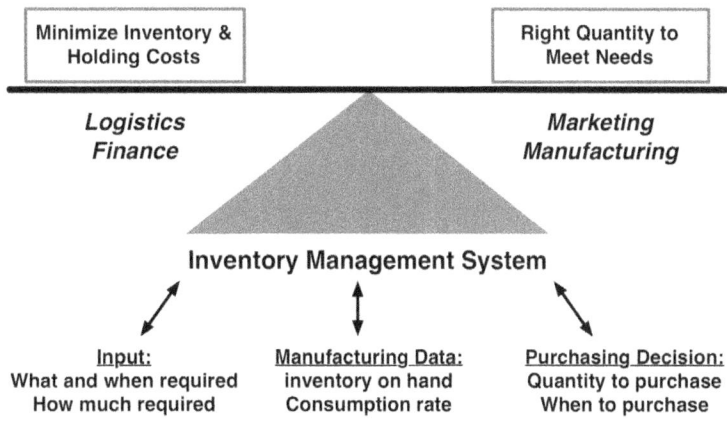

Figure 3.2 - Inventory Balance

there are sufficient quantities of inventory on hand to meet operational needs. To achieve this, the purchasing professional needs data input, such as how many of what items are required when. The purchasing professional also needs real-time or regularly updated information on what inventory is on hand and how fast it is being consumed. From these inputs, the purchasing professional can decide on the quantity to procure and when to procure it.

Maintaining an inventory balance is essential in the globally competitive 21st century manufacturing industry. Today's firms understand that inventory is a cost and they can control this cost using techniques such as *Just in time (JIT)* inventory and *EOQ* models.

ATTEMPTING TO HOLD MINIMUM INVENTORY BY JUST IN TIME

Just in time is a widely used business strategy to reduce in-process inventory and its corresponding carrying costs. The just in time approach is incorporated into today's inventory control systems. It focuses on holding less inventory and instead coordinating supply chains so that desired inventory arrives "just in time" for it to be used. Just in time (JIT) originated in the Toyota Taiichi Ohno automotive plant as part of their lean production process with automobile parts being delivered and received just in time for the manufacturing process. JIT systems are designed to deliver the right item at the right place in the right quantity at the required time. Ideally, JIT eliminates raw material or in-process inventory needs and often results in more frequent deliveries of smaller quantities.

JIT is sometimes described as a **pull system**, in which the downstream process pulls the material from the succeeding step. For example, when a customer purchases a product, this consumption would pull a replacement item from the finished inventory. As the product is removed from the finished inventory, it causes the manufacturer to send another product from manufacturing. This sequence continues through the supply chain until the raw material is reached. For example, when you purchase an automobile oil filter from Otto's Auto Parts and your sale is rung up in the store's computerized **EPOS (electronic point of sale)** system, this information is immediately sent to Otto's supplier, Homer Wholesalers, which pulls the item from its shelves and immediately sends this information to the oil filter manufacturer, Philadelphia Filters, so that they can manufacture and send a new filter. In general, this pull process depends on the quantity consumed in each step in the process, pulling material, pieces, parts, and components from the preceding step just as it is needed.

This is counter to the **push manufacturing supply concept**, in which each step in the manufacturing process pushes its finished product to the next stage, regardless of the subsequent need. Push systems are not based on the quantity needs of the next step in the supply chain but instead on other factors such as historical demand or the rate at which the manufacturer can produce the product. For example, seasonal items such as beach towels and snow shovels may be part of a push system because their orders are determined using historical demand. Because they are not based on immediate demand, push systems can lead to **overstocking**, in which $15 beach towels must be sold off at the end of the summer for $3.99.

From the view of the purchasing specialist, JIT involves the essential need to know precisely what is required and when it must be available for use. In today's environment, to achieve this often requires complex computer programs. These computer programs continually monitor the raw and in-process inventories, consumption rates, and forecasted needs to determine a recommended procurement request. Depending on the organization, the recommended procurement request can be fully automated or manually processed.

CHECK IT OUT!

Check out Chapter 5 for even more information about **just in time** systems!

ORDERING & HOLDING COSTS

In the world of purchasing, there are additional costs associated with getting the right quantity, which extend beyond the actual unit cost suppliers charge you for their product. These other costs are associated with *placing orders* and *holding inventory*. These cost interactions become critical considerations for purchasing when deciding how much to order and when to place the order.

ORDERING COSTS

Every purchase order a company places has an associated cost. The full cost of placing an order is related to a variety of factors, including the different labor rates for each person involved in: the purchasing department placing the order, the warehouse department receiving the order physically, and the accounting department paying the invoice. Other costs may involve other purchasing activities, such as:

- *clerical support,*
- *searching for the right supplier,*
- *phone calls,*
- *negotiation time,*
- *forms,*
- *expediting services, and*
- *order tracking time requirements.*

Ordering costs are all costs associated with placing and receiving an order.

INVENTORY HOLDING COSTS

When the purchasing department makes decisions on the quantity they will order, they must add into their total cost equation the reality that having inventory sitting in a warehouse incurs a cost. This ***inventory holding cost*** is the cost associated with maintaining the physical space, building insurance, heat, electricity, warehouse staff, warehouse equipment, and *inventory shrinkage*. There are also the financial costs associated with the cost of capital (i.e., money) borrowed to procure the material. On top of all these costs are ***lost opportunity costs***, which are the costs associated with using the company's funds to procure the material versus some other needed activity.

> **How are ordering costs calculated? Let's look at an example!**
>
> Don's airplane engine repair shop must order special aircraft parts on a daily basis. Don wants to understand how much these purchasing orders cost his firm on average. Once he has determined his ordering costs, Don intends to use this information in determining his own repair shop's service costs to customers.
>
> Don conducted a time and motion study to determine how long it takes: the purchasing department to plan an order, the warehouse to receive and process the order, and the finance department to check and pay the supplier's invoice. His time and motion study determined that three people are involved in the process of ordering, receiving, and paying for the parts ordered. Each person's fully loaded hourly cost is $45. The time and motion study also revealed that, on average, it takes 15 minutes to place and track an order, another 15 minutes to receive the order at the warehouse and place it into stock, and 30 minutes to check the order and pay the supplier's invoice.
>
> With this information, Don is now ready to determine his average ordering cost!
>
> **Average ordering cost = employee cost per hour x number of hours**
>
> **Average ordering cost = $45 per hour x (15 min + 15 min + 30 min)**
>
> = $45 per hour x (60 min) = $45 per hour x 1 hour = <u>$45 per order</u>

Whenever a firm must hold inventory, a physical environment must be maintained. At the same time, history is quick to show that when material is stored, inventory shrinkage occurs. **Shrinkage** is the loss of inventory due to theft, loss, deterioration, or physical damage such that it can no longer be used. Regardless of the cause of shrinkage, the firm loses the cost of the items that were once purchased but can no longer be used or sold, which plays a significant part in reduced future profits.

Thus, *inventory holding costs* are all costs required to maintain and carry an inventory. Holding costs are often stated as a percentage of inventory value. As we will see in the next section of this chapter, costs of ordering, and holding costs are used in the development of the EOQ model.

> **How are holding costs calculated? Let's look at another example!**
>
> Don's airplane engine repair shop must maintain an inventory of critical items. These items are required to quickly respond to air carriers' immediate needs. Based on historical records, Don has identified that holding costs are, on average, 30% of his inventory material cost per year.
>
> If Don's material cost is $25, what is the average holding cost? Let's calculate!
>
> **Holding cost = average holding cost percentage x material cost**
>
> **Holding cost = 30% per hour x $25 = <u>$7.50</u>**

As we will see in the next section of this chapter, costs of ordering, and holding costs are used in the development of the EOQ model.

WORKINGS OF THE EOQ MODEL

Economic order quantity (EOQ) is the oldest and most commonly known inventory control model. Over many years, it has saved many a purchasing staff countless hours of decision-making frustration as they attempt to answer the time old question: *When and how much should we order?* Two major reasons for the model's successful longevity are its ease of use and its robust nature as a model.

Purchasing professionals find EOQ easy to use because it is based on a clear set of assumptions and its mathematical calculations are simple. The key assumptions that form the foundation for the EOQ model include:

1. *Demand is independent, known, and constant (does not change).*

2. *Inventory receipt is instantaneous and complete.*

3. *Lead time (the time between placing and receiving an order) is known and constant (does not change).*

4. *No quantity discounts are allowed.*

5. *Stockouts (running out of inventory) will not occur if orders are placed when indicated and for the calculated amounts.*

Figure 3.3 below illustrates these various assumptions. First, **demand is independent and constant** is demonstrated by the constant linear reduction of inventory level over time.

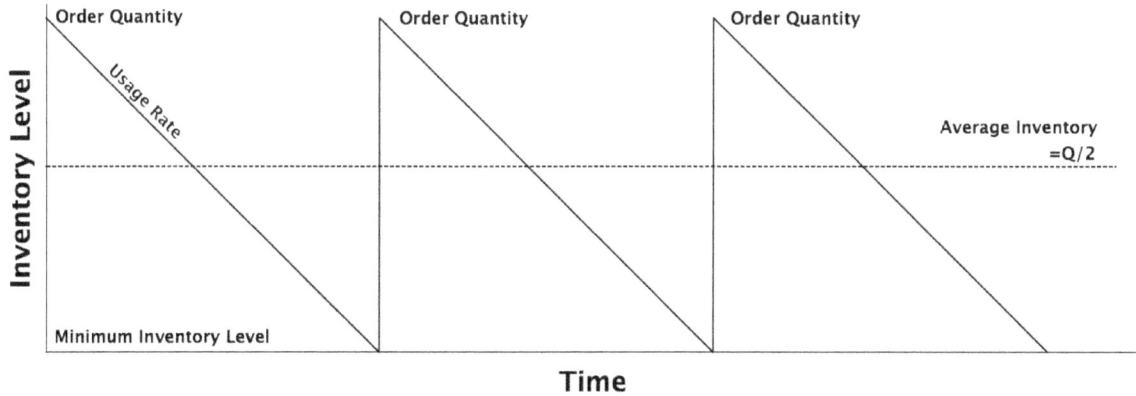

Figure 3.3 - Inventory Usage over Time

Second, the saw tooth shape demonstrates that when the inventory reaches the predetermined minimum level, a new order occurs. Instantaneously, the inventory reaches its predetermined maximum level. According to the EOQ model, ***the full order is received immediately***. While, in reality, inventory may not arrive instantaneously, EOQ's robust capabilities allow this assumption to remain valid. Thirdly, Figure 3.3 also demonstrates that ***lead time is known and constant*** as the cycles are fully repetitive with the same durations from cycle to cycle. No deviations occur due to varying lead times. Fourth, ***no quantity discounts can be negotiated***. Finally, since the inventory is received instantaneously, ***no stockouts occur***. When the last item is consumed, a full order is received. All of the five assumptions stated above are key to the EOQ model's ability to provide a recommended order quantity. These assumptions also support the model's robust characteristics.

The EOQ model can be described as robust because it yields very satisfactory results over a wide range of input variations. For example, while one assumption is that the demand is fully known and constant, the actual data used may show that variation in demand occurs over time. As will be shown later, this change does not affect the model's output. The model's mathematical simplicity allows the user to perform numerous calculations in a short timeframe to test the output based on varying inputs. This is also known as conducting sensitivity analysis. ***Sensitivity analysis*** occurs when the purchasing professional analyzes a procurement decision using various options, such as different ordering costs and holding costs, to determine the impact on order quantity.

To derive an EOQ, the user must know the following information:

Q = Number of pieces per order

D = Annual demand in unit

H = Inventory carrying costs per unit per year

S = Ordering costs per year

With this information, we can calculate ***Q**** or the ***economic order quantity***. Before delving into EOQ mathematical efforts, let's examine Figure 3.4, EOQ Cost Curves, below.

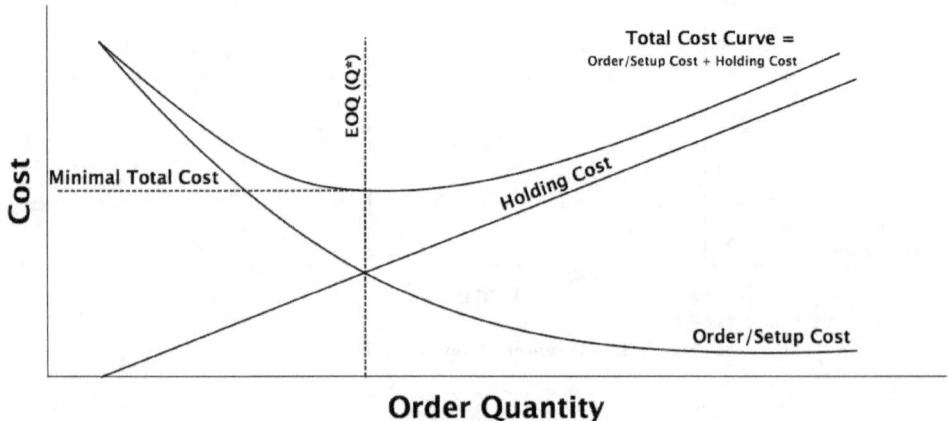

Figure 3.4 - EOQ Cost Curves

Figure 3.4 contains three curves, which indicate order costs, holding costs, and total cost values based on order quantity. The ***order cost curve*** is generally viewed as a decreasing cost curve based on an increasing number of items ordered per order. For example, Equation 1 below shows you the unit order cost when a firm orders this year' needs of a 1,000 units all at once for an order cost of $25 for the one-time annual order. Equation 2 shows you the unit order cost when a firm orders 100 units 10 times per year at an order cost of $25 for each of the ten orders.

EQUATION 1   **Order cost #1 = $25/1,000 units = $0.025/unit**

EQUATION 2   **Order cost #2 = $25/100 units = $0.25/unit**

Comparing equation 1 to equation 2 reveals that *by ordering a greater number of units, the per unit cost decreases*, which is also shown in the order cost curve in Figure 3.4 above. Figure 3.5 below provides another view of how the per item order cost decreases as the number of units ordered increases.

Order Cost = $25 per order	
Units Ordered	**Ordering Cost per Unit**
10	($25/10) = $2.50
100	($25/100) = $0.25
250	($25/250) = $0.10
500	($25/500) = $0.05
1000	($25/1000) = $0.025

Figure 3.5 - Decreasing Ordering Cost per Unit with Increasing Order Size

The ***holding cost curve***, as shown in Figure 3.4 previously, indicates that the cost of holding increases as the order quantity increases. As previously mentioned, holding costs are often stated as a percentage of inventory value. As such, the larger the quantity ordered, the more you will receive at one time and the more it will cost to hold the larger inventory over the same time period. Equations 3 and 4 demonstrate this concept with each $25 and $250 of inventory ordered, with an annual holding cost average of 30%. (Remember: 30% = 0.30)

EQUATION 3   **Holding cost = 30% x $25 worth of inventory ordered = $7.50**

EQUATION 4   **Holding cost = 30% x $250 worth of inventory ordered = $75.00**

Clearly, as the quantity of inventory held in stock increases, the cost of holding this extra inventory increases as well.

The third curve of Figure 3.4 is the ***total cost curve***. This curve is the summation of the ordering and holding cost curves, which means that for every different value of order quantity, the order and the holding cost are added together to get the *total cost* value. This resulting total cost curve is parabolic, or u-shaped, because costs start out at a maximum level, decrease to a minimum level, and then begin to increase again. EOQ takes the various cost relationships into account to derive the *lowest total cost curve point*. This will be the EOQ point that produces the *minimum total cost*.

To clearly understand how EOQ derives the minimum total cost point, an understanding of annual ordering cost, annual holding cost, and their relationship is required. Let's now look at annual ordering cost.

ANNUAL ORDERING COSTS

Annual ordering cost is simply the total number of orders placed per year multiplied by how much each order costs. Equation 5 shows this relationship for a company that places 10 orders a year at a cost of $35 per order.

EQUATION 5   **Annual ordering cost = Total orders per year x order cost**

Annual ordering cost = 10 orders x $35 per order = $350

Often, a company will know how many units were purchased in a year and the minimum order lot size but will be missing the ***total number of orders*** placed in that year. This can easily be calculated using Equation 6, in which a company has procured 14,500 units in the past year and the vendor sells the units in lot sizes of 50 each.

EQUATION 6   **Total number of orders = Annual demand/purchased lot size**

Total number of orders = 14,500/50 = 290 orders

Equation 7 provides the final ***annual ordering cost*** formula using the values used in equations 5 and 6 above.

EQUATION 7   **Annual cost = (Annual demand/order size) x cost per order**

Annual cost = (14,500/50) x $35 = $10,150

As previously discussed, the annual ordering cost is just one part of the equation. Annual holding cost is the other part of the EOQ formula.

ANNUAL HOLDING COSTS

As discussed earlier, ***annual holding cost*** equals inventory costs multiplied by holding cost per unit per year. Since the EOQ assumption requires inventory to be consumed at a steady rate, the annual inventory cost is an average value. This is illustrated in the example to the right, which shows that inventory starts at a maximum level and is consumed at a steady rate over time. Thus, on average, half the time there will be more than 50% of the inventory present and for half the time less than 50% of the inventory is present.

> Frank's Dairy receives boxes of shipping labels twice a year. Each shipment contains 600 shipping label units. Frank's Dairy consumes the labels at a monthly constant rate of 100 units per month. The company's shipping label supplier has zero lead time. Frank's Dairy does not maintain a safety stock. The following chart demonstrates the first six months of label use.
>
> | Month | Labels Issued | Labels in Inventory | |
> |---|---|---|---|
> | late December | | 600 received | |
> | January | 100 | 500 | |
> | February | 100 | 400 | |
> | March | 100 | 300 | *average stock* |
> | April | 100 | 200 | |
> | May | 100 | 100 | |
> | June | 100 | 0 | |
> | late June | | 600 received | |
> | July | 100 | 500 | |

Figure 3.6 - Inventory Usage Over Time at Frank's Dairy

Thus, the annual inventory level is the average of the overall inventory, which can be quickly derived by dividing the maximum inventory level by 2. Our example of Frank's Dairy in Figure 3.6 above shows the relationship of constant usage over time. In this example, March is the middle of the consumed inventory process. For the first three months, Frank's inventory is over 300 and for the last three months, it is under 300. Therefore, Frank's Dairy's average inventory is 300 units. Equation 8 shows how the relationship between the average inventory level and the holding cost per unit per year equals the annual holding cost. For this example, a company orders 600 units per order with an estimated holding cost of $0.16 per unit per year.

EQUATION 8 Annual holding cost =

(Order quantity/2) x annual unit holding cost

Annual holding cost = (600/2) x $0.16 = $48.00

ECONOMIC ORDER QUANTITY

As shown in Figure 3.4 previously, ***EOQ***, or the ***economic order quantity***, occurs when the *annual order cost equals the annual holding cost*. Figure 3.4 also shows that, as the order quantity moves to the left or right of this point, the total costs will increase. If the order quantity decreases below the EOQ point, the order cost per unit increases. This results in an increase in total costs. If the order quantity increases beyond EOQ point, the holding costs increase and cancel out an incremental large order cost savings. This equality is shown in Equations 9 and 10, which show that that annual holding cost equals the annual order cost. Equation 10 shows the abbreviated form of this EOQ relationship.

EQUATION 9   **Annual holding cost = Annual ordering cost**

(ordering quantity/2) x annual unit holding cost =

(annual demand/order quantity) x order cost

EQUATION 10 $(Q/2) \times H = (D/Q) \times S$

Starting with Equation 10, the **order quantity**, Q, can be derived as shown in Equation 11.

EQUATION 11 $(Q/2) \times H = (D/Q) \times S$

$Q/2 = (D/Q) \times S/H$

$(Q/2) \times (Q/D) = S/H$

$Q^2/2D = S/H$

$Q^2 = (2DS)/H$

$Q^* = \sqrt{(2DS)/H}$

EOQ, as represented by the symbol Q^*, is the square root of 2 times the annual demand times the order cost divided by holding cost. Shown below in Figure 3.7 is an example of an EOQ calculation using data from Frank's Dairy on page 38.

Frank's Dairy must decide how many milk cartons should be purchased at one time to minimize inventory cost while optimizing the cost of placing the order. Historically, Frank's Dairy purchases 57,000 milk cartons per year (D). Each time Frank's Dairy places an order, it costs the firm $35 (S). Holding cost is estimated at $0.24 per unit per year (H) based on a per unit purchase price of $0.80 and a holding cost of 30% per unit per year.

With this information, how do we determine Frank's EOQ point?

$Q^* = \sqrt{(2DS)/H}$

$Q^* = \sqrt{(2 \times 57{,}000 \times 35)/0.24}$

$Q^* = 4{,}077.38$ or 4,077 **units** (rounded to a whole number)

Figure 3.7 - Calculating the EOQ Point at Frank's Dairy

Once EOQ has been determined, the firm can then calculate how many orders and how often they should be placed within a year.

ORDERS PER YEAR, REORDER POINT, AND SAFETY STOCK

Answering the question of how many units should be ordered during each purchase is only part of the question. The fuller question is: *How many orders will be required each year and how frequently should the orders occur?* Understanding the annually estimated number of units required and the EOQ allows for the easy calculation of how many orders a year to place. Equation 12 expands on the example from Frank's Dairy to demonstrate how the **annual number of orders** to place is calculated.

EQUATION 12   **Annual number of orders = Annual demand/EOQ = D/Q***

Annual number of orders = 57,000/4,077 = 13.98

In this example, the firm will place approximately 14 orders a year (13.98 rounded to the nearest whole number). Referring back to the formula in Equation 5, Frank's Dairy can expect to spend $490 annually on ordering costs.

Annual ordering cost = Total orders per year x order cost

Annual ordering cost = 14 orders x $35 per order = $490

Yet, now that the number of orders per year is known, *how often should the orders be placed to minimize holding costs?* Returning to the EOQ assumptions, the answer to this question becomes: **the orders should be placed on an evenly distributed annual basis.** Calculating the order frequency requires knowing how many days a year the firm works and how many orders per year will be made. Equation 13 provides the formula for determining how many working days should occur between orders for Frank's Dairy, which works 260 days a year.

EQUATION 13   **Order frequency = Working days per year/annual orders**

Order frequency = 260/14 = 18.57 = 19 working days per order

In this example Frank's dairy will place an order every 19 working days. Figure 3.8 below analyzes the impact of the *number of orders per year* on the company's *total annual holding cost*.

As Figure 3.8 demonstrates, the total cost decreases as the number of orders per year increase – until it reaches a particular point. In this example, that point is fourteen orders, which is where the lowest total cost occurs. From this point on, the total cost increases as a direct function of the increasing cost for each additional order. At this point in time, a firm can easily determine its EOQ, number of orders per year, and how often to place the orders. Each of these formulas can be easily performed on a calculator, entered into a computer spreadsheet, or incorporated into a larger inventory or procurement computer system. One question that remains is: **How low should the firm's inventory reach before an order is placed?** EOQ identifies how many units should be ordered, but how low the inventory can go is not a factor of EOQ. It is instead a factor of the real world issues of delivery lead times and the firm's strategic customer service view, which may or may not allow stockouts to occur, which brings us to the *reorder point*.

NUMBER OF ORDERS	COST OF ORDERS $35 x number of orders	QUANTITY PER ORDER 57,000 per year/number of orders	HOLDING COST PER YEAR (quantity per order/2) x $0.24	TOTAL COST order cost + holding cost
10	$350.00	5,700	$684.00	$1034.00
	$35 x 10 = $350	57,000/10 = 5,700	(5,700/2) x $0.24 = $684	$350 + $684 = $1034
11	$385.00	5,182	$621.84	$1006.84
12	$420.00	4,750	$570.00	$990.00
13	$455.00	4,385	$526.20	$981.20
14	$490.00	4,071	$488.52	$978.52
15	$525.00	3,800	$456.00	$981.00
16	$560.00	3,563	$427.56	$987.56

Figure 3.8 - Ordering, Holding, and Total Costs at Frank's Dairy

REORDER POINT

By definition, the **reorder point (ROP)** is the inventory level at which the purchasing department places an order. The order will restock the inventory to the maximum level, as established by the EOQ order number and ROP level. The two primary inputs to deriving ROP are the firm's *strategic view on customer service* and *product lead time*.

The firm's **strategic view of customer service** includes the decision of whether or not to allow stockouts and, if allowed, how often they will be tolerated. All companies are in the business of satisfying their customers. Achieving 100% customer service is complex and multi-faceted, but one critical factor is to ensure that every customer can purchase what they need from you in the right quantities of every item every time. To achieve this requires the company to stock a large inventory, which, as has been discussed, is a cost to the company. Thus, the firm strives to provide a high level of customer service by maintaining reasonable inventory levels. This controls holding costs but generates a condition where the firm may not always have what the customer wants when they might want it.

After a company's senior management establishes its customer service level, the next critical ROP input is the unit lead time. ***Lead time*** is the amount of time between placing the order and receiving the goods ordered. ROP is the real world acknowledgement that it takes time from when an order is placed until the material arrives at the required location.

Determining the ROP involves understanding daily customer demand and how long it will take to receive the material once ordered. Customer demand is determined using historical information or forecasting. With this information, a reorder point can be established, as shown in Equation 14, in which Frank's dairy estimates a lead time of 10 working days.

EQUATION 14   **ROP = (annual demand/number of working days) x lead time**

ROP = (57,000/260) x 10 = 2,192

Based on Frank's annual demand and number of working days, it is estimated that 219 milk cartons are used each business day. Frank's Dairy's supplier says that they can deliver the EOQ volume within 10 days of receiving an order. To ensure that the production facility does not run out, Frank's Dairy must reorder when inventory levels reach 2,192 cartons.

EOQ is a simple and straightforward robust model. It provides purchasing personnel with the ability to quantify how much and when to place a material order. Each of these decisions ultimately supports the organization's own customer service goals. Yet, while EOQ is a robust model, real world situations exist that generate conditions where the company may run out of critical inventories. Firms minimize this risk through the use of *safety stock*, also called **policy stock** or **buffer stock**.

SAFETY STOCK

Safety stock is extra inventory that provides a buffer for real world events that impact the firm's inventory levels. In the real world, orders are delayed due to floods, storms, human error, or transportation problems. Orders may also be delayed when procurement authorization procedures are delayed in the purchaser's company. Unanticipated customer demand can also dramatically impact inventory levels. In each of these situations, the company is faced with the potential of running out of inventory. As previously discussed, any time a company runs out of inventory, it will, at minimum, lose out on sales.

To minimize this risk, firms implement ***safety stock policies***. Unlike the EOQ model, which provides a definitive order quantity, there are a variety of techniques for calculating safety stock levels to accommodate uncertainty in demand and lead time. With highly independent inventory level needs and customer service satisfaction objectives, each firm must establish a safety stock level that caters to its unique operating environment.

Recognizing that each firm has a unique operating environment, one way to approach safety stock mathematically is to use a ***modified reorder point formula***. Let's begin by restating Equation 14, the reorder point formula.

EQUATION 14   **ROP = (annual demand/working days) x lead time**

In Equation 15 below, we modify Equation 14 to match the firm's unique operating environment by altering the *lead time* to a function of *safety stock*.

EQUATION 15   ROP = (annual demand/working days) x safety stock lead time

The ***safety stock lead time*** factor is the length of time to which the firm wants to change its lead time to minimize the risk of running out of inventory. This resulting increased inventory level can be viewed as insurance. This insurance is acknowledged as costing the firm holding costs above the minimum achievable by applying the EOQ model. Although insurance (in the form of extra holding cost) is a cost, this extra cost is worth the peace of mind that it brings to many companies because they are now covered should problems arise.

Development of the safety stock lead time can be based on historical data, such as how often the supplier has missed their promised lead times and by how much. This historical information allows the firm to predict the inventory level they want to procure as safety stock. As an example, Frank's Dairy faces excessive losses if they run out of milk cartons before they complete the production run. Based on historical data, Frank's Dairy's milk carton supplier often delays deliveries by two days. Thus, *how many days of safety stock should Frank's dairy maintain as insurance against the supplier being late?*

To determine the safety stock levels, Equation 15 incorporates Frank's daily milk carton demands with the potential supplier delay days.

EQUATION 15   ROP = (annual demand/working days) x safety stock lead time

ROP = (57,000/260) x 2 = 438

Based on daily milk carton usage and the potential two-day late delivery risk, Frank's dairy should have an extra 438 milk cartons on hand as a safety stock. This increased inventory level will increase Frank's holding costs but insure against larger losses that a milk carton stock outage would produce. Taking lead-time and safety stock lead-time into account, Frank's reorder point is now 2630, or the *lead time* (2192) *plus the safety stock lead time* (438).

ECONOMIC ORDER QUANTITY & DISCOUNTS

Purchasing professionals use the EOQ as a foundation for minimizing costs of ordering and holding inventory. One example of this is when they **negotiate a quantity discount**. These discounts must be considered at each succeeding point to determine the best quantity to order. Let's consider an example of how a discount structure affects the EOQ. For our example, let's assume the following information:

- Usage per year: 4,000 units
- Order Cost: $40 per order
- Carrying Cost: 10% of unit price
- Unit Cost: $20

We calculate the EOQ using the basic price:

$$Q^* = \sqrt{(2DS)/H} = \sqrt{(2 \times 4{,}000 \times 40)/(20 \times 0.10)} = 400$$

Based on the information above, the EOQ formula tells us that if we order 400 items per order, we will minimize our costs of ordering and our costs of holding inventory. However, if our supplier offers us a bulk discount, which will reduce the cost per item, then we will need to recalculate the EOQ to see if it will be worth ordering the larger quantity. Let's say we order 800 units rather than 400 units because we receive a bulk discount. This will mean that we will have fewer orders issued per year and our unit cost price will be less. However, if our quantity is greater on each order, we will incur extra holding costs. The objective is to assess the range of offered bulk discounts and see if our costs outweigh our savings. The bulk discounts structure for our example is:

- 800-1,599 units per order: 2% discount
- 1,600-3,199 units per order: 4% discount
- 3,200 or more units per order: 5% discount

We can now analyze our data to see if it is worth purchasing fewer orders of larger quantities with bulk discounts offered using the following model shown in Figure 3.9 below.

	ORDER QUANTITY	EOQ 400	BUY 800	BUY 1600	BUY 3200
line 1					
line 2	DISCOUNT PER QUANTITY	zero	2% 2% x $20 unit cost = $0.40 per item	4% 4% x $20 unit cost = $0.80 per item	5% 5% x $20 unit cost = $1.00 per item
line 3	AVERAGE ORDERS PER YEAR usage per year/order quantity	10	5	2.5	1.25
line 4	ORDERS SAVED orders per year for EOQ - line 3	zero	5	7.5	8.75
line 5	ORDERING COSTS SAVED line 4 x order cost	zero	$200.00 (5 x $40)	$300.00 (7.5 x $40)	$350.00 (8.75 x $40)
line 6	EXTRA DISCOUNT PER NEW QUANTITY PER YEAR annual usage x discount amount	zero	$1600.00 (4000 x $0.40)	$3200.00 (4000 x $0.80)	$4000.00 (4000 x $1.00)
line 7	TOTAL SAVINGS BY ISSUING FEWER ORDERS line 5 + line 6	zero	$1800.00 ($200 + $1600)	$3500.00 ($300 + $3200)	$4350 ($350 + $4000)
line 8	EXTRA HOLDING COSTS PER YEAR order quantity x unit price x carrying cost	$800.00 (400 x $20.00 x 0.1)	$1568.00 (800 x $19.60 x 0.1)	$3072.00 (1600 x $19.20 x 0.1)	$6080 (3200 x $19.00 x 0.1)
line 9	TOTAL EXTRA COSTS FROM INCREASED QUANTITY line 8 - holding cost for EOQ	zero	$768.00 ($1568 - $800)	$2272.00 ($3072 - $800)	$5280.00 ($6080 - $800)
line 10	NET GAINS/LOSSES line 7 - line 9	zero	+ $1032.00 ($1800 - $786)	+ $1228.00 ($3500 - $2272)	- $930.00 ($4350 - $5280)

Figure 3.9 - EOQ and Discount Structures

Using the information calculated in the table above, the most economic order quantity to purchase, given the volume discount structure, is 1600 units because there is the greatest gain - $1228. This is the lowest purchase cost where the greatest benefit is gained, when the ordering costs and the holding costs are minimized.

A CLOSER LOOK AT THE EOQ AND DISCOUNT STRUCTURES TABLE

Let's now take a closer look at Figure 3.9 line by line and examine how each of the values are calculated.

line 1	ORDER QUANTITY	EOQ 400	BUY 800	BUY 1600	BUY 3200

Line 1 shows the different quantities we can buy for each calculation. The first value, 400, is the economic order quantity. The next three values - 800, 1600, and 3200 - are the minimum quantities required for each level of discount.

line 2	DISCOUNT PER QUANTITY	zero	2% 2% x $20 unit cost = $0.40 per item	4% 4% x $20 unit cost = $0.80 per item	5% 5% x $20 unit cost = $1.00 per item

The top portion of line 2 shows the discount offered for each quantity ordered. For example, if you buy 800 items, there is a 2% discount. The bottom portion of line 2 shows the actual monetary discount given per item purchased. For example, if you buy 1600 items, you will receive a discount of $0.80 on each item. This discount amount is calculated by multiplying the discount percentage by the item's unit cost.

line 3	AVERAGE ORDERS PER YEAR usage per year/order quantity	10	5	2.5	1.25

Line 3 lists the number of orders you would have to place per year if all of your year's orders were limited to the quantity shown in line 1. For example, if you buy 800 items each time you place an order, you would need to place 5 orders per year. This value is calculated by dividing the number of items you use in a year (4,000 in our example) by the order quantity (line 1).

line 4	ORDERS SAVED orders per year for EOQ - line 3	zero	5	7.5	8.75

Line 4 shows the number of orders fewer you would have to place if you ordered in quantities larger than the economic order quantity value. For example, if you ordered in quantities of 800 items per order, you would have to place five fewer orders per year than in you ordered in quantities of 400 items per order, which is our predetermined economic order quantity. To calculate this value, you subtract the average orders per year in line 3 from the ten orders per year required if you purchased the EOQ of 400 items per order.

| line 5 | ORDERING COSTS SAVED
line 4 x order cost | zero | $200.00
(5 x $40) | $300.00
(7.5 x $40) | $350.00
(8.75 x $40) |

Line 5 now shows how much money you would save in ordering costs by purchasing the items the number of times per year calculated in line 3. For example, if you ordered in quantities of 800, you will save $200 per year in ordering costs. This value is calculated by multiplying the number of orders saved (line 4) by the order cost, which is $40 in our example.

| line 6 | EXTRA DISCOUNT PER NEW QUANTITY PER YEAR
annual usage x discount amount | zero | $1600.00
(4000 x $0.40) | $3200.00
(4000 x $0.80) | $4000.00
(4000 x $1.00) |

Like line 5, line 6 also involves monetary savings by showing how much money is saved by ordering the items at the bulk discount. For example, if you order 1600 items at a time, you would receive a $3200 discount from the supplier. This value is calculated by multiplying the number of items used per year (4000 in our example) by the monetary discount per item as shown in the lower portion of line 2.

| line 7 | TOTAL SAVINGS BY ISSUING FEWER ORDERS
line 5 + line 6 | zero | $1800.00
($200 + $1600) | $3500.00
($300 + $3200) | $4350
($350 + $4000) |

Line 7 shows the total savings experienced as you make increasingly fewer orders with increasingly larger order sizes. For example, if your order quantity is 800, you will save a total of $1800 per year. This value is calculated by adding the ordering costs saved (line 5) and the quantity-based price discount (line 6).

| line 8 | EXTRA HOLDING COSTS PER YEAR
order quantity x unit price x carrying cost | $800.00
(400 x $20.00 x 0.1) | $1568.00
(800 x $19.60 x 0.1) | $3072.00
(1600 x $19.20 x 0.1) | $6080
(3200 x $19.00 x 0.1) |

While lines 5 through 7 showed how much more you would save with increasing discounts and order sizes and less frequent orders, line 8 shows how much more money you would spend in holding costs by placing orders of greater and greater numbers of items. Holding costs would naturally increase because you would have to hold and store more items until they would be used. For example, if you ordered 1600 items at a time, your extra holding costs would now be $3072, up considerably from the $800 holding costs when placing orders in your economic order quantity of 400. This value is calculated by multiplying the order quantity (line 1) by the unit price (our item price of $20 minus the discount shown in line 2) by the carrying cost (10% in our example).

| line 9 | TOTAL EXTRA COSTS FROM INCREASED QUANTITY
line 8 - holding cost for EOQ | zero | $768.00
($1568 - $800) | $2272.00
($3072 - $800) | $5280.00
($6080 - $800) |

Line 9 shows how much extra we would spend with order sizes greater than our economic order quantity. For example, if we were to place orders in quantities of 3200, we would spend $5280 more per year in holding costs than if we were to place orders in quantities of 400, our economic order quantity. To calculate this value, subtract the $800 holding costs for EOQ orders (as shown in the EOQ column of line 8) from the extra holding costs per year calculated in line 8.

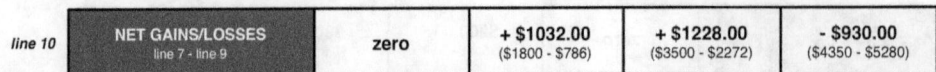

Finally, line 10 shows if we have an overall loss or gain financially when straying from our economic order quantity or 400 items per order. For example, if we order 800 items at a time, we would have a gain of $1032 compared to placing orders of 400 items at a time. This value is calculated by subtracting the total extra costs by volume (line 9) from the total savings by volume (line 7).

Interestingly, if we ordered 3200 items at a time, the quantity that offers that largest discount, we would actually suffer an overall loss of $930 because of the higher holding costs. When dealing with bulk discount structures, it doesn't always pay to go for the biggest discount! Purchasing professional must factor in both the savings and costs of increased order sizes. Line 10 of our shows that the greatest savings can be attained from ordering in quantities of 1600, which would result in an overall annual gain of $1228.

A Final Look at Quantity Considerations

Purchasing personnel are faced with providing answers to the questions:

- *What should be ordered?*
- *How much should be ordered?*
- *When should the orders be placed?*

Answers to the first question can come from a variety of sources. Operations personnel may request specific quantities of a required material. In this situation, purchasing personnel must work with various supplier firms to obtain the best financial deal that meets operations needs within acceptable time frames. Purchasing personnel may also find themselves supporting projects with very specific material procurement requirements. Within this environment, the purchasing department is provided with exact specifications, quantities, and delivery dates which support the project's needs.

In other situations, the purchasing department is faced with the task of developing minimum inventory levels that support the firm's lean systems objectives. This situation requires purchasing personnel to work closely with the manufacturing department to develop communication and procurement methods that support the lean operations.

Other situations occur in which the purchasing department must calculate order quantities that balance order costs and holding costs to minimum levels. In this situation, the longstanding, flexible, and robust economic order quantity model is applied. The EOQ model provides an easy mathematical approach to understanding how many items to order at a single time and when to place the order. Frank's Dairy Summary in Action in the box below illustrates the various formulas presented in this chapter that would assist the purchasing department in identifying the new EOQ value.

With the various methods of deciding how much and when to place orders, the real world may conspire to prevent you from receiving the product early enough to prevent stockouts. To address this risk, firms establish a combination of reorder points and safety stock levels.

Reorder points identify the minimum inventory that the firm will reach before a procurement order occurs. ROP is based on daily demand and lead times. The firm may expand the ROP volumes by a margin referred to as safety stock. Safety stock can be viewed as insurance against the real world challenges of delivering a procured product on or before the promised delivery date. In this real world situation, the firm increases its inventory by a company-specific level. Each firm exists in a unique environment in which the impact of a potential stockout will have different ramifications. Based on the firm's strategic view and customer service policies, an extra inventory may be maintained as insurance against stockout conditions.

In the business world, managers, supervisors, purchasing professionals, and contracting personnel face procurement-based questions. Being able to answer these questions logically is critical to the company's long-term success. This chapter presented several methods that allow you to answer these questions.

Franks' Dairy Summary in Action

Frank's Dairy has the opportunity to support a fourth company by placing the Frank's brand name in the new grocery store's milk aisle. If Frank's Dairy accepts the offered contract, their annual order quantity is expected to increase from 57,000 units to 69,000 units per year.

Frank's Dairy's financial data will not change. They expect the following values to be valid for next year:

- Order cost = $35.00/ order
- Carton purchase price = $0.80/carton
- Holding cost = 30% of purchase price/unit
- Annual number of work days = 260
- Safety Stock lead time = 2 days

Using the formulas supplied, determine the following for Frank's Dairy:

A. new EOQ
B. number of orders per year
C. purchase cost
D. annual ordering cost
E. holding cost
F. total purchase and holding cost
G. safety stock levels

A. EOQ
$Q^* = \sqrt{(2DS)/H} = \sqrt{(2 * 69{,}000 * \$35)/ \$0.24} = 4486$

B. Number of orders/year
Number of orders = annual demand / EOQ = 69,000/ 4486 = 15.38 (round to 15)

C. Purchase cost
Purchase cost = order quantity × purchase price = 4486 × $0.80 = $3588.80

D. Ordering cost
Ordering cost = number of orders per year × order cost = 15 × $35 = $525.00

E. Holding cost
Holding cost = (order quantity/2) × unit holding cost = (4486/2) × (30% × $0.80) = $538.32

F. Total order and holding cost
Total cost = annual ordering cost + holding cost = $525.00 + $538.32 = $1063.32

G. Safety stock
Safety stock = [annual demand/#working days] × safety stock lead time
= [69,000/260] × 2 days = 531 (rounded from 530.77)

Chapter 3 Review Questions

1. What are the consequences when purchasing professionals buy too much of an item? What are the consequences when they buy too little of an item?

2. Where is inventory held in the supply chain?

3. What must a purchasing professional balance when determining desired inventory levels?

4. What is the difference between a *push system* and a *pull system* of inventory management? Provide an example of each type of system with your answer.

5. What are some examples of *inventory shrinkage*? In your opinion, what businesses or types of companies face the problem of shrinkage?

6. What is the *EOQ model* and when might a purchasing professional want to use it?

7. What information must you know to derive an *economic order quantity*?

8. What should happen when a company reaches a *reorder point* for a product?

9. Why is its *lead time* important in setting a product's reorder point?

10. Is the following statement true or false: *Based on the EOQ model, the greatest savings for a company are always attained by discounts on the largest quantities*? Explain your answer.

Chapter 3 Case Exercise

EOQ with Discounts at Myers of Michigan

Myers of Michigan is a distributor of small heaters used in manufacturing plants, warehouses, and other industrial facilities. The company's market area encompasses eastern Ohio, most of Pennsylvania, and all of New Jersey. You work for a national manufacturing firm and the Vice President of Logistics has asked you to determine the optimal number of heaters to purchase per order from Myers of Michigan based on the information and discount structure provided below. You currently order 200 heaters at a time, five times a year.

Annual Demand (heaters used per year): 1,000 heaters

Order Cost: $20 per order

Inventory Carrying Cost: 20% of unit price

Unit Cost (price per heater without discount): $5

Discount Structure:

- 400-799 units per order: 2% discount
- 800 or more units per order: 4% discount

INSTRUCTIONS:

1. Looking back to the Equation 11 and Figure 3.7 in this chapter's section on "Workings of the EOQ Model," first determine the EOQ without discounts for your annual order of heaters from Myers of Michigan.

2. Next, using the newly calculated EOQ and the information provided above, complete a table similar to the one provided in Figure 3.9 to determine the order quantity that will provide the greatest savings to your company. Your table should include calculations for the EOQ quantity, 400 units, and 800 units. (Remember: 400 and 800 are the starting points for each of the discount levels.)

Chapter 4

The Right Quality in Purchasing

Dr. Morgan Henrie

When the space shuttle lifts off for another trip into space, on board are a crew and a cargo hold full of very expensive material. As the February 2003 disaster of the space shuttle Columbia demonstrated, space travel carries a risk – a risk that if something goes wrong, loss of life is a real result. To minimize this risk, extensive engineering, detailed construction processes, extensive testing, and exhaustive training have all been combined into a holistic program designed to deliver the highest safety factor for each space trip.

Highly involved and intricately linked throughout each and every step of the space shuttle's design, engineering, construction, and maintenance are purchasing professionals. These highly skilled professionals bring millions of parts from around the world in the right quantities to the right place at the right time and of the right quality to achieve this complex system called space travel.

As discussed in Chapter 3, purchasing professionals contribute to this complex system as they continuously face the need to make right quantity buying decisions. It is their responsibility to ensure that the right part of the right quantity is delivered to the right place at the right time. They also face the additional responsibility of ensuring that the part delivered is of the right quality. This chapter explores the purchasing professional's role in obtaining the right quality level for the procured material.

When the space shuttle lifts off, an airplane takes off, or you take your family for an automobile ride, the safety and health of everyone onboard relies not only on the designers, engineers, and manufacturers but also on the quality procurement decisions of the many purchasing professionals involved in the design, engineering, construction, and maintenance of the shuttle, an airplane, or your car. To make these decisions requires the understanding that getting the right quality carries quantitative and qualitative attributes that must be met, which all have a variety of associated internal and external costs.

> **Take a minute to see if you can remember a case where different suppliers' prices appeared to be related to quality. Are higher priced cars selling for prices higher than their competition based on their perceived quality?**

As we will discuss later in the chapter, purchasing professionals can trade off a part's purchase price with various levels of quality. If they demand the highest quality possible, the procurement price may increase. This may result in the final product price being too high for the customer to purchase. If, on the other hand, the purchasing professional accepts the lowest quality part for a low purchase price, the final product may not meet the customer's minimum quality standards. Failing to meet the minimum quality standards will result in lost sales, customer warranty claims, and potential product liability lawsuits. Balancing material procurement price with quality requirements is one of the procurement professional's critical jobs.

Being able to balance and measure the cost of procuring the right part at the right time at the right price in the right quantity of the right quality is critical to the company's long- term success. This chapter presents a series of methods that help purchasing personnel address this challenging issue.

STRATEGIC VIEW: QUALITY & THE PURCHASING PROCESS

Today's firms deal in the global marketplace where suppliers and customers might be located anywhere in the world. The global procurement market is an international supply chain where different laws, rules, customs, and cultures coexist and collide on a daily basis. In this turbulent world, the purchasing professional faces the challenge of obtaining the right quality level item at the right price.

The company's strategic position drives its quality requirements. This strategic view starts with the company's desire for long-term financial viability and its need to satisfy the end user. Customers that are satisfied with both the quality and price of a company's products will keep coming back for more. Quality can support or hinder a company's strategic view as it contributes to the company's reputation, legal implications, and the global market's acceptance of its products or services.

Each firm must realize that its reputation is a direct result of meeting its customer's needs and wants. As will be discussed later in this chapter, when considering potential suppliers, all customers have a minimum quality bar at which their needs and wants are satisfied. This minimum bar is referred to as ***order qualifiers***. There is yet another bar, called the ***order winner***, which is reached when the customer buys your product. Often the difference between order qualifiers and order winners is the product's quality. If a company continually meets the order winner bar, the firm's sales will continue and its reputation will remain high.

Often closely coupled with the firm's reputation are product liability implications. **Product liability** is the area of law in which manufacturers, distributors, suppliers, retailers, and others who make products available to the public are held responsible for the injuries those products cause. For example, the Ford Motor Company faced a serious gas tank quality design problem in the Ford Pinto that resulted in loss of life, permanent injuries, and millions of dollars of liability costs. In most recent years, children toys and various food products have faced extensive recalls. Each of these events can be directly linked to poor quality. Aside from liability costs, legal costs, and lost sales, each of these events also impacted the various firms' reputation and global standing.

Any loss of reputation due to poor quality subsequently cascades throughout the company's global marketplace. Because most firms operate in a competitive environment, the customer's ultimate purchasing decision is driven by many variables, including the supplier's reputation and capability of delivering a quality product. If the customer feels or believes that one company has a good reputation for supplying quality products and another competing company does not, the company with the positive reputation will probably make the sale, regardless of price. Quality is a global supply chain company attribute that starts at the strategic level and permeates throughout the organization.

DEFINING QUALITY & SPECIFICATIONS

Quality is essential to a firm's survival. But what is *quality* in the business and supply chain setting? To answer this question, let's take a look at the history of quality, starting with the origins of quality standards and processes at the end of World War II. At this time in history, the United States was essentially the only manufacturing nation that remained intact. As the world rebuilt critical infrastructures and recovered from the devastation of war, there was a tremendous demand for all manufactured products with global supply capability predominately limited to the United States.

In this lopsided demand and supply equation, with greater demand than available supply, quality wasn't a major driver for purchasing decisions. Instead, the driver was quantity: *Can we buy enough parts to ensure sufficient material is on hand to keep things moving?* The waste, lost money, and other problems associated with poor quality parts was just a cost of doing business. If quality existed, it was in the form of quality control. **Quality control (QC)** is a process of inspection and rejection, ensuring that products meet preset standards and so not have any noticeable defects. (Think back to times when you have purchased something and a little slip of paper falls out of the packaging which reads, "Inspected by number 7.")

Out of the busy and hectic post-WWII manufacturing environment, today's modern quality movement sprang roots. In its desire to rebuild its society, infrastructure, and fiscal resource capabilities, Japan had to find a way to compete with the rest of the world. They achieved this through the early adoption of a quality management program developed and taught by Dr. W. E. Deming.

Dr. Deming was an American statistician, author, consultant, college professor, and quality leader who drafted an overarching 14-point quality program that extended beyond a QC inspect-and-reject mentality and encompassed the organization as a whole. Unfortunately, U. S. manufacturing firms did not readily accept Dr. Deming's 14-point program, believing that a new holistic program was unnecessary and instead preferred to sell everything they could, regardless of potential quality defects. The prevailing attitude in the U.S. was: *the system is not broken, so why should we fix it?* With little U. S. support or success, Dr. Deming went to Japan with his holistic quality program. The Japanese quickly saw how it could enhance their products, improve overall quality, and even lower their manufacturing costs. In the end, Dr. Deming's 14-point program became a resounding Japanese national success as the quality of the country's manufactured products quickly escalated and surpassed that of most other countries. The world took note in the later part of the twentieth century and global customers started to buy these superior quality products, especially in the automotive and consumer electronics industries.

Today's holistic quality program is the culmination, but not conclusion, of this emerging quality learning process. In post-WWII days, quality was a QC-based inspect-and-reject process. From these rudimentary beginnings, quality expanded into a *statistical process control (SPC)* program to a *total quality management (TQM)* program. From this came the *total quality control (TQC)* program and, finally, today's global quality version of *lean manufacturing*.

One method used in modern enhanced quality systems is **quality circles**, which are small, often volunteer, teams assembled from the same work area. These small teams meet approximately once a week to discuss and determine action plans that will help increase safety levels, improve or resolve quality issues, increase productivity, or develop cost saving initiatives.

Modern companies now include procurement professionals in these quality circle teams because the raw material received must meet and sustain certain quality levels. If the necessary quality levels of materials procured are not met, the firm's overall productivity will decrease while manufacturing costs increase. To help minimize or eliminate raw material issues, the procurement professional works with the quality circle team as they develop methods, tools, and processes to ensure that the highest quality product is produced at the lowest cost.

While many types of quality programs exist and are in use, how can we define quality? While many definitions for quality exist in business, management, and purchasing publications, a quick and easy definition of **quality** is: the level of fitness a product has for customer use. Is a product fit for its customers' intended use? Unless your product or service is of good enough quality to be used by the customer the way the customer want to use it, no one will want to buy your product and a customer base will not exist, leading to no sales and no reason for your company to exist.

QUALITY SPECIFICATIONS

To say that something is a "quality product" or "quality service" implies that metrics exists to measure and compare it to its competitors. If there is no metric with which to compare the product or service, how can you say that product or service meets, exceeds, or fails to meet the quality metric? Measuring quality is essential to organizational survival.

Quality metrics may be either quantitative or qualitative in nature. A ***quantitative metric*** has some measurable physical attribute, such as weight, length, width, depth, color, power output, power consumption, speed, or industry-recognized standards. For example, a procurement department may receive a request to procure a set of computers. One quality requirement may include the specification that each computer must contain a Nationally Recognized Testing Laboratory (NRTL) electrical safety certification. This metric is an industry-recognized quantifiable standard that can be measured very accurately. The product either has the certification or it does not.

Conversely, the procurement professional may receive a request to procure a new fleet of vehicles. The specification says that the paint and final finish must be of "high quality." Unfortunately, this specification of "high quality" is not numerically measurable. The specification does not include a color; it just says it must have a high quality finish. This is a qualitative judgment that does not appear to have a quantifiable metric associated with it. In the case example below, Frank's Dairy faces a similar situation.

> **QUALITY AND THE CASE OF FRANK'S DAIRY**
>
> Frank's Dairy produces a full set of dairy products, including cottage cheese. The company's product engineers have established very specific quality metrics for the production facility. As part of the manufacturing process, various metrics are statistically measured to ensure that a manufactured product of acceptable quality is released for sale.
>
> Frank's Dairy's marketing department wanted to find out how their clients view their cottage cheese. A survey of randomly selected customers was conducted of customers buying cottage cheese at supermarkets. This survey included customers who bought Frank's Dairy's brand of cottage cheese as well as those who selected other brands. A key survey question was: *Why did you not buy Frank's Dairy cottage cheese?* A very common response was that their selected product was of higher quality.
>
> Since Frank's Dairy uses exacting quality manufacturing metrics, how can the cottage cheese buyers rate the quality of their product selected as higher than Frank's?

For manufacturing firms, quantitative quality measurements tend to be absolute. Either the product meets the established metric or it does not. Conversely, establishing ***qualitative metrics*** and consistently measuring them is more flexible and less absolute. The challenge with qualitative metrics is that quality is often in the eye of the beholder.

The purchasing professional has an "eye of the beholder" or gatekeeper role. As Figure 4.1 demonstrates, the purchasing professional views quality from the perspective of a buyer, with metric input from engineering, and from the perspective of a seller to internal operations, manufacturing, and maintenance groups. The purchasing professional controls the gate of who can and will supply products and services to the firm while promoting long-term supplier relationships to support the company's strategic and tactical views.

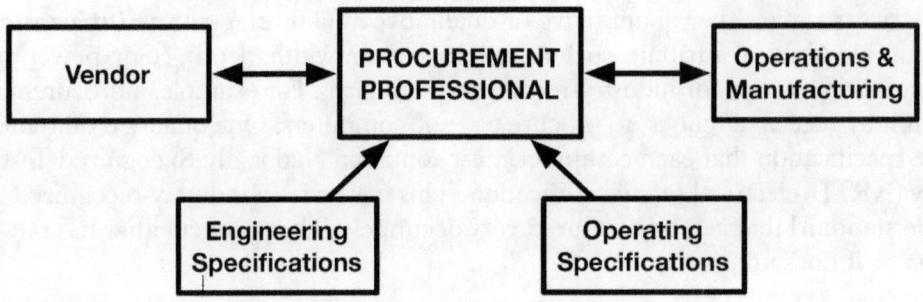

Figure 4.1 - Role of the Procurement Professional

QUALITY SUPPLIER IDENTIFICATION

The purchasing professional is the essential link between an organization's internal needs and the external suppliers of those needs. The purchasing professional is an essential link because he/she:

- *Receives the organizational material and service requests;*
- *Conducts industry surveys to identify potential sources;*
- *Evaluates the various potential sources' competitive advantages;*
- *Negotiates favorable terms; and*
- *Issues financial procurement agreements.*

As we examined in Chapter 2, the overall procurement process begins with a request from within the organization. This request can originate from many possible sources, such as engineering, inventory re-stock, operation and maintenance, or special projects requests. Regardless of the requesting source, the purchasing professional must be supplied with some very specific data and information before they can ensure they purchase the correct quality products or services.
To assist procurement in purchasing the right quality, the information needed includes the following:

- Specific item make and model numbers (with the item description) for off the shelf purchases.
- Specific shipping and handling instructions if goods are of a fragile nature.
- Specific industry recognized standards, such as ISO standards.
- Specifications and standards specific to our company.
- List of potential sources who have previously supplied the right quality.

An organization's purchasing department is typically able to identify a set of suppliers across the world that are able to meet its needs and wants. With a global market, a purchasing professional's quality assurance challenge is to identify the key elements that differentiate the higher quality suppliers from all others. One method of differentiating potential qualified suppliers is to identify those who have received internationally recognized quality standard certification.

The only internationally recognized quality certification is issued by the ***International Standards Organization (ISO)***, made up of 91 member nations that established the ISO 9000 series of quality standards in 1987. The ISO 9000 series is a set of standards that defines how firms should establish their quality programs, which should include the attributes of clear leadership roles and responsibilities, policies, procedures, documentation requirements, record keeping, and explicit work instructions. The ISO 9001 is a related set of quality standards and requirements that organizations must fulfill in order to become an ISO 9001 certified supplier. Purchasing professionals can use this ISO 9001 supplier certification as an indication that the firm will produce a quality product or service based on a documented and supported quality program.

THE COSTS OF POOR QUALITY

One principal tasks of the purchasing professional is to obtain quality products in the right quantity at the right time delivered to the right place. Part of this task is quality supplier selection using techniques such as the Supplier Certification program. This process is designed to ensure that the product or service meets all requirements prior to it arriving at the procuring firm's location.

Ensuring that a quality product arrives on site is important to both the supplying firm's and the purchasing firm's financial bottom line. From the supplying firm's perspective, providing quality products means that few items are rejected for failing to meet all their customers' quality requirements. Each product that is rejected is a product which costs the supplier to produce but for which they are not being paid. Either the rejected product must be reworked or a replacement supplied. From the purchasing firm's financial perspective, there are substantial costs involved in testing materials received and rejecting poor quality items.

The most significant negative financial impact can occur if the poor quality product actually enters the firm's manufacturing process. The earlier the poor quality is detected, the lower the overall negative cost of reworking or scrapping the product will be. In either case, rework or scrap, the firm has spent financial resources to produce a product they cannot sell. In an extreme case, the firm's internal quality program may not detect the defective raw material problem until after the product is in the end user's hands. In this case, the firm faces a range of negative results from product recalls, negative press, and reputation damage to legal action due to faulty products. Ford automobile and their tire supplier, Firestone, is a classic example of how a supplier's poor quality product can significantly impact the firm if the defective product makes it to the end user.

Ideally, the supplier will provide quality products 100% of the time. This saves everyone time and money. Yet, unless the supplier and purchaser carry out 100% product testing, some defective items may still enter the supply chain. Identifying these defective parts, measuring quality, and monitoring suppliers' performance will be explored in the section to follow.

Measuring Quality: Statistical Quality Control

Essential to the procuring firm's total quality program is the ability to monitor supplier performance to: *identify when defective parts arrive, identify trends indicating that a quality problem is occurring,* and *take early corrective actions*. Key to the total quality monitoring program is a method known as ***statistical process control (SPC)***. SPC uses a set of tools to monitor and measure the raw products to ensure that they are within established specifications. SPC also allows the firm to detect problems as they develop and take corrective action before the product strays outside of established control limits.

SPC originated in the work of Dr. Walter A. Shewhart of Bell Telephone Labs in the early 1920's. Dr. Shewhart identified that production variations come in two forms, natural and assignable. ***Natural variation*** is the type of process change which has no identifiable cause. These changes occur naturally and can never be eliminated. Examples of natural variations include temperature, humidity, and machine vibrations. ***Assignable variations***, on the other hand, are variations that have a root cause that can be identified and corrected. For example, a drill bit wearing out and producing holes outside of design specifications would be an assignable variation. Dr. Shewhart showed that, by using SPC techniques, a firm could separate natural variations from assignable variations. Clearly identifying the different variations allows the firm to focus on what can be controlled and ignore those areas that cannot be controlled. In a quality program, the focus is the elimination of all assignable variations before the product fails to meet all required specifications.

SPC CONTROL CHARTS

Statistical process control is, as the name implies, a statistics-based methodology used to monitor a process. Without going into an in-depth statistical discussion, SPC relies on the ***central limiting theorem*** as the foundation for its various control charts. According to the central limiting theorem, for a given population of interest, the distribution of data will tend to follow a normal bell curve as the number of samples increases. A normal bell curve, as shown in Figure 4.2 below, has a center point that is the average value of all samples taken. At this center point, 50% of the data taken is greater than the average value and 50% of the data is less than the average value.

Statistically, it can be shown that 99.73% of all sample values (data) will occur within plus and minus three standard deviations, as indicated in the area along the curve between the -3 and +3 x-axis locations in Figure 4.2. The case study on the next page demonstrates how procurement professionals utilize statistical techniques to monitor inbound material quality at Frank's Dairy.

Purchasing professionals working with the Quality Control department can use various Statistical Process Control tools to assist their firms in identifying whether or not received products are within specifications. They can also help identify if a problem is starting to develop before it becomes a costly problem. The pages to follow highlight a few SPC tools that graphically identify and quantify the state of the system.

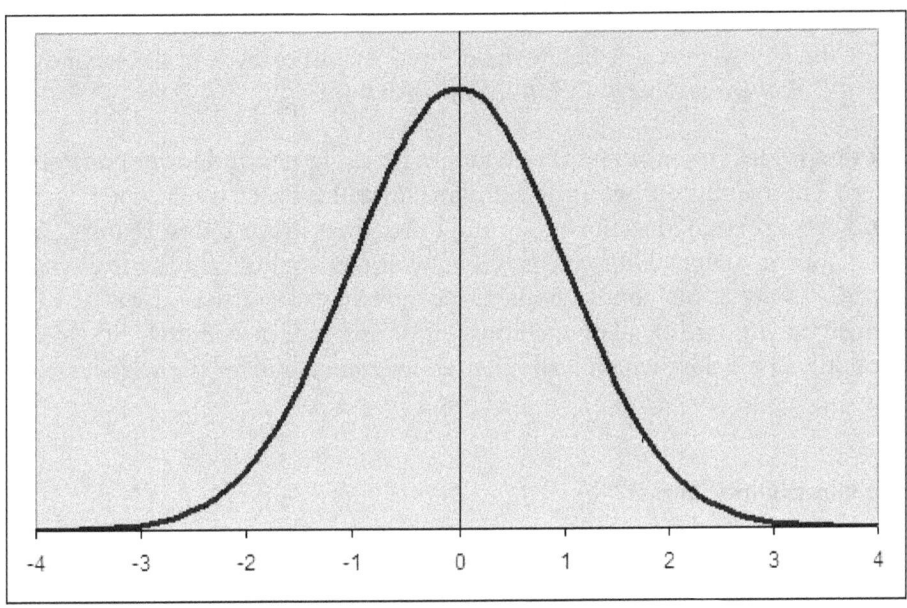

Figure 4.2 - A Normal Bell Curve

MEAN CHARTS

One key SPC tool used in examining quality is the **control chart**. Control charts represent changes in a particular aspect of product quality over time. These aspects measured may be *variables* or *attributes*. **Variables** are product characteristics that have an infinite range of values and can be measured continuously, such as weight and temperature. **Attributes**, on the other hand, are product characteristics that are measured in binary form, which means that the product either passes the test or not. This is a yes/no, pass/fail, or similar either/or analysis. Control charts plot the various results of random samples to see if the measured variable or attribute falls with the respective control chart limits. One common variable control chart is the *mean chart*.

Mean charts, also called **x-bar charts**, are control charts that show the average values of a variable product characteristic over time. A mean chart has five essential characteristics. First, the x-axis represents time with subsequent sample periods plotted to the right of the previously taken samples. Second, the vertical y-axis is the sample average measurement range. The third characteristic is the center line, which is the desired average sample value. This center line is often called the **mean value** or **process average value**. The fourth characteristic is the **upper control limit (UCL)**, the line at which everything located above is out of normal variation control. The fifth and final characteristic is the **lower control limit (LCL)**, the lower limit to which the sample can be measured at and still be within the design standards.

Figure 4.3 is an example of a standard SPC mean chart. The quality control mean value is the center line with the average measurement value of approximately 30.4. In this case, the measurements in our SPC mean chart were from Frank's Dairy. One of the company's products is a fruit yogurt with a target weight of 30.4 ounces. Grocery stores are concerned about getting yogurts that are consistent in their volume and not under-filled or over-filled. Frank's Dairy takes multiple measurements of the fruit yogurt tubs it produces every hour and calculates an average of these measurements every hour. As you can see from the SPC chart in Figure 4.3, the average measurement of the fruit yogurt was below the desired weight of 30.4 in the second hour of measurements and above this desired weight in the fifth hour.

To ensure that the product is within required quality limits, upper and lower control limits have been established. These limits are set using standard formulas based on accepted statistical foundations and are represented as the upper and lower lines in the chart. Frank's Dairy has determined that approximately 30.0 ounces is the lower control limit for the fruit yogurt tubs and approximately 30.8 is the upper control limit. Over the twelve hour period, Frank's Dairy has done well because the average of all of the hourly averages is approximately 30.4 ounces, as shown in the middle line below, which is the desired average value for the yogurt weight.

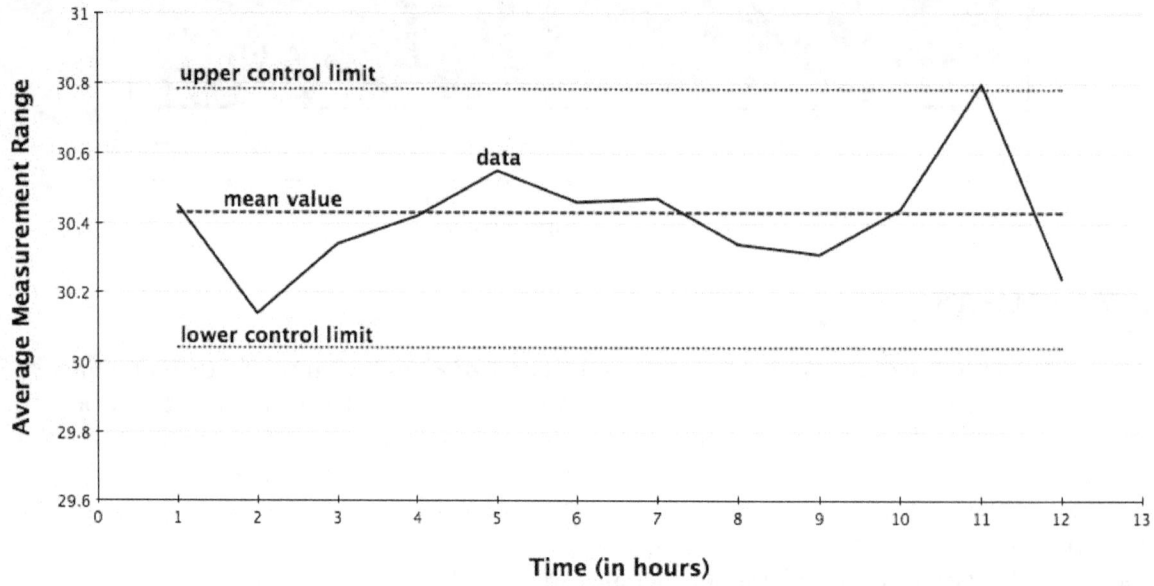

Figure 4.3 - Standard SPC Mean Chart

With mean charts like Figure 4.3 above, quality control or receiving professionals monitor the incoming material sample data line to see if any data point occurs outside the control limits. Any value that falls outside the control limits indicates an assignable variation has occurred and corrective action is required. The reviewing individual also uses the chart to look for trends. If the data shows trend in one direction is occurring for three or more data samples in a sequence, this would indicate an assignable variation may be occurring and corrective action must be taken. In our chart in Figure 4.3, we can see that the average weight measurement of the fruit yogurt tubs was above the upper control limit in the eleventh hour, which may mean that further investigation is needed on the production line.

Mean charts do not present a complete picture of product quality, however, because they indicate if the sample's *average* is within the established quality standards. While this is an important piece of information, looking at sample averages can mask individual product values above and below the upper and lower control limits respectively. As such, another control chart must reviewed: the *range chart*.

RANGE CHARTS

Range charts, or ***R-charts***, track the spread of values of a particular aspect of product quality. The R-chart specifically looks at the difference between each sample set's highest and lowest measurement to derive the sample range. To determine each measured sample range value, the quality reviewer identifies the highest and lowest measurement for each sample taken. The lowest measured value is subtracted from the highest measured value to generate the sample set range. Once each of the sample ranges has been determined, an average of the range values is calculated. For example, Frank's Dairy found that the average range over the twelve-hour period was 0.51 ounces. The company was concerned about its r-chart findings during the fifth hour, however, because the highest measurement was 30.99 ounces and the lowest measurement was 30.00 ounces, resulting in a range of 0.99 ounces. This range was much higher than the other ranges measures over the twelve-hour period and may require further investigation.

Using a combination of mean and range charts allows the receiving or quality personnel to establish if the material is within quality standards. It also allows the reviewers to identify when a quality problem is developing so corrective action can be taken before the received product is out of specifications. Overall, this process both prevents receipt of inferior products and prevents downstream system costs associated with lost productivity, wasted time, and wasted financial resources to produce a product using procured material of a poor quality.

P-CHARTS

P-charts provide a visual indication of quality *attributes*, the binary yes/no, pass/fail analyses of the incoming materials. Attribute quality examples would include: lights work or not, computer starts or not, or received flour moisture is below a certain percentage or not. In each case, the decision is whether the measurable attribute meets the standard or not. There isn't a gray area or a continuum of possible outcomes. The product meets the measurement or it is rejected. P-charts provide an SPC method that allows an operator to monitor the received product quality.

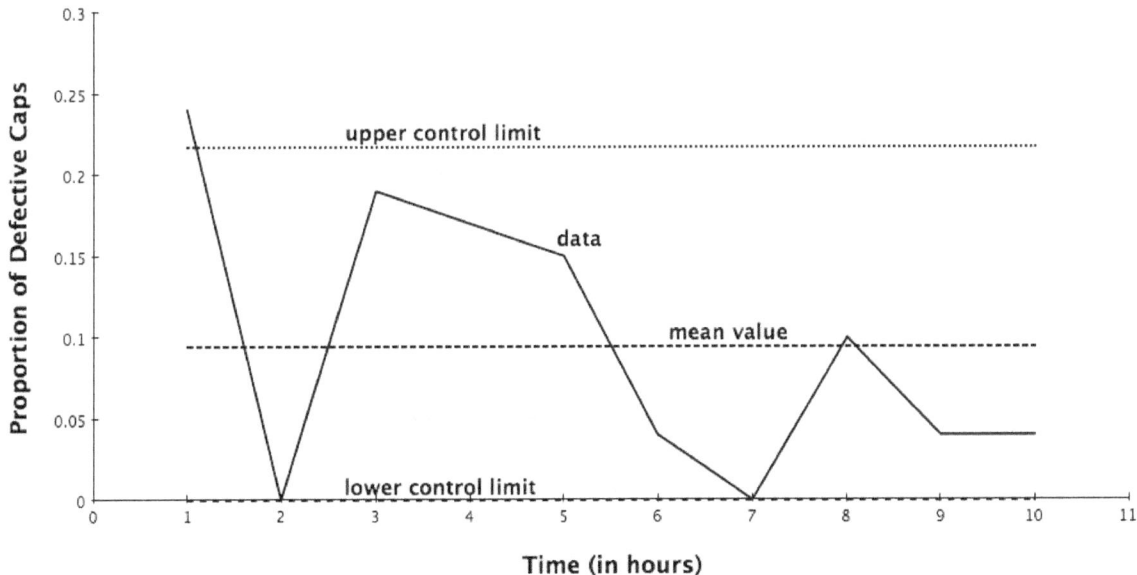

Figure 4.3 - Example of Frank's Dairy P-Chart

To achieve the desired results, P-charts graph the proportion of defective parts received. As with the mean and R-charts, P-charts have a targeted proportion with corresponding upper and lower control limits. Figure 4.4 above demonstrates a P-chart from Frank's Dairy for the proportion of defective milk carton caps (y-axis) over a set of ten sample sets of data collected each hour (x-axis).

In Figure 4.4, the range of data falls outside the acceptable quality range during sample period one. Further evaluation at Frank's Dairy found that, as the day progressed, the proportion of defective parts decreased throughout the shift. Quality personnel at Frank's would use this data to investigate why the high number of defective parts occurred early in the work schedule.

Whether the received quality metric is a variable or attribute, a statistical process control chart is available to monitor the received material quality. These charts are developed using well-established statistical tools and methods. The charts help to identify if the system is within statistical process control, if there are indications that the system is drifting out of specifications, and when a part must be rejected if it fails to meet the quality design measurements. The charts help to separate random system variations from assignable system defects. Using these charts and corresponding analysis, quality personnel support the procurement professional to ensure that only quality products are introduced within the manufacturing supply chain

QUALITY FOR THE PURCHASING PROFESSIONAL

The purchasing professional can be viewed as the gatekeeper god of Roman mythology, Janus, who simultaneously faces two directions. Facing both ways at once allows Janus to control who comes and who goes. In their quality assurance role, purchasing professionals are also gatekeepers facing two opposing directions. They are face outward from their firm as the gatekeeper of supplies ordered from outside vendors. At the same time, purchasing professionals face inward and must be aware of and support their firm's internal operations so they meet quality requirements. This internal view is exemplified in the purchasing professional's participation in the firm's quality circles. Both the external and internal views of the purchasing professional are critical and essential to a company's long-term viability.

To ensure long term viability, the purchasing professional is charged with the complex system task of providing the right quantity of parts to the right location at the right time, ensuring that all required quality measurements are met. In modern industry, this is a significant challenge that has a direct impact on the firm's profitability. If the quality of the raw material received meets or exceeds all requirements, the firm can produce quality, value-added products at the lowest possible costs. Conversely, if the firm receives materials that do not meet its quality requirements and the poor quality material is not rejected, the firm will not be able to produce a quality, value-added product. In this case, each poor quality product will increase the firm's overall cost in the form of rejected final products, wasted time and material, and potential liability lawsuits. Quality monitoring and control process are used to ensure receipt of quality products involve monitoring, measuring, and tracking specific quality characteristics of raw materials.

Meeting quality standards means that specific quantitative and qualitative characteristics must be met. Achieving these quality metrics allow a firm to provide the means to ensure that when the space shuttle lifts off, an airplane takes off, or you take your family for an automobile ride, everyone on board has the best chance for a safe ride. In these instances and many others, the end user relies not only on the designers, engineers, and manufacturers but also on the quality procurement decisions of purchasing professionals.

As previously discussed, purchasing professionals can trade off an item's purchase price for various levels of quality. When they demand the highest quality possible, the material price can increase. If, on the other hand, the purchasing professional accepts the lowest quality part for a low purchase price, the final product may not meet the customer's minimum quality standards. Failing to meet the minimum quality standards will result in lost sales, customer warranty claims, and potential product liability lawsuits. Balancing procurement price with quality requirements is one of the procurement professional's critical jobs.

To achieve this balance, procurement professionals rely on the firm's engineers, operations personnel, and others to provide them with quantifiable quality metrics for the required raw material. The purchasing professional relies on these internal inputs as key data to guide them during the search and ultimate selection of a specific supplier. These same internal inputs are then used to evaluate the received raw material quality.

Several tools and techniques exist to support monitoring the received raw material quality. These tools typically fall within the area of statistical process control. SPC involves many techniques, including the mean chart, R-chart and P-chart tools. In each of these SPC methods and tools, a specific raw material characteristic is measured using a random sampling process. The results of these random samples are graphed to provide a visual reference of the material quality.

Each SPC chart has upper and lower control limits, within which the characteristic of the raw material measured must remain. These limits provide an indication of whether the quality measurement of the material received is varying due to natural random variations or assignable variations. Random variations are naturally occurring differences with no identifiable cause. Naturally occurring random variations cannot be fixed or changed. Assignable variations, on the other hand, are those changes that can be traced to a specific cause and corrected. Quality's goal is to identify assignable variation and take corrective actions as soon as possible.

Before we delve into issues of time and place in the next chapter, let's remember that in the world of purchasing, obtaining a quality product is not just an option. It is instead an essential element of the purchasing process.

Chapter 4 Review Questions

1. What do we mean when we say the a purchasing professional can often *trade off* an item's purchase price with various levels of quality? Do you do this when you make personal purchases? Why or why not?

2. What is the difference between an *order qualifier* and an *order winner*?

3. What effect does poor quality have on an organization's image and bottom line? Describe a time when poor quality impacted your purchasing decisions.

4. What is a *quality circle*? Why should a purchasing professionals be part of one in their organization?

5. What is the difference between *qualitative* and *quantitative* metrics? Give an example of each.

6. Why might a supplier want to become *ISO 9001 certified*?

7. What happens when poor quality products enter a company's manufacturing process undetected?

8. How does *statistical process control* help the purchasing professional?

9. Why is the *upper control limit* important on an SPC chart?

10. How are *p-charts* and *r-charts* different? How might they each be used in a purchasing setting?

CHAPTER 4 CASE EXERCISE

Joe Jones and the ISO 9000

"This was too good an offer to pass up. Three month's supply of one of our key manufacturing inputs, even with customs charges and transportation, cost us 40% less! The products arrived on time, to the right place and in the quantity," pleaded Joe Jones, the new purchasing officer at Cabin Cove Engineering. "The supplier assured me that their product's quality matched our quality specifications to a T!"

"But," said Susan Sparks, the production manager, "although the products looked good, they were made from a low grade alloy and did not meet our specifications. They failed our most basic quality test. I know your predecessor used to buy internationally, but he always checked that the supplier was ISO 9001 certified. At this stage, it does not matter whether or not we can sue the supplier. I just do not have enough parts to finish a production run!" Sue Sparks then angrily stormed out of the meeting. Joe Jones was speechless. He was new to purchasing and had never hear of the ISO or the ISO 9001 standard.

Joe quickly left to call Jackie, a new friend he had met at last month at his first Institute of Supply Management annual conference. Jackie was an experienced buyer and Joe was sure she could give a bit of information about the ISO and the ISO 9001 standard.

To prepare for his talk with Jackie, Joe wrote down the following questions:

- *What is the International Standards Organization?*
- *Specifically, what is this ISO 9001 standard*
- *What does the ISO 9001 mean to the supply chain?*
- *How would ISO 9001 have helped me in selecting an international supplier?*
- *How could I have confidence that the supplier meets ISO 9001?*
- *If I had selected a supplier that is ISO 9001certified but does not end up meeting my quality requirement, what can I do?*

Unfortunately, when Joe called, Jackie was busy but told Joe she would call him back later in the afternoon. She suggested that, in the mean time, Joe should check out the ISO website because it explains everything you need to know about the ISO and ISO standards. She also suggested that Joe search the site for a brochure entitled, ISO 9001: What does it mean in the supply chain?

INSTRUCTIONS:

1. **Go to the ISO website (www.iso.org). Search the site for answers to Joe's first two questions for Jackie.**

2. **Next, find the brochure, *ISO 9001: What does it mean in the supply chain*, on the ISO website and find the answers to the remaining questions there.**

Chapter 5

Looking at Time and Place

Dr. Philip M. Price

In our earlier chapters, we talked about the Five Rs of purchasing. So far, we've explored the first and second R's: the *right quantity* and the *right quality*. We're now ready to look at the third and fourth Rs of purchasing: the *right time* and the *right place*. In this chapter, we will examine how purchasing professionals work to get goods to where they are wanted when they are wanted.

The needs of the user are the critical elements a purchasing professional must consider when placing an order for goods or services. Once a requested item has been identified and a supplier has been selected, the purchaser must make sure that the user gets this item when and where he or she wants it.

For example, during the 2nd week in May, the marketing department at Poppi's Pool Supplies in Palo Alto, California has requisitioned the purchasing department for a massive printing job. They would like to find a high quality printing service that can print a variety of promotional materials for the annual Poppi's Pool Supplies Summer Sale. The advertising material is required the first week in July. One month is the generally accepted lead-time for a print job of this size among printing firms. Poppi's purchasing manager spends two weeks engaged in supplier selection and, in the end, finds a printing service, Go-Go Graphics, with exceptionally high quality printing machines offering services at a third of the price of its competitors and jumps immediately at this cost savings. The purchase order is placed with Go-Go Graphics in the first week of June. On the first of July, an expediter contacts Go-Go Graphics to check on the status of the order and, much to their horror, they find that the order was dispatched at the end of June to the wrong location! Go-Go Graphics had sent the completed job, not to Poppi's Pool Supplies in Palo Alto, California but instead to another customer, Poppi's Reindeer Rides in North Pole,

Alaska. Go-Go Graphics decides to reprint Poppi's order rather than pay the costlier express shipping costs from North Pole. However, the second Poppi's printing job is delayed primarily because Go-Go Graphics' low prices are creating too much business for the mom-and-pop business. In the first week of August, Poppi's finally receives the entire order at an additional discount for their inconvenience. All of these savings are worth nothing, however, because Poppi's did not receive the goods where it wanted them (in Palo Alto), when it wanted them (July 1st, in time for the summer sale).

TIME AND PLACE IN MANUFACTURING

All purchasing professionals must ensure that their suppliers are able to deliver their goods and services to the right place at the right time. This is especially critical, however, when goods are procured for manufacturing. Manufacturing departments operate on strict planning schedules that require not only the exact quantity and quality of an item, but also that the item be at the correct place within the production line at a specific time. Shipping delays or delivery of an item to the wrong place can cause a manufacturing plant to shut down, costing a company thousands of dollars or more in lost production time and unhappy external customers.

Planning where inventory must be and when it must be there is of supreme importance in the manufacturing environment. Manufacturing companies use a variety of tools and techniques to help them stay organized and operate at optimum efficiency. These companies manage information about inventory for the manufacturing process using systems such as: a *master production schedule (MPS)*, *materials requirement planning (MRP)*, the *inventory records file*, and a *bill of materials (BOM)*.

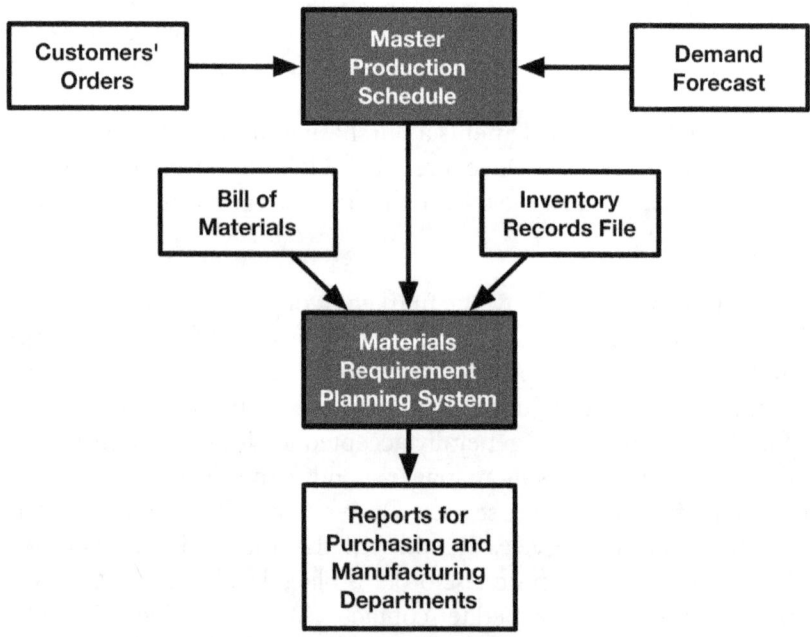

Figure 5.1 - Purchasing and the Master Production Schedule

An ***MPS***, or ***master production schedule***, lists in detail exactly what finished items the manufacturing system must produce, how many of each item they must produce, and the exact date on which these finished items are needed. The MPS is usually based on customers' orders and demand forecasts and is typically organized by week or month.

Materials requirement planning (MRP) is an information technology, time-phased requirement planning system to help an organization minimize inventory-holding costs. It is essentially a computer-based common sense approach to coordinating the purchase and use of materials with the needs of complex production schedules. With MRP, a manufacturing organization can know exactly when and where inventory is needed so that it doesn't need to hold extra or unnecessary inventory.

As shown in Figure 5.1 above, the purchasing department gets its information from three sources:

1. *The Master Production Schedule (MPS)*.

2. *The Bill of Materials (BOM)*. The ***BOM***, or ***bill of materials***, is a structured directory that lists all of the items or parts required to manufacture a finished product. In addition to listing the items and parts needed, the BOM lists the amount of each needed and the dates by which they are needed for the manufacturing process. In some companies, the BOM is also called an ***RMR***, or ***report of materials requirements***.

3. *The **Inventory Records File***, which is a complete record of each item held in inventory. Before a production run, the MRP system calculates the total quantity of each item that needs to be ordered along with their lead times. The MRP system can then generate a report for the purchasing department outlining: the items that need to be ordered, the quantities to be ordered, and order date for each item. The MRP system also generates inventory reports for the manufacturing department that help them decide what, when, and how many items to produce.

Let's now look at an MPS, and MRP system in practice as we consider time and place issues in the case of the Luxury Lamps Limited and the Alcatraz Hotel.

CASE STUDY: LUXURY LAMPS, LTD. AND THE ALCATRAZ HOTEL

The Alcatraz Hotel in San Francisco, California is currently undergoing major room renovations. Known for its austere, prison-like setting, the Alcatraz is looking to update its image to become a luxury hotel for the nouveau riche. The hotel's interior designer has just informed the Alcatraz purchasing department that, in order to complete the hotel's honeymoon suites, it "must, must, MUST" order thirty Serendipity model lamps (item code 1111) from Luxury Lamps, Ltd. The designer also said that, if these lamps do not arrive by November 29th, ten weeks from the date of order, the hotel's remodeling venture will not be finished on time and that the honeymooning couples booked to stay in the rooms starting November 30th will have to suffer the tragedy of garish lighting.

The Serenity lamp (item code 1111) is a handmade specialty item and is not part of Luxury Lamps' normal production line. Because of their significant expense, Luxury Lamps does not carry any inventory and the company's purchasing department orders all of the parts to manufacture the lamp as orders are placed by customers. The Luxury Lamps, Ltd. manufacturing facility is in Buffalo, New York and their distribution center for all west coast distribution is in Fresno, California. When all of the lamps arrive in Fresno from New York, the Fresno distribution center completes the final assembly by fitting bulbs and electrical plugs before delivering the completed lamps to the final customer.

For all specialty lamps, such as the Serenity (item code 1111), it takes one week to assemble lamps at the New York Luxury Lamps manufacturing facility, one week to ship the lamps from New York to Fresno, one week to fit a bulb and plug at the Fresno distribution center, and one week to deliver goods from Fresno to the final customer. To assemble and deliver these important lamps to the Alcatraz Hotel by November 29th, the purchasing department at Luxury Lamps, Ltd. must consider both time and place as they make their procurement decisions for all of the parts that go into making the Serenity lamp.

First, the purchasing department at Luxury Lamps, Ltd. must consider when they need to order parts from suppliers to ensure that they arrive at the New York manufacturing plant in time for assembly. When placing the order, the purchasing department must also consider their supplier's **_lead time_**, or the time it takes from placing the order until the item has been received, inspected, and ready to issue to the manufacturing department. Next, the purchasing department must consider a variety of additional time considerations including the assembly time at the New York plant, the distribution time to Fresno, the time needed to fit the bulbs and plugs in Fresno, and the time it takes to deliver the Serenity lamps assembled in Fresno to the customer in San Francisco, all of which must be completed by the November 29th deadline. Finally, the purchasing department must consider place throughout, keeping in mind that some items ordered will be needed in the Buffalo, New York manufacturing facility and others will be needed in the Fresno, California distribution center.

Master Production Schedule (MPS): Determining the weeks when the parts need to be assembled in New York and Fresno to ensure that the quantity of 30 finished unit are delivered to San Francisco on November 29th

Item #1: Lampshade	Weeks									
	1	2	3	4	5	6	7	8	9	10
Must assemble in **New York** in week 7 for delivery to Fresno by week 9							Assembly scheduled in NY: 30 units			Delivery to Alcatraz: 30 units
Must finish assembly in **Fresno** in week 9 for delivery to customer by week 10									Final assembly scheduled in Fresno: 30 units	

Figure 5.2 - Master Production Schedule

In Figures 5.3 and 5.4 below are two examples of the ways in which a BOM can help the Luxury Lamp's purchasing department understand the time and place requirements for this specialty lamp order.

Item Number	Part Needed	Quantity Required for One Lamp	Supplier Location	Lead Time	Place Required
1	Lamp shade	1	Montreal, Canada	3 weeks	Buffalo, New York
2	On/off switch	1	Freeport, Maine	2 weeks	Buffalo, New York
3	Lamp base	1	Tempe, Arizona	4 weeks	Buffalo, New York
4	Light bulb	1	Helena, Montana	5 weeks	Fresno, California
5	Electrical plug	1	Sarasota, Florida	2 weeks	Fresno, California

Figure 5.3 - Bill of Materials - Items Needed to Assemble Lamp Code 1111

Item Number	Part Needed	Gross Requirement	Inventory on Hand	Net Requirement	Lead Time
1	Lamp shade	30	0	30	3 weeks
2	On/off switch	30	0	30	2 weeks
3	Lamp base	30	0	30	4 weeks
4	Light bulb	30	0	30	5 weeks
5	Electrical plug	30	0	30	2 weeks

Figure 5.4 - Bill of Materials - Requirements for Assembling 30 Units of Lamp Code 1111

Figures 5.3 and 5.4 above are both examples of a BOM that might be used by Luxury Lamps, Ltd. In Figure 5.3, the BOM shows supplier locations, lead times, and the required delivery location for each of the lamp's component parts. In Figure 5.4 the BOM includes the suppliers' lead times but also focuses on the hotel order's requirement and any inventory of component parts that may already be held in the warehouse of the Luxury Lamps manufacturing facility. In this case, because 30 Serenity lamps have been ordered, 30 units of each item (or component part) are needed. Because the Luxury Lamps warehouse does not carry any of these items in its inventory, the **net requirement**, or amount to be ordered from each supplier, remains 30.

Let's now look at a **materials requirement plan**, or **MRP**, for this order. As shown in Figure 5.5 below, an MRP is organized chronologically. In this case, the MRP is broken down into a ten-week period with the order placed from the Alcatraz Hotel in Week 1 and the final product delivered to the hotel in Week 10.

Item #1: Lampshade	Weeks									
	1	2	3	4	5	6	7	8	9	10
Must order in week 3 for week 7 assembly in New York			Order 30 shades	Lead time 3 weeks			Assembly in New York	Delivery to Fresno	Fresno assembly	Delivery to Alcatraz

Item #2: On/Off Switch	Weeks									
	1	2	3	4	5	6	7	8	9	10
Must order in week 4 for week 7 assembly in New York				Order 30 switches	Lead time 2 weeks		Assembly in New York	Delivery to Fresno	Fresno assembly	Delivery to Alcatraz

Item #3: Lamp Base	Weeks									
	1	2	3	4	5	6	7	8	9	10
Must order in week 2 for week 7 assembly in New York		Order 30 bases	Lead time 4 weeks				Assembly in New York	Delivery to Fresno	Fresno assembly	Delivery to Alcatraz

Item #4: Light Bulb	Weeks									
	1	2	3	4	5	6	7	8	9	10
Must order in week 3 for week 9 assembly in Fresno			Order 30 bulbs	Lead time 5 weeks to Fresno					Fresno assembly	Delivery to Alcatraz

Item #5: Electrical Plug	Weeks									
	1	2	3	4	5	6	7	8	9	10
Must order in week 6 for week 9 assembly in Fresno						Order 30 plugs	Lead time 2 weeks to Fresno		Fresno assembly	Delivery to Alcatraz

Figure 5.5 - Materials Requirement Plan for Lamp Code 1111

By following the charts in the MRP above, the purchasing department at Luxury Lamps, Ltd. can ensure that all of the component parts needed to assemble the Serenity model lamp can arrive at the right time and at the right place. For example, because the lampshades, on/off switches, and lamp bases are assembled in Week 7, they must arrive in New York by the end of Week 6. Similarly, the light bulbs and electrical plugs must arrive in Fresno by the end of Week 8 for assembly in the Fresno distribution center in Week 9.

COMPLEXITY OF MATERIALS REQUIREMENT PLANNING

In the previous example of Luxury Lamps and the Alcatraz Hotel, the number of component parts needed to assemble the Serenity model lamp was relatively small. Imagine, however, the number of component parts needed to produce larger or more complex goods, such as a computer or automobile. For these goods, there could be tens or even hundreds of component parts, with all of them often from different suppliers in different locations with different lead times. It might take reams and reams of paper to print out all of the bills of materials and master production schedules for these products, confusing a poor purchasing department to distraction! Thanks to information technology and materials requirement planning, this information can easily be managed and accessed to help the purchasing department understand the time and place requirements of complex orders.

JUST IN TIME (AND AT THE RIGHT PLACE, TOO!)

The MRP concept of scheduling inventory ordering and delivery to coordinate with manufacturing schedules to minimize inventory holding is taken a step further with a concept that we first became acquainted with in Chapter 3 - *just in time (JIT)*. At its core, JIT is both a philosophy and inventory control practice, which aims to ensure that the right item of inventory is at the right place and time and that no unnecessary inventory is held.

Three decades ago, traditional approaches to purchasing and inventory management in a manufacturing environment rested heavily in holding extra safety inventory *just in case (JIC)* something went wrong. While the JIC idea provided a buffer against inefficiencies in the manufacturing process, costly levels of inventory were required to be held. From the 1950s through the 1980s, Japanese manufacturers developed the inventory management and control approach we now call *just in time*. The JIT approach sees excess inventory as wasteful and seeks to eliminate it. In JIT systems, the amount of inventory held is reduced by reducing transits times and having smaller quantities delivered more frequently. All manufacturing requirements (i.e., items which were previously held in inventory) are thus produced *just in time* instead of *just in case*.

RULES FOR A SUCCESSFUL MANUFACTURER-SUPPLIER RELATIONSHIP WITHIN A JIT SYSTEM

1. **Establish and nurture long-term relationships.**
2. **The relationship must be mutually beneficial.**
3. **The supplier must be able to guarantee its products' quality with zero defects.**
4. **Technical competence of both the manufacturer and supplier must be continually examined.**
5. **Both the manufacturer and supplier must be located within the same geographic area to ensure reliable delivery.**

For JIT systems to be effective in ensuring that goods are delivered at the right time and place, an organization and its suppliers must work seamlessly and to the same JIT standards. Not only does an organization use a JIT system to reduce its inventory of raw materials, work-in-process, and finished goods within its own facility and distribution chain, but it must insist on similar reductions in its suppliers as well. With JIT, suppliers are seen as an extension of an organization's own plant and thus part of its manufacturing team. Suppliers receive special requests and special containers and are expected to make several deliveries per day. Suppliers must also guarantee the quality of their products so that goods can be delivered directly onto the manufacturing line with no quality control inspections carried out. Because of this close, interdependent relationship with suppliers, organizations with successful JIT systems tend to use ***single source purchasing***, i.e., purchasing specific items or a range of items from a single supplier.

Over the past twenty years, JIT systems have garnered much attention for their ability to drastically reduce inventory holding levels, create better relationships with suppliers, highlight potential problems in manufacturing efficiencies, increase manufacturing efficiency as a result of fewer defective products from suppliers, and create a multifunctional workforce. Although it is very useful for inventory reduction, JIT does present a range of challenges for time and place goals, including: problems resulting from late, incorrect, or insufficient deliveries; difficulties posed by single-source relationships; and shortages of skilled JIT staff. Despite its challenges, JIT has grown to become one of the most effective and popular inventory control techniques worldwide.

Because of the close bond between buyer and suppliers in JIT relationships, purchasing professionals must be ready to navigate this fast-paced environment and remain in constant contact with their suppliers. Purchasing professionals must also hone their communications and "people skills" to handle these highly important relationships effectively. (Later in Chapter 11, "The People Side of Purchasing," we will explore some of these important skills.)

HOLDING INVENTORY: CONSIDERING TIME & PLACE

Earlier in this chapter, we explored MRP and JIT systems that aim to reduce or eliminate inventory held because of the great expense an organization incurs when it holds inventory. Seeing that holding inventory is so expensive, why do organizations bother to hold any at all? Why not operate solely under Just-in-Time style conditions in which inventory is received from the supplier only when it is needed and only in the exact quantities needed? Believe it or not, in certain circumstances when done properly with an efficient inventory control system, the seemingly expensive practice of holding inventory can be extremely advantageous and even cost effective.

Purchasing professionals are often key sources of information in determining whether or not it is advantageous to hold inventory. Because they work closely with the suppliers of much-needed inventory, members of the purchasing department can help their organization determine when inventory might need to be held to ensure that finished products are delivered to the right place at the right time. Some of the many reasons organizations choose to hold inventory include:

✦ **Unreliable inventory deliveries**. Purchasing professionals often find it difficult to rely on all of their suppliers to deliver every order exactly on time every time an order is placed. (Remember Go-Go Graphics and Poppi's Pool Supplies?) By keeping tabs on the reliability and timeliness of suppliers, purchasing professionals can help an organization assess which suppliers' items should be held in inventory. In addition, even the most reliable suppliers are challenged to claim they have never had shipments delayed by strikes, transportation difficulties, their own supplier problems, bad weather, or administrative errors. Therefore, holding inventory ensures that an organization will have adequate stock to maintain operations, even when a supplier's shipment has been delayed.

✦ **Bulk discounts**. By holding more inventory than is needed for one manufacturing cycle (such as a week or a month), an organization is able to buy goods in larger quantities. Thus, the Purchasing department can "buy bulk" and may be able to obtain a lower per unit price. In a company that spends millions of dollars every year on inventory, such discounts can have a significant positive impact on overall profit levels.

✦ **Reduced purchase order processes**. Before the supplier delivers an item to inventory, one process that must occur is the purchase order process, as shown in Figure 5.6 below. When an organization holds very little inventory, it must perform this process frequently, resulting in purchasing and warehouse departments' increased time and labor costs. When an organization holds greater amounts of inventory, however, it performs the purchase order process less often, which can result in significant cost savings. An organization's purchasing department can provide invaluable information about the cost and frequency of the purchase order process to help determine whether inventory should be held to reduce their frequency.

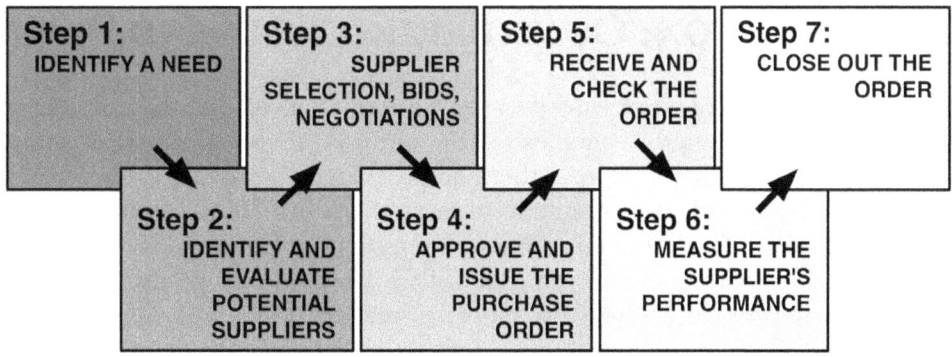

Figure 5.6 - The Purchase Order Process

✦ **Inventory value appreciation**. When higher quantities of goods are held in inventory, an organization can deflect the burden of price inflation for those goods. For example, an automobile manufacturer buys six-months-worth of tires and, suddenly, there is a shortage of rubber worldwide, causing tires to double in price. Because it is holding such a large tire inventory, the manufacturer has successfully deflected the current drastic tire price hike for six months! To assess whether or not to hold inventory because it may increase in value, the purchasing department must keep a keen eye on the changes and trends in the market prices of needed goods and services.

✦ **Low seasonal prices**. Some products, especially agriculturally based raw materials, are more readily available at some times of the year than at others. The purchasing department can help an organization determine whether or not it should purchase its annual needs of such products when their prices are the lowest to reap price savings benefits.

- **Reduced risk to manufacturing operations**. When extra inventory is not held, the risk of a "nil inventory" situation increases, in which inventory of an item runs out and manufacturing is halted until more inventory can be delivered. The cost of halting manufacturing operations can be very high because, in addition to fixed costs, it creates a loss of profit, a loss of sales, a diminished reputation among customers, and an increased labor cost of employees waiting around and doing nothing until the inventory arrives. Therefore, an organization's purchasing department must listen to and work closely with its manufacturing department to ensure that a costly nil inventory situation does not arise.

- **Increased output flexibility**. When an organization holds higher levels of inventory in reserve, it is better able to increase production output levels should the need or demand arise. Again, purchasing and manufacturing professional must work in concert to ensure that manufacturing flexibility is maintained.

As seen here, there are many positive benefits for holding inventory. The purchasing professional must work closely with all involved to adequately balance the cost of holding inventory with its potential benefits to achieve the correct inventory level needed.

TRANSPORTATION: CONSIDERING TIME AND PLACE

Part of the goal of effective purchasing is to get the goods delivered at the right time to the right place. An important piece in this complex puzzle is transportation. Most organization's suppliers are not located right next door to each other and purchased goods must often travel many miles across states, countries, and even continents to reach the buyer. For example, take a minute to look at the labels of all the clothes you are wearing right now. Did they all come from a clothing manufacturer right down the street from you? Unless you live in the garment district of Hong Kong or Shanghai, your clothes were probably manufactured in a range of countries across Asia, Europe, and Central America, even though you may have purchased them at the mini-mall down the street. So how did your clothes make their way from the manufacturer to your local retailer? Using transportation, of course!

Transportation is the act of moving goods or people from one place to another. It is also the key to ensuring that goods are delivered at the right time and to the right place! In the purchasing world, transportation is more often referred to as the movement of goods, not people, to a desired location. Transportation of goods forms the critical bridge between areas of abundance, such as manufacturing or warehousing facilities where the goods are located, and areas of scarcity, such as the immediate customers' locations where the goods are desired.

One of the roles of a company's purchasing department is to coordinate and control the buying or outsourcing of the company's transportation needs, often for both the inbound goods from suppliers for manufacturing and the outbound finished goods to the immediate customers. The relationship between transportation and purchasing extends far beyond simply establishing the cost of transporting goods and incorporating these costs into the cost of goods purchased. Transportation decisions made by an organization's purchasing department play a significant strategic role in determining supply chain costs and levels of service. Two primary decisions a purchasing department must make that have a significant impact on the final cost of goods are:

- *Who will handle the transportation?*
- *Which mode of transportation will be used?*

WHO MOVES THE GOODS?

When an organization is purchasing goods, these goods must be moved from one location to another to arrive at the right time and place. Before it even places the order, the organization's purchasing department must first decide who will physically move these goods: the organization itself or a **carrier**, i.e., a second company that transports goods. An organization typically uses a carrier when it must move goods a great distance or use specialized transport modes, such as by airplanes, railroad cars, or ocean cargo ships, which most companies are not likely to own. A single carrier may use any combination of one or more of the five modes of transportation (road, rail, water, air, and pipeline). Carriers also may own or lease the vehicles and vessels they use.

Most raw materials and consumer goods today are not only moved across countries, but also across oceans. To navigate the murky and complex waters of transportation management, companies often turn to **third party logistics service providers**, also known as **3PLPs** or **3PLs**, to provide some or all of the transportation and transportation management services needed. 3PLPs typically bundle a range of these services under one cost structure. Some of the transportation management activities covered by a 3PLP might include:

- *planning shipments and selecting transport carriers;*
- *keeping track of shipments in transit;*
- *determining freight costs prior to shipping;*
- *checking and paying carriers' freight bills;*
- *filing claims with carriers for damaged goods;*
- *transportation budget planning and management;*
- *transportation administration and human resource management;*
- *monitoring and maintaining service quality;*
- *conducting carrier rate negotiations;*
- *keeping up with local, state, federal, and international transport regulations;*
- *planning and handling transport information systems; and*
- *conducting transport systems analysis.*

For most organizations that manufacture or sell goods, members of the purchasing department must become familiar with the costs, services, and reliability of a variety of carriers and 3PLPs. When armed with this knowledge, purchasing professionals are invaluable members of the strategic team that must decide whether or not an organization will outsource its transportation and transport documentation needs.

MODES OF TRANSPORTATION

When a company's purchasing department is deciding who will transport its goods, it must also decide the mode by which its goods will be moved. In the world of logistics and physical distribution management, a **mode of transportation** is the physical means across or through which the goods are carried. These five modes of transportation - *road, rail, water, air,* and *pipeline* - each have different costs and limitations associated with them and offer different advantages and disadvantages. To make effective transportation decisions, purchasing professionals must be familiar with all of the costs,each of these five modes of transportation.

Modes of Transportation: ROAD

Unless you live far within the Brazilian jungle or deep within the earth among H.G. Wells' Morlocks, you probably already know that a **road** is a surfaced route used by vehicles for moving goods or people. Within most countries around the world, road is, by far, the most commonly used mode of transportation. For example, according to the 2007 *U.S. Census Commodity Flow Survey*, which is conducted every seven years, road is the primary mode of transportation for goods transported within the United States. A total of 71% of goods by value and 70% of goods by weight are transported by road across the U.S.

The primary advantage of using roads as a mode of transportation is that, within most countries, more locations are accessible by road than any other mode of transportation. For example, in the United States, the National Highway System measures approximately 160,000 miles! On road networks, vehicles can also operate 24 hours a day, 7 days a week. Compared to other modes of transportation, roads offer more cost-effective movement for smaller deliveries and shorter distances. They are also highly flexible and allows for last minute changes and adjustments. For example, if there are production delays at a factory, it is far easier to change a delivery schedule when containers of goods are being moved by road than when they are being moved by a prescheduled barge.

Although flexible and highly accessible, roads also present disadvantages as a mode of transportation. Traffic jams, congestion, and adverse weather can all affect road delivery times. Labor costs are also higher because the number of drivers or operators required per amount carried is much higher than for other modes of transportation. For example, one truck driver can transport one or two container loads of goods while a crew of five people can transport over 1000 forty-foot containers via cargo ship.

Weight also plays a factor in road transport. The per-ton-mile cost of road transport is higher than those of rail or water. Also, size and weight limitations on national road networks limit carrying very heavy items and large pieces of machinery.

Modes of Transportation: RAIL

The transportation mode of **rail** is commonly used to transport large, heavy, and bulky items and large quantities for long distances. Although rail offers the advantage of transporting large and heavy goods cost effectively, in general, rail is not used as frequently as road transport. According to the 2007 *U.S. Census Commodity Flow Survey*, which is conducted every seven years, rail is used to transport 4% of the total value of all U.S. goods and 15% of all goods by weight.

The primary advantage of rail is that rail cars can accommodate very large, heavy items and it is a less expensive mode of transportation for larger volumes over longer distances than road. Rail also offers greater reliability than many other transportation modes because it is less likely to experience traffic delays (common for road transport) or adverse weather delays (common for air and sea transport). Furthermore, most maritime cargo ports are connected to rail networks, making rail a vital element of global supply chains.

The primary disadvantages of rail are its geographic and time limitations. Rail networks are in limited, fixed locations. Also, rail carriers typically operate only at specific times, making them less flexible than road-based motor carriers. It is also not a suitable mode of transportation for fragile goods nor is it cost effective for small quantities moving short distances. Finally, there are sometimes very long transit times when using rail.

Modes of Transportation: WATER

Water is a mode of transportation used to transport large quantities of nonperishable and bulk goods both domestically and internationally. In domestic trade, goods travel by water within and along the United States through inland and intra-coastal waterways. According to the 2007 *U.S. Census Commodity Flow Survey*, water is the domestic mode of transportation used for 1% of all goods by value and 3% of all goods by weight. In international trade, the majority of goods travel by ocean and enter/leave through container ports. According to the 2011 *U.S. Water Transportation Statistical Snapshot* from the U.S. Department of Transportation Maritime Administration, U.S. foreign container trade increased by 10.1% from 2006 to 2011.

One of the primary advantages of using water transport is that massive quantities of goods and bulky items can be carried at one time. It is also reliable and does not suffer the traffic-related delays of road transportation. Water can also be less costly because it is far less expensive than air for international trade and there are no costs for using ocean waterways.

Water is, however, perhaps the slowest mode of transportation, making it less viable for shipping perishable or time-sensitive goods. These long transit times also increase the insurance costs of goods. Scheduling can also be limited with water transport. Ships sail on fixed schedules, limiting delivery scheduling flexibility, and fog or sever weather can easily cause sailing cancellations.

Modes of Transportation: AIR

Air is the mode of transportation more commonly used for perishable and time-sensitive goods. According to the 2007 *U.S. Census Commodity Flow Survey*, ***air*** is used to transport 2% of the total value of all goods within the U.S. and less than 0.04% of goods by weight.

The primary advantage of air is that, over long distances, it is the fastest mode of transportation available, which can dramatically reduce delivery times. Because of the shorter delivery time, it is suitable for perishable goods, reduces the risk of damage, and requires less packaging of goods. Also, as long as airports are available, air transport can be used to move goods to anywhere in the world.

With air, all of these great advantages come at a price, however. Air transport is very costly, especially compared to other modes of transport. Like water, air also allows for less scheduling flexibility. Flights are generally at fixed times and adverse weather can delay flights and cause transportation delays. Furthermore, airplanes are strictly limited in the weights and item dimensions they can carry.

Modes of Transportation: PIPELINE

Pipeline is the mode of transportation used to carry goods from point to point through a steel or plastic pipe. While oil and natural gas are the goods most commonly transported by pipeline, any form of liquid, such as water or sewage, can be carried via pipeline. Amazingly, even solid goods such as coal can be transported by pipeline.

Although expensive to construct, pipelines yield extremely low transportation cost. According to the 2007 *U.S. Census Commodity Flow Survey*, pipeline systems are used to transport 3% of the total value of all U.S. goods and 5% of all U.S. goods by weight.

THE TRADE-OFF PRINCIPLE

In deciding which mode of transportation to use to ensure that time and place needs are met, purchasing professionals must consider the ***trade-off principle***, in which the advantages and disadvantages of purchasing decisions are considered and evaluated based on the degree of change in the following three criteria: *cost*, *resource use*, and *customer service*. The advantages and disadvantages offered within each of these three areas are weighed against one another to see if the decision under consideration would be an advantageous one.

Expanding on the idea of the trade-off principle, transportation decisions are often made by striking a balance between the advantages and disadvantages offered within the following six criteria:

1. **Cost**. Obviously, transportation costs increase as delivery distances increase, making cost a central factor in determining the geographic limits within which a product can be purchased or sold cost-effectively.

2. **Speed**. For many products or situations, a speedy delivery time may be more important than delivery cost. For example, speedy delivery is essential for perishable goods (such as Maine lobster and Alaska King crab, both of which must be flown to their hungry customers) and goods immediately essential to a large manufacturing operation (such as a spare part needed to repair an ice cream producer's freezer, which will be flown in as quickly as possible before too much product melts).

3. **Safety and Security**. An organization's finished goods are often its most substantial financial assets. In order to protect the value of these assets, the organization must ensure that the transportation system handling its goods keeps them safe from damage and secure from theft at all times. Safety and security are especially important criteria for transportation decisions involving high-cost or hazardous goods.

4. **Convenience**. For a transportation plan or system to be the successful backbone of any logistics or supply chain, it must be convenient to all members of the chain.

Transportation decisions made must consider how easy it is for customers, retailers, wholesalers, distribution centers, warehouses, and manufacturers to interface with those transporting goods. Consider a furniture retail store in Hawaii that needs to ship goods from Los Angeles to Honolulu. If the proposed transportation agent, which is slightly cheaper than other transport agents, does not offer en route communication about the approximate time of shipment delivery, the furniture store would be less likely to consider selecting it because it does not offer the convenience of keeping customers informed of changes in delivery times.

5. **Reliability**. Even when costs are low, deliveries are fast and convenient, and goods are kept safe and secure, a transportation system is no good to an organization when it is not reliable. If transportation can't consistently and reliably get goods where they need to be when they need to be, an organization loses the time and place advantage that reliable transportation provides.

6. **Flexibility**. For organizations that must transport a wide range of goods of different sizes, weights, and handling needs, a flexible transportation system is essential. For example, the transportation system of warehouse-style retailers carrying goods from regional distribution centers to individual stores would need to be flexible enough to handle a wide range of goods within one shipment, from dish detergent to televisions to king-size mattresses.

Throughout this chapter, we examined the importance of time and place in the world of purchasing. We explored the role manufacturing, MRP, and JIT play in getting goods to the right place and at the right time. We also considered the impact that holding inventory and selecting modes of transportation have on time and place considerations. Although time and place are important considerations in world of purchasing, in the next chapter, we will see that equally important is the concept of "getting the right price."

Chapter 5 Review Questions

1. What happens on a manufacturing line if the required inputs do not arrive at the right time or place? If you were the manager of Poppi's Pool Supplies in the example at the beginning of the chapter, how might you have handled the situation differently?

2. How does *MRP* help the *MPS* achieve success?

3. In the Luxury Lamps case study earlier this chapter, if the light bulbs had been delivered to Fresno one week late, how would the delivery of the lamps been affected?

4. Why might a manufacturing organization consider *JIT* in its inventory control system?

5. *Just in time* is a tried and tested concept to reduce inventory held. Under what conditions or circumstances might it be beneficial for a company to hold its inventory?

6. What critical bridge does *transportation* provide between customers and suppliers? Provide an example of this with a company and product that you know.

7. What activities and services might a *3PLP* provide? What are some examples of 3PLPs that you use in your life?

8. What are the *five modes of transportation*? What are the advantages and disadvantages of each? What products might you transport with each mode of transportation?

9. Which mode of transportation is used the most in the United States? Which is used the least? Why?

10. What are the criteria you would consider when weighing the advantages and disadvantages of each mode of transportation?

CHAPTER 5 CASE EXERCISE

Time for a Repeat Purchase of Luxury Lamps by the Alcatraz Hotel

The Alcatraz Hotel in San Francisco, California was so impressed with the quality and the customer service provided by Luxury Lamps, Ltd. that the hotel has decided to buy 100 of a different lamp. They had previously purchased model 1111 and are now interested in the larger, twin bulb model number 1149 called "the Serenity lamp." The hotel's purchasing manager orders the lamps on January 1st so that they will be delivered within 10 weeks to San Francisco.

About the Model 1149:

The base (one required per lamp) and lamp shades (two required per lamp) for the Model 1149 are both hand painted and purchased from Mexico, with a lead time of 5 weeks and there is currently no inventory in the warehouse. Each lamp requires two bulbs, purchased in Sarasota, Florida and has a lead time of 2 weeks. Luxury Lamps, Ltd. currently has 500 bulbs in inventory at their Fresno distribution center. The on/off switch (two per lamp) are purchased in Phoenix, Arizona and have a lead time of 3 weeks. There is currently an inventory of 100 on/off switches held at the Fresno facility. The bulb holders (two required per lamp) are purchased from Vancouver, Canada with a lead time of 5 weeks. Luxury Lamps holds a current inventory of 50 bulb holders. Electric plugs (one required per lamp) are purchased in Knoxville, Tennessee, have a lead time of 2 weeks, and a current inventory of 50 plugs at the Fresno facility.

The Luxury Lamps, Ltd. manufacturing facility is in Buffalo, New York and their distribution center for all west coast distribution is in Fresno, California. All the lamp parts (except bulbs and electrical plugs which are required and fitted in Fresno) are held and assembled in Buffalo.

When all of the lamps arrive in Fresno from New York, the Fresno distribution center completes the final assembly by fitting bulbs and electrical plugs before delivering the completed lamps to the final customer. It takes one week to assemble lamps at the New York Luxury Lamps manufacturing facility, one week to ship the lamps from New York to Fresno, one week to fit the two bulbs and plug at the Fresno distribution center, and one week to deliver goods from Fresno to the final customer.

As they make their purchasing decision, the purchasing manager at Luxury Lamps, Ltd. must consider:

- when and where the parts are required at their respective assembly points
- their suppliers' lead times, and the quantities of inventory already available
- the assembly time at the Buffalo plant (1week)
- the distribution time to Fresno (1week)
- the time needed to fit the bulbs and plugs in Fresno (1 week)
- the time it takes to deliver the Serenity lamps assembled in Fresno to the customer in San Francisco (1 week)
- the completion deadline of the 2nd week in March, which is 10 weeks from the receipt of the order

<u>Instructions:</u>

Using the models shown in Figures 5.2, 5.3, 5.4, and 5.5 as a presentation guide, prepare a Master Production Schedule, Bill of Materials, and a Materials Requirement Plan for item 1149. You must take into account all the constraints mentioned above.

Chapter 6

Understanding the Right Price

Dr. Morgan Henrie & Dr. Philip M. Price

Way back in Chapter 4, we explored how the purchasing professional can calculate the right quantity to ensure inventory is available when needed. We examined the case that when it comes to materials, having too much or too little inventory can be detrimental to any company. Too much excess inventory increases overall operating costs because it causes holding costs, insurance costs, and shrinkage losses to increase. However, with too little inventory, a company may run out of required parts or material and may not be able to meet its obligations to its customers. This can impact immediate revenue streams and cause the loss of future business. This chapter will examine the factors involved in determining the right or *fair price*.

GETTING STARTED WITH GETTING THE RIGHT PRICE

Obtaining materials and service for your organization at a fair and reasonable price has a significant impact on its ultimate success or failure. If you pay more for goods or services than is a fair price, you lower the overall profitability of your organization. Conversely, if you drive such a hard bargain that the supplier fails to make a profit on the sale, they will be hesitant or unwilling to do business with you in the future. Ultimately, it is best for all concerned that the purchasing professional obtains the company's needs at a fair price so that all concerned can make a profit and stay in business.

When it comes to increasing a firm's profits, there are two primary methods to achieve this goal. First, the firm can generate more revenue and subsequently more profits by increasing its sales, which results in an increase in market share. This revenue-increasing method faces a range of challenges, including global, national, and local competition. Competing companies are all trying to increase their own market share and every market has a finite number of participants. In a stagnant or decreasing market, for a firm to increases its market share, another firm must lose some market share. Although many companies try, increasing profit by concentrating solely on increasing market share is difficult to achieve.

The second method for increasing profits is to reducing overall costs while maintaining current sales figures. If the **revenue stream**, or money coming in from sales, remains constant while production costs decrease, profits go up. Purchasing professionals have the greatest opportunity to reduce their companies' operating expenses and subsequently increase profits by reducing the costs of materials and services purchased. Getting goods and services at the right or *fair price* can mean the difference between success and failure for many organizations. But what does it mean to obtain a ***fair price***? As previously mentioned, a fair price must be a price that allows the purchasing firm to obtain a profit while also allowing the supplying firm to obtain a profit. If either firm fails to make a profit on the overall deal, the resulting price is not a fair price.

When purchasing professionals receive a request to obtain a product or service they need to determine if the requested item is a commodity item or not. ***Commodity items*** are those parts or services that have: *several sources or suppliers, a minimum acceptable quality level common across all sources*, and *suppliers that compete on price*. With commodity items, if your primary source fails to or is unable to meet your demand, switching to another supplier is easy and has minimal to no additional costs. For many firms, paper products, cleaning supplies, and office supplies are examples of a commodity item.

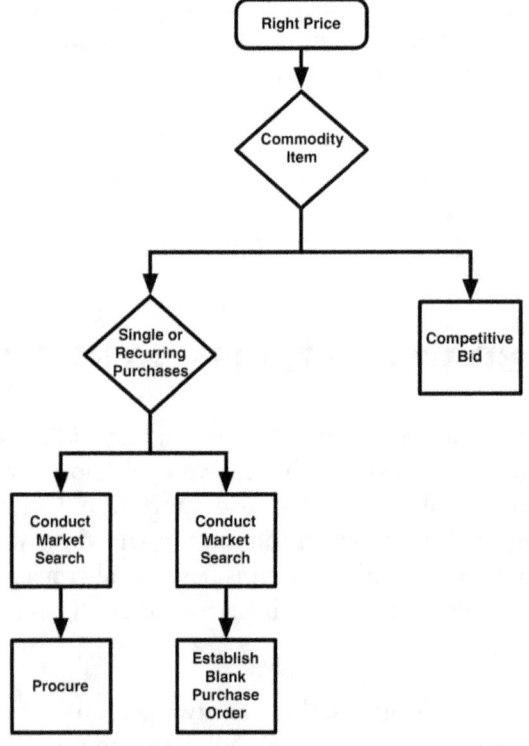

Figure 6.1 - Decision Making in the Purchasing Process

As shown in the flowchart in Figure 6.1, if the requested item is a non-essential production input and a commodity item, the purchasing professional must then determine if this is a ***single*** or a ***recurring purchase***. If this is a single purchase, the purchasing professional will make a quick market survey to identify where the item can be obtained. With a single purchase, the purchasing professional does not usually take the time to conduct a competitive bid or enter into protracted negotiations. The cost of a single, non-essential, production input commodity item purchase does not warrant the costs of the competitive bidding or negotiation process.

If the current purchase request is one of many to come, the purchasing professional may negotiate a long-term procurement agreement with the supplier. This agreement can take the form of a blanket purchase order. A ***blanket purchase order (BPO)*** is an agreement between buyer and supplier that establishes the pricing structure, invoicing requirements, and payment methods, all before an order is placed. The BPO then allows the requesting firm to initiate a recurring request simply and expeditiously.

On the other hand, if the purchasing professional receives a request for an item or service that is not a commodity item but is instead a ***special item*** or ***unique need***, a different procurement path is followed. This different path usually involves developing and implementing a competitive bid process that results in obtaining a negotiated fair price.

COMPETITIVE STRUCTURES IN THE SUPPLY MARKET

Every purchase occurs within specific supply and demand environments. In their most basic form, the three types of supply and demand environment are: *perfect competition*, *oligopoly*, and *monopoly*. Each of these types of supply and demand environment impacts how fair prices are obtained.

PERFECT COMPETITION

An environment of ***perfect competition*** is a market condition in which several firms provide homogenous material or services and no single firm can or does influence the price of goods. In an environment of perfect competition, each firm offers its product at the lowest price possible that still allows them to recoup their costs and remain in business. At the same time, no single entity has a majority of the market share and purchasers of the product or service are free to switch easily between suppliers at any time.

An economist might describe an environment of perfect competition as firms offering their output where the ***marginal costs***, or the change in cost when more than one item or service is produced, are equal to ***marginal revenues***, or the increase in revenue when more than one item or service is sold. In this environment, a firm would not be able to lower its offering price and still recover its internal costs because it would be operating at a loss. Since no firm will operate at a loss for long, competition does not occur by lowering prices for long. Conversely, in a perfect competition market, a firm will not raise the price of their product or service either. The controlling factor here is there are many existing competitors who offer identical units. If one firm raises their price, competing firms will continue to offer the product or service at a lower price, which will increase sales for these firms while reducing sales for those who raised their prices.

In reality, an environment of strictly perfect competitive does not exist. Firms do increase and decrease product prices for many reasons. The market does respond to the changes, but a time lag and other factors tend to keep the market moving towards a state of perfect competition, even though perfect balance may never be achieved. While an environment of true perfect competitive does not exist, purchasing professionals can leverage the close approximation of this environment because they can rely on price competition and the ability to easily switch between suppliers.

OLIGOPOLY

An *oligopoly* is a market environment in which a small set of firms dominates the overall market. In this environment, there are significant barriers to market entry that limit the ability of other firms to enter the marketplace. All companies are very well aware of other competing firms and the actions they take in the marketplace. Thus, decisions and actions taken by one firm generate a fast response from its few competitors.

In this environment, pricing of products and services is based more on what the competition is doing rather than on the firm's own internal costs. Oligopoly firms operate at a profit margin much higher than commodity-based or perfect competition environments because they try to compete on value-added product or service attributes instead of price.

An example of a near-oligopoly market is one in which two or three airlines provide service to a specific area. The number of suppliers is limited and each firm has a very strong understanding of their competitor's pricing structure, internal costs, and value- added features. This extensive competitor knowledge allows each firm to focus on value-added features over price structures in buyer-supplier negotiations.

MONOPOLY

A *monopoly* is a market environment in which a product or service is provided by a single entity. There is no competition or alternative source from which the purchasing professional can obtain the product or service. A prime example of a monopoly is the municipal water and sewer service most of us utilize. In this situation, the only entity that can and does offer fresh water to our homes and businesses is our local municipal water service. You either avail yourself of these services or you go without fresh water.

Monopolies can occur when an extreme barrier to market entry exists. Over time, the railroad, electric companies, natural gas suppliers, and telephone companies all held a monopoly on their services. In each of these environments, the cost of entering the market, i.e., building a new rail or water pipe infrastructure, was so high that it effectively blocked out anyone from entering the marketplace. In an effort to protect the consumer, a variety of laws and regulations have been enacted. These laws and regulations are designed specifically to prevent firms with a monopoly from reaping unrealistic profits by taking unfair advantage of the consumer.

BASIC PRINCIPLES OF SUPPLY AND DEMAND

In a market-based economy, sellers and buyers are free to interact at will. In theory, sellers can set any price they want for the products or services they provide. At the same time, buyers are free to procure products and services from whomever they want to at whatever price they agree to. While sellers and buyers are free to sell and buy at any price structure, in reality, a free marketplace operates within the ***law of supply and demand***. In a competitive, free market economy, the price for an item will fluctuate based on the availability of supply and the levels of consumer demand until it reaches an equilibrium. If there is an increasing demand for an item and an unchanging supply level or if there is an unchanging demand and and decreasing supply of the item, equilibrium is reached at a higher item price. Conversely, if there is a decreasing demand for an item and an unchanging supply level or if there is an unchanging demand and and increasing supply of the item, equilibrium is reached at a lower item price.

While the market place tries to ensure price equilibrium, the market is in continuous motion. At any point in time, supply may exceed demand or demand may exceed supply. These forces will tend to drive the price of the product or service price either up or down, depending on which side of the market is out of balance and which market environment is supplying the product or service.

So how does understanding the basic fundamentals of the law of supply and demand and the market environment help purchasing professionals perform their job successfully? To start with, a knowledgeable purchasing professional has a significant leverage over an uniformed purchasing professional. If the purchasing professional is informed of how the law operates and they are monitoring the supply and demand environment, they can make informed decisions. Part of the decision process is to establish purchasing strategies that assist them in obtaining the right quantity at the right place at a fair price, all based on how the law of supply and demand might be out of balance. For example, if you know that supply is greater than demand, you can try to obtain a better price. If demand is outpacing supply, it might be the wisest decision to wait and see how the market moves before purchasing the required items. In the end, knowledge is power and informed decisions outperform uninformed decisions.

We will discuss where we can find suppliers in Chapter 7, "Supplier Selection."

GETTING A FAIR PRICE

The process of getting the right or ***fair price*** is influenced by the attributes of the requested part or service, the supplier environment, and the buying company's purchasing policies. Some of the most popular methods for establishing a fair price are: *accepting the list or posted price, negotiating a discount, competitive bidding,* and *engaging in a reverse auction*.

For commodity-based items, such as cleaning supplies, nuts and bolts, or other occasionally purchased lesser-value items, a fair price is often set as the suppliers' list or posted price. On a normal day, anyone can procure the item at this price. With items of a very small value and when only a small quantity is required, suppliers will rarely negotiate on price and the posted price will be very similar from one supplier to another. In this situation, the purchasing professional can easily switch from one supplier to another with virtually no penalty or risk.

A posted price might also be accepted when the purchasing professional does not need to procure a large quantity, or ***high volume***, of the item. In this situation, the firm does not require sufficient quantities to warrant the time and energy trying to negotiate a lower price. However, if procurement needs are very large, even for items of lesser value, the firm then has sufficient clout to negotiate a discount price. For example, because of its massive purchases worldwide, Walmart negotiate bulk discounts on even its least expensive items. Unless the quantities required are very large, there usually is no merit in trying to negotiate a lower price because negotiation time and effort costs will far out weigh any potential price reductions that may occur.

While a firm may not have the purchasing clout of Walmart, it may still have sufficient needs that warrant entering into negotiations. For example, a company may establish a ***preferred supplier agreement*** with a supplier. This preferred supplier agreement would be guaranteed that the purchasing firm would order a set or group of required materials or services over a set period of time and that the preferred supplier would offer these items at a negotiated discount.

A ***negotiated discount*** is another option for purchasing professionals seeking a fair price. (Remember our bulk discount in our "EOQ & Discounts" example back in Chapter 3?) When larger orders are desired, a supplier is often willing to negotiate a lower price in exchange for a firm commitment for this larger order. This commitment allows the supplier to negotiate from its supplier's favorable raw material prices. A manufacturing firm can often reduce the per unit variable costs based on producing large quantities of identical items during a fixed time frame. Understanding these conditions allows the purchasing professional the ability to know when negotiating bulk discounts is possible or not. There are times when it is worth negotiating rather than accepting the supplier's list price. There are other times, however, when a company's policies will dictate that negotiations must occur, such as when government organizations are engaged in procurement.

When a *competitive bid process* must take place, purchasing professionals lead the process. **Competitive bid processes** are usually linked to company policies or specific attributes of the requested product or service. For example, a company may have a policy that anything with a total value of over $5,000,000 must be competitively bid. Such policies prevent the purchasing professional from entering into an agreement with a single source without first engaging in a competitive bid process, thus protecting both the company and the purchasing professional. The company is protected because they leverage competition to obtain a fair price. The purchasing professional is protected because it is much harder to unduly influence a purchasing professional during competitive bidding than during sole or single source procurement.

A request to potential suppliers for a competitive bid can take many forms, including a *request for information (RFI)*, *request for proposal (RFP)*, or *request for quote (RFQ)*. The steps in most competitive bidding processes include:

1. *Develop detailed specifications and requirements documents*
2. *Develop detailed bid request documents*

3. *Issue the request to an identified set of suppliers or as an open solicitation so anyone qualified can bid*

4. *Receive supplier bid responses*

5. *Compare the received bid responses*

6. *Negotiate*

If the competitive bid process begins with an **RFI**, the intent of the request is to determine which suppliers are interested in participating further. In this situation, the requesting firm is trying to identify the number of available and interested suppliers to assess whether or not competitive bidding would be possible.

When an **RFP** is used in the competitive bidding process, a company asks the responding supplier organization to provide a solution to the purchasing company's needs. In this process, the requesting firm has a need that can be supplied by several different methods or processes. For example, a firm has a need to transport 75 people between two locations three times a day. The purchasing professional provides an RFP that outlines the requirements of when, from where, and to where people must be transported along with a series of special requirements for passengers, such as the availability of free water and a selection of sodas. All potential suppliers are asked to submit a proposal that meets these requirements and the price they will charge to meet the needs.

In this example, a supplier could propose using a yellow school bus, several small vans, a luxury coach bus, or some other creative method. The key here is that the purchasing professional has a need that can be solved in more than one way. In this situation, the supplier is asking potential suppliers to determine the most economical way to meet these needs and propose the solution and associated costs. The firm will then select the best package that meets the request's requirements at a fair price. (Remember that "best" does not necessarily mean lowest price.)

An **RFQ** is different from an RFP in that the RFQ request specifically states how the supplier will meet the purchasing professional's needs. The requestor has a specific solution that they want or need and that solution is the only acceptable response. For example, a purchasing professional has received a request for an on-site security guard at the gate of a new building, 24 hours a day, 7 days a week. Due to internal company policies, security personnel's skill sets, certifications, and training have been precisely defined. Because more than one security firm can meet these requirements, the purchasing professional issues an RFQ to initiate the competitive bidding process in order to find a supplier offering a fair price.

In this RFQ, the purchasing professional does not ask the potential suppliers to propose any one of a range of options. The request is to provide a price to supply personnel meeting the detailed requirements and specifications provided. If multiple firms all meet the minimum requirements, selecting the preferred supplier is predominately driven by who is offering the fairest price.

Competitive bidding takes time and costs money. For unique, large quantity items or for very expensive items, competitive bidding provides a means to obtain the product or service at a fair price. The obtained fair price is usually lower than list prices, as the potential suppliers know they are in competition with others and part of the selection criteria is price. Meeting or exceeding the purchasing professional's needs, all at the lowest price, increases the potential that a supplier will win the bid.

A fairly new competitive bid structure has recently entered the world of purchasing and has become quite popular in the past few years. This new competitive bid structure, called a **reverse auction**, is an online processes that is either controlled by a third-party website or the purchasing professional's internal intranet reverse auction software. In a reverse auction, the buying firm posts online a complete description of the product or service they are trying to procure. The buyer then provides a selected set of potential suppliers access to the reverse auction webpage. The suppliers then have access to the requesting documents and the online location to which they can provide their bid. The supplier's **bid** is the price at which they are willing to sell the requested product or service as specified in the reverse auction site.

During the reverse auction process, all potential suppliers can see the lowest offered price at any time. The potential suppliers cannot see who made the offer; they just know what the lowest and most current bid offered. Based on this information, the competing suppliers can decide if they want to make a lower price offer or drop out of the bidding process. The ultimate objective is for the purchasing professional to obtain the requested product or service at the lowest cost using this new online auction process.

METHODS OF PRICING PRODUCTS & SERVICES

An effective purchasing professional must understand how suppliers establish prices for their products and services. This knowledge allows the purchasing professional to make informed decisions on whether to buy something at list price, enter into negotiations, or conduct a competitive bid process. Knowledge is essential to making informed decisions. Suppliers us a variety of pricing methods, including:

- *Cost-based pricing*
- *Demand-based pricing*
- *Value-based pricing*
- *Market-based pricing*

The most traditional method of establishing product pricing is **cost-based pricing**, which can be defined by the formula in Equation 1 below:

EQUATION 1   **Price = Fixed cost per unit + variable cost per unit + fixed profit percentage**

As Equation 1 shows, the supplying firm must determine what proportion of its total fixed operating costs will be allocated to each unit, the variable cost associated with producing each unit, and how much profit each unit should bring in based on a percentage of the total cost. This establishes the selling price.

Cost-based pricing is a very common and straightforward pricing structure. What it fails to take into consideration, however, is the law of supply and demand. Equation 1 contains no factors for competitors' pricing, market share objectives, or other factors that may ultimately set the actual price consumers may be willing to pay. Establishing cost-based pricing for new products or services is also difficult as the full cost of producing the new item is not fully known until after the product has been produced through a few manufacturing runs.

With ***demand-based pricing***, suppliers focus on attributes such as *quality* and *customer characteristics* rather than costs, such as firms that sell goods that are perceived as high quality or upper class products. In this price-setting strategy, the supplier forecasts the number of units that can be sold at various prices levels. The final price is set based on the revenue levels the firm wants to achieve and the forecast that indicates how many products may be sold at different price structures. In the end, the supplier must have an excellent understanding of its customer base and what its customers are willing to pay. This knowledge allows the supplier to establish a selling price based on forecasted demands.

Value-based pricing is similar to demand-based pricing in that it sets the selling price based on the *value* the selling firm believes the customers place on its product or service. If the customer places a higher value on a perceived higher quality of goods and is willing to pay the higher price, suppliers can use value-based pricing. For example, paying for a first class airline seat is a type of value-based pricing. The customer perceives that the first class service is of higher quality and worth more than sitting in the rear of the airplane. In this example, all airline seats arrive at the same location, at the same time; it is the perceived quality of service difference that determines the selling price.

Market-based pricing is a pricing method in which the seller uses three distinct components that establish the final selling price, as shown in Equation 2 below:

EQUATION 2   Price = cost + minimum profit + price range

The primary difference between market-based pricing in Equation 2 and cost-based pricing in Equation 1 is the price range. The ***price range*** is the range of perceived value that the firm estimates their customers place on the product or service. As this customer-perceived value increases or decreases, the selling firm can adjust the selling price and still maintain an acceptable profit level. With the dynamic nature of market-based pricing, the selling firm can enter into a tradeoff between market share and price per unit which means that it can try to increase market share by lowering the price or try to maximize the per unit revenue stream by increasing the unit price but at the risk of losing market share.

A selling firm uses several methods to establish the price of its products and services. The final price is driven by a variety of factors, such as the cost to produce the product, the firm's market share objective, perceived quality, competition, customer perceived value, and the supplier's desired revenue stream. Depending on the type of product or service, one or more of these variables may determine the pricing method and control the final selling price.

DISCOUNTING STRUCTURES

The previous section discussed several way firms establish the selling price of a product or service, but the pricing process doesn't end there. To increase the complexity of establishing a final price, sellers and buyers often negotiate discounts that are lower than the list price. There are many discount structures that can be used singly or in combination with each other. Some of the more popular types of discounts offered are based on:

1. *cash payment,*
2. *geographic location,*
3. *seasonal sales,* and
4. *promotions.*

Cash discounts are provided as an incentive to pay for the item when the order is placed or possession of the item occurs. For example, if a local gas station will sell you a gallon of gas for $0.04 less per gallon when you pay with cash instead of a credit card, you have received a cash discount. This 4 cent discount is associated with the price the credit card company charges the gas station for handling the gasoline purchase. (Yes, credit card companies do charge sellers for handling the money exchanges as well as charging buyers for using their credit card.) The gas station would prefer that you use cash and are willing to pass on a portion of their cost savings. Cash-based business saves a company money because it doesn't have to deal with handling charge accounts, invoicing costs, and accounts receivable costs.

Are cash discounts worth the hassle? Let's look at... The Case of Tucker the Trucker!

Tucker is a long distance truck driver who owns and operates his own truck. As part of his hauling contracts, Trucker must cover the cost of all diesel fuel consumed. Since this is a direct cost to him, he is always on the lookout for the lowest diesel price. On a recent trip, Tucker saw two truck stops with the following diesel prices posted:

Truck Stop #1: $3.15 per gallon (credit card or cash)

Truck Stop #2: $3.20 per gallon (credit card) and $3.14 per gallon (cash)

Should Trucker go to Truck Stop #1 or #2 if he buys 100 gallons of diesel?

For this small purchase, we can elect to ignore factors such as opportunity costs and leveraging and instead focus on the actual transaction. The following shows Tucker's costs for the three ways he can procure the diesel.

Truck Stop #1: $3.15 per gallon x 100 gallons = $315.00

Truck Stop #2: $3.20 per gallon (credit) x 100 gallons = $320.00

Truck Stop #2: $3.20 per gallon (cash) x 100 gallons = $314.00

Paying cash at Truck Stop #2 will save Tucker $6 over using the credit and it will save him $1 over the Truck Stop #1 credit card purchase. Therefore, he should go with Truck Stop #1 and pay cash. While a dollar savings might not seem like very much, if Tucker was able to save $1 per fill up for the 200 times per year that he fills his tank, he would save $200 per year. As an independent owner/operator, $200 per year is real money!

Tucker's mom, Talia, owns a fleet of 100 trucks and currently purchases diesel from Truck Stop #1. How much could she save if she were to follow her son's example?

Quantity discounts are another popular discount structure. The "EOQ and Discounts" example way back in the Chapter 3 was a prime example of a quantity discount. Rather than place ten order of 400 units each, it was more cost effective to place fewer orders of 1600 units each.

Do quantity discounts really work? Let's look at... The Case of Kathy's Cab Company!

Kathy's Cab Company operates a fleet of 100 cabs. The firm performs routine maintenance once a month where they replace several items on each cab, such as air filters. The lead mechanic knows that they must replace 100 air filters each month. Historically, they have purchased 100 air filters every month. This order covers the expected needs for the next month.

Kathy's supplier has offered to provide air filters at a range of costs depending on the quantity ordered. If Kathy's firm continues to order 100 units at a time, the price remains $25 per unit. If 200 or more units are ordered, the price is reduced by 10%. Kathy's lead mechanic can maintain an inventory of up to 200 units.

If there are no extra inventory holding costs, should Kathy's lead mechanic order 100 air filters twice or 200 units at once?

Order 100 units twice = ($25 x 100) x 2 = $5,000

Order 200 units once = ((0.9 x $25) x 200) x 1 = $4,500

Savings = $5,000 - $4,500 = $500

Kathy's Cab Company can save $500 by ordering 200 units at once. The average air filter cost is now $22.50 per unit instead of the original price of $25.00 per unit.

Firms are often very agreeable to selling larger quantities at a lower price. Several factors drive this agreeability, such as larger orders that allow the supplier to maximize equipment utilization, which reduces per unit fixed costs and variable costs. Large orders also reduce the costs of handling orders at every stage in the exchange process. It costs the firm money to handle and process each order from the time the order is received, when an invoice is generated and the accounts receivable enters the received amounts. If one order can be placed rather than 3 orders, the overall cost of order handling has been reduced by 66%. Reducing an activity cost by 66% is usually worth doing.

Other factors that must be taken into consideration when negotiating quantity discounts are **inventory-holding costs** (see Chapter 3) When you procure more of an item than can be immediately consumed, the extra items received require storage, physical tracking, and insurance costs. Storing extra items creates an inventory of that product, which can have a broad impact on the firm.

Holding inventory requires the firm to maintain an active list of what is currently available and conduct periodic counts to verify the physical assets match the listed assets. These activities all cost time and money, which form part of the company's inventory carrying costs. Total inventory costs not only include the accounting and tracking functions but also include capital costs, shrinkage losses, carrying costs, physical control and security costs, insurance costs, and lost opportunity costs.

While actual inventory costs vary by industry, the average range of inventory costs per year is 20-30%. Equation 3 below illustrates what an inventory cost would be if it is figured at 25% based on a $1,000,000 average inventory value.

EQUATION 3   Inventory cost = average inventory value x inventory cost %

Inventory cost = $1,000,000 x 25% = $250,000

This equation shows that it will cost the firm $250,000/year to carry an average inventory worth $1,000,000. Understanding the *tradeoff* between inventory cost and quantity discounts is critical when deciding whether or not to pursue a quantity discount.

Another discount some firms offer is the **geographic location discount**. This discount is usually associated with the physical proximity of the supplier and purchasers' locations. If your firm is within so many miles of the supplier, they may charge a lower cost or provide additional services. For example, a location discount offered could be free delivery if you are within 50 miles of the supplier's warehouse. We encounter geographic location discounts in our daily lives when we order pizza for home delivery. Some pizza places will deliver your pizza for free if you live within a specific mile radius of their store. If you live outside this area, they may add an extra charge for delivering. This extra charge is supposed to cover the additional time and costs for driving further to make the delivery.

Many commercial firms have established the same consideration in their pricing structure. If the supplying firm is in California, they will provide free shipping to purchasers in a predefined geographic location, such as the seven western states. For firms outside this location, such as in Alaska or Florida, they will add a delivery charge to the final price.

Other common discounts include *seasonal* and *promotional* discounts. One form of a **seasonal discount** is the markdown of winter clothes as spring and summer approach. In this case, the store is trying to sell products that will have minimal demand for several months. It is better to sell the product at a lower profit, or even a small loss, than paying the inventory costs of carrying a product through the season, to only be out of style the next winter.

Promotional discounts involve special offerings from the supplier as an effort to bring in new customers. If you've opened up a new store and want to entice people to come to your shop, you might offer a discount on products during a preset introductory time period. This approach also applies to offering a new product or service versus a new location. In this case, the new product or service price is discounted as an effort to encourage people to buy it so the firm can increase its market share.

From this discussion, it is clear that suppliers can and do provide a range of discounts. Which discount may be available is driven by a variety of factors, such as the need to reduce inventory, leverage increased efficiencies, reduce direct order handling costs, physical location, and the need to increase market share. Understanding these dynamics allows the purchasing professional to make informed decisions on how to leverage potential discounts in establishing a fair price.

PRICE STRUCTURE	PROS	CONS
Firm Fixed Price, a contract that gives the subcontractor full responsibility for performance costs and resulting profit/loss	Final price is fully agreed. Limits **buyer's** financial risk Lower administration costs.	**Seller** has increased financial risk if product or service costs more than originally estimated.
Firm Fixed Price with Escalations, a fixed-price contract that provides for upward revision of the stated price if pre-defined price fluctuations occur	Establishes a definition on how the agreed to price can change. Reduces the **supplier's** financial risk for an agreed set of escalations.	Increased **buyer's** risk as agreed escalations increase the final costs Increased administration costs.
Firm Fixed Price with De-escalations, a fixed-price contract that provides for downward revision of the stated price if pre-defined price fluctuations occur	Establishes a definition on how the agreed price can change. Reduces the **supplier's** financial risk for an agreed set of de-escalations. Reduces **buyer's** financial risk as the price can decrease based on agreed terms.	Increased administration costs.
Firm Fixed Price with Redetermination, established as a firm fixed-price contract for an initial period, after which, subsequent contract pricing is subject to renegotiation	Establishes a definition on how the agreed price can change.	Increased administration costs. Increased **buyer's** risk as agreed price may increase. Increased **seller's** risk as agreed price may decrease.
Firm Fixed Price with Incentives, a contract which includes additional incentives based on achieving excellence in quality, timeliness, ingenuity, or cost management	Limits **seller's** risk as an agreed profit or incentive price structure and formula is agreed.	Increased administration costs. Increased **buyer** risk as a final, full price is not established at the contract signing.
Cost Plus Incentive Fee, a contract in which the contractor is paid the total target cost plus an agreed fixed fee plus a percentage of the difference between the target cost and actual cost	Limits **seller's** risk as they are to be compensated for all costs incurred plus an incentive for providing the product or service at an amount lower than the contract's total costs. Limits the **buyer's** risk as it encourages the seller to provide a final product or service at a lower cost than the upper contract limit.	Increased administration costs. Determining actual costs is historically difficult. Raises **buyer's** risk in that the seller 'includes' a broad range of costs. Raises **seller's** risk in that they fail to account for all allowable costs.
Cost Plus Fixed Profit, a contract in which the contractor is paid the total cost plus a stated fixed percentage of profit	Limits **seller's** risk as they are to be compensated for all costs incurred plus an agreed fixed profit margin.	Increased administration costs. Increased **buyer's** risk as a final, full price is not established at the contract signing. Increased risk as determining actual costs may be difficult.
Cost Sharing, a cost reimbursement contract in which the subcontractor absorbs a portion of the costs in the expectation of substantial compensating benefits	Limits **buyer's** risk as seller's profit margin is based on meeting specific efficiencies.	Increased administration costs. Increased **seller's** risk as no profit is obtained if specific efficiencies are not met.
Time and Material, a contract in which the contractor is paid a specific price for different elements of the work	Pay only for time and material consumed.	No maximum amount that may be invoiced and **buyer** carries a higher cost base risk level.

Figure 6.2 - Negotiated Purchasing Structures

Understanding Cost in an Enforceable Contract

In simple purchasing processes, the supplier offers a product or service at a listed price and the purchasing professional agrees to buy it at that price. The product or service is exchanged and the purchasing professional's company pays the supplier the agreed price. This is a very straightforward process that is easy to understand and follow. When the firm enters into a negotiated contract, however, the pricing structure can, and often does, become more complex.

Contract pricing structures come in many forms. The table in Figure 6.2 on the previous page highlights just some of the many negotiated pricing structure agreements that a purchasing professional may encounter through the course of their duties. Each of these negotiated commercial terms is intended to develop a fair price for a product or service within a specific contractual environment. No pricing structure is perfect, however, and each has its pros and cons. Selection of the best pricing structure for a given purchase will be driven by the specific product or service, the purchaser's and seller's company policies, and the market environment.

There are many ways that a seller and purchaser can come to terms on a negotiated fair price. All parties involved must remember that each pricing structure will have both positive and negative implications, which must be fully understood by both parties. Some pricing structures may favor the seller while others may favor the buyer. The objective is to develop a pricing structure that doesn't penalize either firm but that instead establishes a fair price for both the buyer and the seller.

Total Cost of Ownership Theory

Total cost of ownership, or ***TCO***, is the complete set of costs associated with an asset over its entire life cycle. For materials that are specifically purchased as parts or components of the firm's products or service, the total cost of ownership is very limited. The item is purchased, incorporated into the product or service, and passed on when the final product or service is sold. If the item is priced correctly, the firm not only recovers the cost associated with the original raw material purchased but also the costs associated with development of the product or service. In this case, the firm actually makes money off the life cycle within a short period of time.

The total cost of ownership looks quite different for purchased capital items that are used over long periods in the firm's daily business. Such items include the firm's buildings, mechanical equipment, computer systems, and software applications. Each of these items has a definitive life cycle with associated costs. The sum of all of these costs, from initial investment to final disposal, is the item's life cycle total cost of ownership.

Figure 6.3 is a simplified view of the total cost of ownership concept for a capital item used in an organization's daily business. TCO starts with the initial purchase price and associated project costs. These costs are usually incurred as a project takes the original need and develops a final system that the organization can then use for its intended purpose. During the initial purchase and implementation of an item, specific decisions are made which ultimately affect the organization's daily operation and maintenance costs. Because of the ultimate impact of an item's

TCO on the company's ultimate profits, the ultimate system owners, users, and maintenance personnel should be actively involved in the initial decision-making portion of the purchasing process.

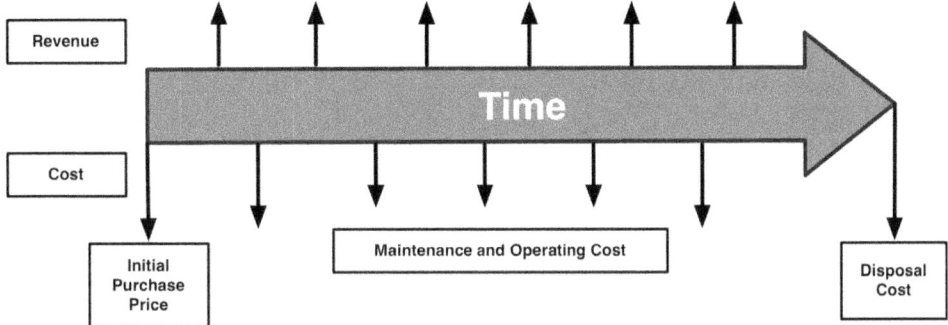

Figure 6.3 - The Total Cost of Ownership Line

After the system, such as a manufacturing or computer information system, has been commissioned and turned over for use, the firm should start to receive a revenue stream directly related to the system. This is shown as the positive, upward-facing arrows on the TCO timeline in Figure 6.3. This recurring revenue stream will continue until the system is removed from service.

After the system becomes operational, TCO operational costs and maintenance costs start to occur. These costs are shown as the negative, downward-facing arrows on the TCO timeline in Figure 6.3. Operational costs can include operators' labor hours, electricity costs, and insurance costs. Maintenance costs would also include the cost of repair parts, system upgrade costs, labor costs to fix the system, and preventative maintenance costs. Other costs that are often included in TCO are lost capital opportunity costs, fees and taxes, depreciation costs, and some corporate overhead costs. In essence, purchasing and operating a system has an overall cost associated with its life cycle.

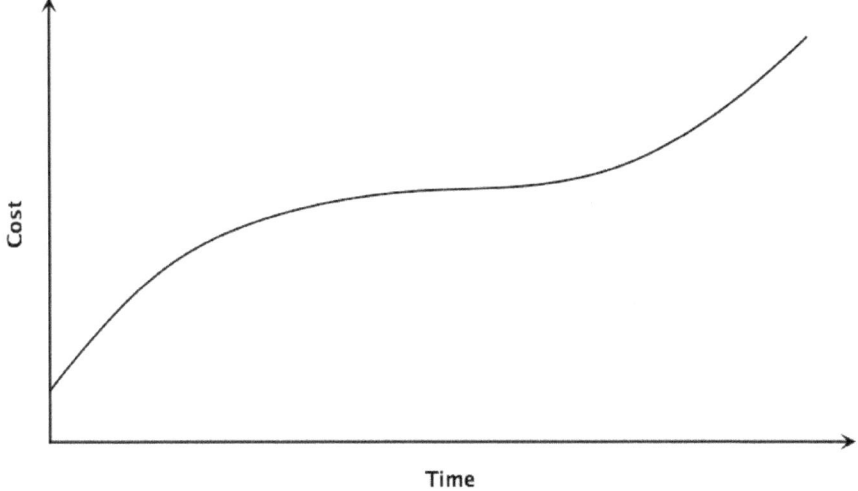

Figure 6.4 - The TCO Cost Curve

All systems have a life cycle consisting of four stages: initial purchase, implementation, utilization, and final disposal. Throughout this life cycle, there are specific costs directly related to the system. The sum of all life cycle costs determines the TCO.

Figure 6.4 above is a representative cost curve based on the Total Cost of Ownership Line in Figure 6.3. At initial investment, or time = 0, the firm incurred an initial investment cost. As time progressed, the system continued to incur a cost, which is indicated as a cumulative cost. Finally, the system is disposed of and the TCO cumulative curve ends at some maximum level.

TCO costs should be included in the initial analysis of any new system purchase. It isn't uncommon for systems with the lowest initial costs to actually generate the highest TCO overall. This is driven by the fact that, while the initial system purchase cost may be less than 10% of TCO, these early decisions can generate 80% of future operating and maintenance costs. For example, although the initial purchase price of a 20-year-old clunker car may be low, you may pay far more in maintenance and repair costs than you would for an initially more expensive used car.

LEGAL CONSIDERATIONS

While the free market environment tends to be a self-correcting system over time, organizations and individuals have engaged in improper or immoral pricing activities. For example, a few oligopoly organizations may come together and collectively agree to a pricing structure that maximizes their profits to the detriment of their customers and other competitors. Another example occurs when a monopoly exists and the monopoly, again, maximizes its profit margin at the cost to the consumer. To address these various improper pricing issues, government agencies have enacted a set of laws and regulations in an effort to protect the consumer from unfair practices.

The history of pricing regulation in the United States government can be traced back to the railroad monopolies of the nineteenth century. In the late 1880s, John D. Rockefeller, Sr. was given an unfair price advantage by the railroads when compared to his competition. This abuse and its impact on consumers resulted in the creation of the ***Interstate Commerce Commission (ICC)***, since replaced by the ***Surface Transportation Board***, established to regulate interstate commerce, such as railroad pricing, and protect the consumer from unfair interstate transportation pricing structures.

Other regulatory agencies have since been established to oversee, control, and, theoretically, protect the consumer. These newer regulatory bodies include the Federal Power Commission, the Federal Communication Commission, and the Security and Exchange Commission. Each agency is given the task of protecting the consumer and ensuring that a fair price is available to all.

Two specific regulatory acts of which all purchasing professionals must be aware are the Sherman and Robinson-Patman antitrust laws. The ***Sherman antitrust law*** is one of the very first Untied States antitrust laws. It specifically addressed preventing entities from combining their resources or knowledge in such a manner that it is harmful to the competition, such as the creation of monopolies or cartels. In the end, the law attempts to prevent artificial price increases by restricting trade based on inter-firm agreements that could and have resulted in monopoly, cartel, or oligopoly environments. In short, the law states that firms cannot come together to establish pricing.

The origin of the **Robinson-Patman antitrust law** is associated with chain stores that could leverage their buying power to obtain products at a lower price than anyone else. In the early days, this pricing structure allowed large chain stores to price their products so low that they drove their smaller competitors out of business. The Robinson-Patman Act is intended to protect all firms by ensuring that discriminating pricing does not occur and that sellers cannot provide additional goods or services to one client and not the same to a comparable client. In short, similar clients must be treated to similar pricing and benefits.

For purchasing professionals, it is essential to obtain a detailed working knowledge of the various regulations and laws that apply to this wide world of purchasing. The Sherman and Robinson-Patman Acts are just a small taste of the many that apply to the big wide world of global procurement.

Chapter 6 Review Questions

1. If you were the Purchasing Manager for Nordstrom or another high end clothing retailer, what might happen if you purchased your store's stock of this season's handbags for a price that was unreasonable high?

2. In your own words, what is a *commodity item*? Give five examples of commodity items a furniture manufacturer might purchase.

3. Which *supply and demand environment* might be more desirable for a purchasing professional new to the market and concerned with reducing costs? Explain your answer.

4. What role does knowledge play in the *law of supply and demand*?

5. What is a *reverse auction* and how does it work? If you were a manufacturer with extra stock of an item with high holding costs, would you use a reverse auction? Why or why not?

6. What is *value-based pricing*? Provide three examples of goods whose prices might be determined using value-based pricing.

7. What are the four discount structures? Provide an example from your life when you have received a discount for each of them. If you have never received a discount for one or more of them, create an example of when you might receive such a discount in the future.

8. What impact do *inventory holding costs* have on the amount of an item an organization can purchase?

9. In what situation might a purchasing professional prefer a *firm fixed price contract* over a *cost plus fixed price contract*? In what situation might it prefer the reverse?

10. Thinking about the *TCO cost curve* and presuming you have the finances, why might it be more cost effective to purchase a new BMW for $50,000 than a 1989 model for $5,000?

CHAPTER 6 CASE EXERCISE

Centralized Purchasing, Discounts, and the No-Tipsy Bar Stool

The Simpson Production Company (known as Simp Co for short) manufactures a range of commercial and residential furniture. One of their best selling products is the No-Tipsy Bar Stool. Simp Co sells 1,000,000 of these bar stools per year. The company has four production facilities, each strategically located to support this demand. Historically, each Simp Co production facility has produced 250,000 bar stools and has independently procured all material inputs required for their manufacturing. Each production facility has their own purchasing department and each buys the bar stool inputs (wood, screws, leather) independently from the supplier Savage Industries. With their current purchasing practice, each facility pays Savage industries $8 per stool for their No-Tipsy Bar Stool inputs.

Jeb Jones is a purchasing officer at the Simp Co production facility in Abilene, Texas. Jeb has just completed a Purchasing class at his local University, where he was introduced to the concepts of centralized bulk buying and the potential it offers for lower costs. Jeb has just decided that he will try to implement this centralized buying concept across all of Simp Co's four production facilities. Because he is only responsible for purchasing at one facility, he will need to make a case for centralized bulk buying to Simp Co's Vice President of Supply Chain Management. Jeb is ready to set out on his journey of analyzing whether or not money could be saved if all purchasing for the No-Tipsy Bar Stool was centralized.

Jeb gathers the following information internally from Simp Co and externally from the supplier, Savage Industries:

- The current discount structure for bar stool from Savage Industries is as follows:
    - Material cost of inputs at a quantity of 350,000 or below are $8.00 per unit.
    - Material costs of inputs at a quantity between 350,001 and 700,000 are 5% less per unit.
    - Material costs of inputs at a quantity greater than 700,000 are 10% less per unit
- Production Labor costs per bar stool is $4.00.
- Machinery costs for each bar stool is $4.00.
- Corporate overhead per bar stool is $2.00.
- The selling price per bar stool is $20.00.

INSTRUCTIONS:

Pretend that you are Jeb Jones. Using the information in the "Getting a Fair Price" section of this chapter, prepare an analysis for the Vice President of Supply Chain Management covering the following:

1. Compare the unit price paid with the present system and the unit price possible by bulk buying through a centralized purchase.

2. How much extra profit per year can be generated by deciding to centralize the purchasing of the bar stool inputs?

3. How many extra bar stools would Simp Co need to sell to match the increase in profits if it did not switch to centralized purchasing?

4. Discuss the possible reactions of the purchasing departments in Simp Co's other three purchasing facilities to Jeb's centralized purchasing proposal. What could Jeb do to ensure that their response would be positive?

5. Based on the first five chapters you have studied, what other possible recommendations could Jeb make to Simp Co's senior management to improve its purchasing processes?

Chapter 7

Supplier Selection

Dr. Morgan Henrie & Dr. Philip M. Price

This chapter focuses on the essential role of selecting the right supplier. The ***right supplier*** is the one who provides a company with the right quantity of the right quality material (or service) at the right time at the right place and at the right price. For the purpose of this chapter, when we refer to the right supplier, we mean those suppliers external to the organization. While this chapter focuses on the *external* supplier, the right supplier may also be available *internally*, especially if your organization is a member of a national or international group of companies.

Selecting the right supplier is essential to a company's efficiency, effectiveness, profitability, and long-term survival. Our natural inclination may be to go for either the cheapest goods or for the most expensive because of their perceived quality. However, careful, costly, and sometimes time-consuming studies of suppliers, their products, and their range of value-added services can save us money and future headaches.

Throughout this chapter, we will explore what the *right supplier* means and how to identify and evaluate one. We will also examine different approaches to sourcing and the involvement of suppliers in product design and development.

DEFINING THE *RIGHT SUPPLIER*

All around the world, the majority of manufacturing organizations and service suppliers rely on other companies for raw materials, semi-finished components, finished goods, and other general supplies. This reliance on others is the pivotal point where purchasing professionals will need to interact with suppliers. A ***supplier***, also know as a ***vendor***, is someone who provides parts or services to another company. The right supplier continuously provides the necessary part or service in the right quantity of the right quality at the right time and place for the right price.

WHY SELECTING THE SUPPLIER IS CRITICAL

Selecting the right supplier is critical to an organization's success and survival. Many of us have heard of the saying, "garbage in equals garbage out." While this phrase was coined for the computer system, it also applies to the purchasing professional's selection of suppliers. Selecting a supplier who does not meet your input needs can result in a ***failure*** on your final product. In 2000, National Highway Traffic Safety Administration alerted both the Ford Motor Company and its tire supplier, Firestone, about the high incidence of tire failure on SUV models fitted with Firestone tires. The tire tread separated from the tire at high speeds, causing the SUV models to roll over, which resulted in more than 250 deaths and 3000 injuries. After a long and ugly public relations battle between Ford and Firestone in which each blamed the other for the failure and subsequent deaths, both companies lost millions of dollars and Firestone ultimately severed the 100-year-old supplier-purchaser relationship.

Your situation doesn't have to be as dire as the Ford-Firestone relationship for a supplier to fail you. For example, the supplier can fail to deliver on time. Its product can fail to meet the minimum acceptable criteria for quality. It can fail to deliver the right item. It can fail to deliver it to the required place. Finally, it can fail to deliver you the product at a fair price. If the right supplier is selected, however, and this supplier keeps its promises, it can contribute directly to an organization's positive market place share, profitability, and consumer image.

The right supplier can also bring greater value to its buyers by assisting in new product development, supporting lean organizational needs, and providing key technical support needs.

TYPES OF SUPPLIES

When selecting a supplier, we must also consider the nature of the supplies we are purchasing and their potential impact on the purchase. Two primary categories of supplies that impact the supplier selection process are: *commodity items* and *specialty items*.

A ***commodity item*** is a standard item that is available from a wide range of suppliers. It will be the same good of similar quality, no matter who supplies it. Examples of commodity items include oil, wheat, milk, and paper. With commodity items, the purchasing professional has a high level of assurance that these items can be procured from many sources at extremely competitive prices and the item quality will be standard from supplier to supplier. If one source is out of inventory or fails to meet the buyer's requirements, the purchasing professional can quickly and easily select a new supply source.

Conversely, ***specialty items*** are unique items that may only be available from a single supplier or small range of suppliers. While it may be similar to other products, a specialty item can have very specific or unique specifications, functions, or other attributes that sets it apart from similar products. For example, a television may not sound like a specialty item because televisions are available from multiple suppliers. However, a 52" flat screen, high definition television that ranks first in its class in consumer ratings is a specialty item that is likely to be available from a limited range of suppliers.

Procuring specialty items requires more of the purchasing professional's time, attention, and expertise. Not only might the supply source be limited, but the item can also have very specific or unique specifications. If the wrong item or an item of substandard quality is received, it may not be possible to run to the local hardware store to find a replacement.

INTENSITY OF SEARCH

With their very busy workday, purchasing professionals need to balance the time needed for comprehensive supplier selection with the importance of the item or service to be purchased. The amount of time and resources spent on finding the right supplier is based on three criteria:

- *Is the item readily available from a number of sources?*
- *Does the item need to be specially made for your organization?*
- *Is the item needed essential for your finished product?*

Is the item readily available from a number of sources?

As previously discussed, commodity items are available off the shelf from a range of suppliers. If the requested item is a commodity item, it is readily available through many suppliers at competitive prices. Because there are several options for purchasing a commodity item, the purchasing professional does not need to spend an extensive amount of time in selecting the right supplier. In a worse case scenario, the selected supplier might fail to deliver, but the purchasing professional can quickly get a replacement supplier that will be cost competitive and capable of supplying the commodity item required.

For example, if the purchasing professional receives a request to purchase brooms for the janitors in a hot tub manufacturing facility, there are many suppliers for this non-strategic commodity item. Though important for the cleanliness of the facility, the brooms are not a critical input into the finished product, i.e., the hot tubs. If the first supplier fails to deliver, the purchasing professional can switch to another supplier very rapidly, with minimal effort and no disruption to the manufacturing of the final product.

A purchasing professional can often use internal supplier information databases to select a commodity supplier to find out where the brooms were purchased before. If the purchaser is selecting a new supplier, a few phone calls or a quick internet search would suffice.

Does the item need to be specially made for your organization?

If a purchasing professional needs to find a highly specialized, unique, and complex part or service, she may have to carry out an extensive search. In this situation, she would expend lots of time and costly resources. She might also use a defined and detailed supplier selection process for final award of the contract. An extensive and exhaustive search might be necessary because selecting the wrong supplier has the potential for significant negative financial ramifications. If the selected supplier fails to deliver, the purchasing firm faces significant financial impacts, loss of critical time, and lost resource productivity. Getting it right the first time is not an option but a requirement.

The case study below discusses one complex purchasing process that took over two years and in excess of $250,000 to reach a contract.

> **Case Study: A Costly Purchasing Process**
>
> A crude oil pipeline company is under federal and state regulatory requirements to use highly specialized leak detection technology capabilities. This is a very specialized, unique, and complex purchase requirement. Before the purchasing professional was able to enter into a final contract, a very detailed, scripted, and time consuming process had to be followed.
>
> This process included the major steps of:
> - *Developing a detailed functional requirements document*
> - *Determining the set of potential suppliers*
> - *Issuing a request of interest solicitation to potential suppliers*
> - *Issuing a request for proposal for a proof of concept demonstration*
> - *Selecting a set of organizations to provide the proof of concept demonstration*
> - *Conducting and analyzing the proof of concept demonstration*
> - *Selecting the two top technical organizations who demonstrated capability to meet the technical requirements*
> - *Developing and issuing a final and best request for proposal to the top organizations*
> - *Analyzing the request for proposal responses for the best overall proposal*
> - *Contract negotiations*
> - *Issue of contract*
>
> The overall process, from initial request to contract signature, took two years at an estimated cost of $250,000. This is a significant percentage of the overall $3,500,000 contract price.

Are the required products important inputs into your finished product?

If these inputs were not available or delayed, would it prevent your finished product for being completed in time to meet your customer's needs? In this situation, an intense search would be carried out. The time and effort we spend in selecting a supplier is related to whether the item we require is an important input into our final product or service.

SELECTING A NEW SUPPLIER FOR A CRITICAL ITEM

As previously discussed, selecting a new supplier for a critical production item involves more than just finding out if they can supply the goods at a competitive price. It can often involve a major evaluation at the potential supplier's site by a ***specialized cross-functional team*** from the purchasing organization. This team can involve people from a range of disciplines including: manufacturing, quality control, design, marketing, finance and purchasing.

Often, this potential supplier analysis can take considerable time and expense to carry out. Potential suppliers must also be truly interested in developing the relationship before they would allow you to carry out such an extensive analysis on their capabilities. Listed below is a series of factors considered by the cross- function supplier selection team:

- ***Supplier's financial stability.*** Do they have the financial resources to meet our requirements now and in the future?

- ***Technical ability.*** When organizations are involved in innovative product development and design, they may select suppliers who have technical competencies that compliment their products. Can the suppliers be co- opted to the purchasing organization's product development teams?

- ***Production facilities and methods.*** How modern is the supplier's manufacturing facility? Do they have skilled operators? Do they carry out sufficient scheduled maintenance on their equipment to ensure that they will continue to manufacture products according to the purchasing organization's standards?

- ***Make or buy.*** Do they make or buy their inputs into the products they are negotiating with you to supply? If they outsource the majority of the items that are critical to your organization, it may be necessary to complete a supplier analysis on their suppliers.

- ***Management.*** What are the skills, knowledge, and experience of their management team?

- ***Transport.*** Do they have their own transport or do they use an external carrier? If they outsource their transport, it may be necessary to analyze their transport supplier's efficiency.

- ***Information technology.*** Do their computer systems integrate into your systems?

MANUFACTURER OR DISTRIBUTOR?

Suppliers can also fall within the classifications of *direct manufacturing source* or *distributor*. Depending on the actual item of interest, the supplier may have the option to purchase from a distributor, from the manufacturer, or a combination of both.

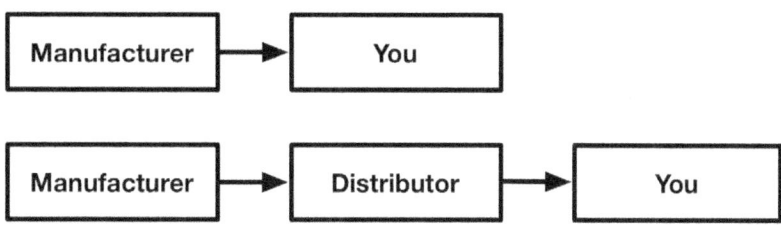

Figure 7.1 - Channels of Supply

Companies often buy needed items from a distributor. A ***distributor*** is a company with a formal agreement between one or more manufacturers to sell their products to end-users. A distributor can be viewed as a middle firm, which brokers the transfer of material from the manufacturer to the end user or another manufacturing firm. The distributor's profit is the difference between what they pay the manufacturer and their selling price.

At other times, the purchasing professional may be able to buy the product ***directly from the manufacturer***. In this case, the distributor and their profit margin have been eliminated. A manufacturer may also offer the added advantage of a higher technical support capability because they have engineers and technical personnel who deal with their product or system on a daily basis. A potential down side to dealing with the manufacturer is the lack of personal attention that a local distributor can provide and a chance of being just another company in a long list of buyers versus an important local customer for a regional distributor.

The purchasing professional needs to weigh the potential positive and negative outcomes when deciding which supply channel they will use, manufacturer or distributor. This choice is often influenced by the industry or item itself. For example, when purchasing a car, buyers can gain far more attention and service when buying from a local distributor/dealer. When purchasing a passenger airplane, however, a buyer is more likely to go directly to the manufacturer because of the customization that might need to be done and because of the availability of technical specialists from the aircraft manufacturer.

FINDING THE RIGHT SUPPLIER

As we've already learned earlier in this chapter, the successful purchasing professional must balance the intensity of their supplier search with the strategic importance of the item being purchased. Items that are strategically important and technically complex will need greater attention when selecting a supplier, while non-critical commodity items may only require a single phone call. Regardless of the intensity of the supplier search, there are a variety of factors to consider when selecting the right supplier.

HOW DO YOU FIND SUPPLIERS?

When procuring items, purchasing professionals often make a list of potential suppliers, using a variety of sources to construct this initial list. Two major sources of information regarding potential suppliers include: *internal purchasing databases* and *internet supply sources*.

The Internal Purchasing Database

Historical internal purchasing data is an important source of information when searching for the right supplier. Information on past and present suppliers provides the purchasing professional with a good starting point to begin their search. This source is sometimes referred to as the ***purchasing information database***. The purchasing information database contains current and past information about suppliers, including: company name, physical location, contact information, parts and services supplied, delivery history and accuracy, delivery timeliness, item quality history, and pricing information.

In today's electronic world, purchasing information data usually exist as a standalone database or part of the firm's Enterprise Resource Planning (ERP) system. At the other end of the spectrum, however, the information might exist in a combination of Rolodex card files and a stack of printed catalogs.

Internet Supply Sources

With the world wide web available to virtually every organization, searching online for the right supplier is becoming both common and useful. Some organizations are even moving towards **e-procurement**, in which the exchange of purchasing information occurs over secure internet connections. No paper is ever exchanged! Regardless of whether or not a firm has adopted e-procurement, using the internet is still an extremely useful tool in identifying the right supplier.

Surveying the internet for potential suppliers allows the purchasing professional to identify organizations that appear to provide the product or service required. After a potential supplier has been identified, the purchasing professional then reviews the supplier's website to obtain more information on the firm. After this initial website review, the purchasing profession then investigates other information available online about the potential supplier, such as: parts catalogs, specification sheets and drawings; financial information in Security Exchange public filings; and buyer/consumer reviews on third party sites.

Although the internet is a great source of information when selecting a supplier, it must be used with a level of caution. Unfortunately, not everything found and available online is factual. Purchasing professionals must use caution, good sense, and cross references to verify the information and avoid the less-than-scrupulous online sources that lurk about.

Other Sources for Potential Suppliers

In addition to internal purchasing databases and Internet supply sources, purchasing professionals have a wide range of sources at their fingertips to help them identify potential suppliers. Some of these sources include:

- *Trade Shows.* Many suppliers use trade shows as ideal opportunities to market their product and meet potential purchasers.

- *Current Trade Magazines.* Many industries have magazines that cater to their needs. These magazines provide the dual benefit of keeping people connected to what is going on while also acting as an ideal place for suppliers' advertisements.

- *Membership in Purchasing Professional Organizations.* Membership in professional organizations provides an excellent resource for contacts that can lead to finding the right supplier. Two such important organizations for the purchasing professional are the Institute of Supply Management (www.ism.ws) in the United States and the Chartered Institute of Purchasing and Supply (www.cips.org) in the United Kingdom.

- *Interviews with Current and Potential Suppliers' Sales Representatives.* Sales representatives can give you current information and, in many cases, can inform you of developments in their products that may be of future interest to you.

- *Personal Contacts.* A great way to locate a potential supplier is to ask one of your personal purchasing contacts for a reference. Professional contacts usually will not recommend someone they would not use themselves. The key to these relationships is the bi-directional manner that should be followed. When your colleague calls for a reference, you should reciprocate as well.

WHERE IS THE RIGHT SUPPLIER LOCATED?

With a multitude of ways to identify potential resources, the purchasing professional will typically be faced with how to narrow the final selection down. One consideration in selecting the right supplier is the supplier's location, i.e., should the supplier be a local firm or a national firm or should you go with an international firm?

Purchasing from Local Sources

Because they tend to be smaller operations, local supplier often stock smaller quantities, but they may have a broader range of items to meet the urgent needs of the local market. They may also be able to be very responsive to smaller quantity purchases with a short delivery time and they may have a competitive price structure when total costs of ordering are considered.

For the local supplier, all that may be required is for them to deliver the product across town or the purchasing firm may actually pick it up rather than have it delivered. In this case, the delivery cost would be much less expensive than if the item were ordered from a national or international company that would have to ship the item. Other advantages of purchasing locally include:

- *The local firm's ability to support a "just in time" delivery need.*
- *The ability to develop a close purchaser and supplier working relationship.*
- *Local support services and faster responses to rush requirements.*
- *The effect on the local economy and its community.*

Organizations often have a policy that favors purchasing from local suppliers or producers, even though the local supplier's price is often above the national or international cost. The extra costs are usually justified as the organizations contribution to building and supporting the local community.

Purchasing from National Sources

National organizations are often able to provide larger quantities than local sources because they maintain much larger inventories and often have a broader set of support services and technical knowledge available.

Purchasing from International Sources

We live in a global economy where production inputs, commercial goods, and a wide range of services can be obtained from around the world. Current e- procurement technology provides the means to purchase something globally with a few clicks on the computer mouse. The global supply chain stretches buying opportunities to the earth's far corners. Having the ability to purchase production inputs, commercial goods, and various services from suppliers around the world opens up many options but adds to the purchasing professional's complex decision process.

When purchasing internationally, the purchasing professional still must answer the basic question: *Can this firm provide the right item, of the right quantity, at the right time and place, in the right quality, and at a competitive price?* As we will see in greater detail later in Chapter 10, having the ability to purchase items and services internationally provides the purchasing professional with many new opportunities and many new challenges.

SINGLE OR MULTIPLE SOURCES

When it comes to selecting potential suppliers, organizations often have very specific policies on whether they will use *sole*, *single*, or *multiple sources*. In some situations, only a sole supplier, or **sole source**, may be available for the item you need, perhaps because of a monopoly or the unique nature of the item you need. In this sole source situation, there is limited opportunity to negotiate prices or extra services. Often the only choice open to the purchaser is to pay the price and meet the conditions asked by the supplier. This is in contrast to where there are many suppliers but the organization decides to purchase from only one supplier, i.e. a **single source**.

Single sourcing occurs when the firm elects to purchase the requested product from only one of many different possible sources. In this situation, there are several potential suppliers, yet the firm elects to award one supplier the total contract. A buyer may select a single source for a variety of reasons, including:

- *Improved economics of scale opportunities.* There may be a lower cost per unit for larger purchases from a single supplier.

- *Just in time (JIT) delivery control.* Coordination of a single source supply when and where needed can assist JIT methods.

- *Reduced shipping cost.* Better shipping rates can be negotiated when larger orders are placed and shipped as a single unit.

- *Opportunity to negotiate improved support agreement.* Larger orders to a single supplier provide opportunities to obtain or negotiate preferred service agreements and improved supplier-purchasing professional relationships.

- *Selection preference.* Your order may be processed ahead of the smaller, one-of-a-kind order.

- *Higher attention to emergency orders.* If you are a regular major purchaser, suppliers may tend to respond to emergency requests faster.

As the list shows, there are many positive reasons why a purchasing professional would want to select a single source supplier. However, there are also disadvantages that should be considered when implementing a single source purchase strategy, which include:

- Changing from one supplier to another will take time. Depending on the type of item, changing suppliers can take extensive time and resources to achieve, particularly if the item is a non-commodity and a very important input into your product's final assembly.

- Single supplier's problems will cascade into the purchasing firm's processes. Problems such as industrial action at your supplier's plant or their suppliers letting them down will spread to your production line and cause delays. This could force a production line shutdown that may prevent you from meeting your commitments to your customers.

- Contractual obligations hinder switching organizations. Some single source purchasing contracts limit how the organizations can cancel the contract. This could severely limit the purchasing professional's options if other opportunities for better prices or services occur.

- When technology or production processes are constantly changing, your organization's development may be hampered if your single source supplier is not keeping up with emerging technology, new materials, or new processing methods being developed within your industry.

Unlike single sourcing, ***multiple sourcing*** occurs when an organization has decided that it will award contracts for its requirements to multiple suppliers. Deciding to award purchase contracts to two or more suppliers helps mitigate some single source purchase supplier risks. With multiple sourcing, if one supplier has problems, the purchasing firm will continue to receive products from the other suppliers. The other suppliers may even be able to increase the number of items they can deliver to take up any slack caused by the first supplier's problems.

While single sourcing seems like a simpler option, multiple sourcing can offer distinct advantages. Multiple sourcing helps to address the need to change from one supplier to another. For example, when seeking to replace problematic Supplier #1, supplies continue to stream in from reliable Supplier #2. Multiple sourcing also tends to support ongoing competition. When all of the suppliers involved are aware that you are purchasing identical items from other organizations, they are more diligent in ensuring their service levels and promises are constantly met. Multiple source purchasing produces an environment in which suppliers continue to be competitive and responsive to your needs in an effort to win a greater percentage of your total purchase.

Another advantage of multiple sourcing is that using two or more suppliers allows the purchasing firm to assist small, disadvantaged, or minority organizations. It can accomplish the dual efforts of obtaining the required items by selecting multiple suppliers where one is a small business and the other is a larger firm with more resources to draw from. The purchase orders are placed to maximize, but not over extend, the small business entity while allocating the remaining items required to the larger supplier.

Despite its advantages, purchasing professionals must remember that multiple sourcing presents an increased workload when managing two or more suppliers. The decision to invest this increased time must be balanced against the positive aspects that multiple sourcing brings.

PURCHASING RELATIONSHIPS

Every purchase involves a relationship between the supplier and purchaser. Associated with these relationships is the good will that develops between the supplier and purchaser. **Good will** is often referred to as a win-win or mutually beneficial relationship, which we will learn more about later in Chapter 8. Good will arises after the transaction is completed and: *the supplier feels that they have received a fair price that allows it to make a fair profit* and *the purchasing firm feels they have received a quality item or service at a fair price*. While all transactions should result in goodwill, the amount of time taken to foster this goodwill varies depending on the type of relationship entered into.

Relationships between the supplier and purchaser can take the form of a single transaction, a short-term interaction, or a long-term interaction. **Single transaction** relationships involve only one transaction between the purchaser and supplier. The purchasing professional places a single order, the supplier delivers the product, and the two never engage in further transactions. In a single transaction relationship, each firm receives the mutually agreed benefits and a level of good will is established. In the single transaction process, the amount of time the purchasing professional spends in developing a supplier-purchaser relationship will probably be minimal. The purchaser will treat the supplier fairly, equitably, and honestly but will not be motivated or need to understand the supplier's business. Similarly, the supplier is not motivated to understand the purchasing firm's intricate inner workings. A single transaction interaction does not require each side to develop those next layers of deeper understanding and relationship-building that are found in short-term or long-term relationships.

In **short-term relationships**, the purchaser and supplier are looking to be engaged for more than a single purchase. Short-term relationships may last from a few weeks to a year. In this situation, developing the supplier-purchaser good will to the next level is required for improved chances of success for both organizations. Building the next relationship level involves understanding how each firm's business and processes impact or are impacted by the other part of this relationship. Increased good will between the supplier and the purchaser is a desirable and needed component of a short-term relationship because both will be working together for a period of time in which actions by *both* can either have a positive or a negative impact on the other. Developing deeper working relationship and understanding of the other firm's needs and wants can increase the possibility of positive outcomes for each firm while minimizing or mitigating any potential negative outcomes.

Many supplier-purchaser relationships are formed to last more than one year. These are called **long-term relationships**. Two types of long-term relationships are *repetitive delivery contracts* and *partnerships*. **Repetitive delivery contracts** establish a legal agreement to purchase the product for a long period of time, at least a year. Contractually, both organizations agree to supplying and purchasing a product over a period of time at agreed contract terms.

In the world of purchasing, a **partnership** is a relationship formed between a supplier and purchaser in which both make a commitment to work together over a longer timeframe to achieve mutually beneficial results. This relationship, which may or may not imply a legal or contractual agreement, is also known as a **strategic alliance**. For a partnership to be successful, it is important that both parties have a clear understanding of each other's expectations, communicate openly, share information, provide the basis for mutual trust, and have an agreed vision for the future direction of their partnership.

For example, a production organization can form long-term partnerships or strategic alliances with a transport and distribution organization. In this relationship, the transport company could take control over the collection of all the production organization's inbound production inputs and could then distribute all of their finished products. This allows the production organization to concentrate on its core competency (manufacturing goods) by placing their transport needs with an organization whose core competency is transportation.

Long-term relationships require a continuous commitment to work on supplier- purchaser good will. The long-term relationship expands on the short-term relationship's benefits through a process of greater supplier-purchasing integration. It is also characterized by each firm developing a deep understanding of the other's business, processes, and needs. This deeper understanding also allows the free flow of ideas and suggestions from firm to firm so each can improve the overall supply chain's success to the mutual benefit of both organizations.

SUPPLIER INVOLVEMENT

New product development can be a very complex process that involves a wide range of resources over an extended period of time. Yet, new products are the lifeblood of the organization. It is in every organization's best interest to take appropriate steps to minimize the cost, time, and risks associated with developing new products. One way organizations minimize the risk associated with new product development is through the early involvement of suppliers as part of the new product development team.

The supplier and purchasing organizations often have distinct areas of technical knowledge and expertise. Bringing the suppliers and our own expertise together in one working group reduces the time to answer design questions, provides an opportunity to expand on ideas through collaborative design, and provides direct link between the designers, production lines, and quality control processes. In the end, this joint technical knowledge sharing process can result in an improved product that can be manufactured more easily, often at a consistently higher quality and a much-reduced cost.

One disadvantage of including the supplier in the new product development team is the potential to lose competitive advantage through loss of proprietary information. While every relationship is entered into in good faith, some organizations or specific individuals may leverage the inside knowledge gained to enhance their own product or opportunities to the detriment of the other.

Evaluating the Current Supplier

The sales staff of some suppliers can make promises throughout the negotiation stage but later leave these promises unfulfilled. Late deliveries, wrong quantities, and poor quality can all create problems at the purchaser's end. If there is a significant breach of the contract, the purchaser can file a legal action. However, suppliers can fulfill the bare minimum of their promises at a level of service that is far below standard. To prevent this from happening, purchasing professionals now implement wide-ranging performance indicators to measure a range of performance criteria that impacts its own organization's effectiveness and efficiency.

During the negotiation stage, it is important that the purchaser and the supplier agree on evaluation criteria and how the supplier's performance will be evaluated. After the transaction is completed, the next step is to evaluate the supplier to assess how well it performed against the agreed performance levels. To achieve this end, many purchase orders specify the way the supplier's performance is measured. These performance measures are commonly called **key performance indicators**. Key performance indicators, or **KPIs**, outline the supplier's expected performance criteria against which their actual performance will be measured. KPIs often have rewards and penalties associated with them. The rewards are issued when the supplier exceeds the established criteria, while the penalties kick in when the supplier fails to meet the requirements.

While there are many types of KPIs, a few important ones related to suppliers and the world of purchasing include:

- ***Quality performance*** - the ratio of rejected products received to the total products delivered.

- ***On-time delivery ratio*** - the ratio of how often the product was not received when required in comparison to the total number of deliveries or how close to a predefined delivery time was the product received.

- ***Right quantity delivered***.

Performance evaluation is vital when the purchasing professional is dealing with a long-term supplier relationship. It provides the purchaser quantitative data after each transaction on how the supplier is actually performing compared to their promises. When negative deviations occur, corrective action can be implemented immediately. The converse is also true; superior performance can be recognized early and rewarded.

KPIs are often used in ***weighted evaluations*** of suppliers in which the purchaser doing the evaluation can decide if some criteria, or KPIs, are more important than others. The more important KPIs are given a higher weight in the evaluation process. In the example below, the *right quantity delivered* is viewed as a more important evaluation criterion than *rejected parts ratio* or *delivery within 15 minutes*. Therefore, it is given a greater weight, or in this case, 45 out of 100 percent. Using this method of weighted evaluation, purchasers can make sure that the suppliers who are best at the KPIs most important to them can be identified. In the example below, the company assessed received a poor score (2 out of 4) for the KPI *right quantity delivered*. Because this KPI is weighted heavily (at 45%), the weighted score is greatly impacted, resulting in 90 out of a possible 180 points.

From our example in Figure 7.2 below, the purchaser will use the total weighted score to evaluate the supplier's performance. For example, if the supplier has predetermined that an acceptable total weighted score is 260, Supplier 1 from our example is not performing up to standard.

| SUPPLIER 1 ||||
Weight (out of 100%)	KPI	Raw Score from 0 (worst) to 4 (best)	Weighted Score
30	Rejected parts score	4	120
25	Delivery (within 15 minutes) score	1	25
45	Right quantity delivered score	2	90
		TOTAL WEIGHTED SCORE:	**235**

Figure 7.2 - Weighted Evaluation of Supplier 1

When purchasing professionals use multiple suppliers to provide the same item, they can also use weighted evaluations with KPIs to measure, evaluate, and control these multiple suppliers. This may be especially useful to help identify which suppliers to drop if fewer quantities of the item are needed or if the purchaser wishes to narrow its field of suppliers. When weighted scores are used, purchasers select the key performance indicators that are the most important to them and give them greater weight in the evaluation. This ensures that the supplier performing highest on that particular indicator is given the greatest weight. In our previous example, the *right quantity delivered* KPI was given the greatest weight: 45%. With a raw score of 2 out of 4 points, the supplier rated in our example received a low score for that KPI. Let's now examine a second supplier receiving a higher raw score in the *right quantity delivered* KPI and a lower raw score in the *rejected parts* KPI.

| SUPPLIER 2 ||||
Weight (out of 100%)	KPI	Raw Score from 0 (worst) to 4 (best)	Weighted Score
30	Rejected parts score	2	60
25	Delivery (within 15 minutes) score	1	25
45	Right quantity delivered score	4	180
		TOTAL WEIGHTED SCORE:	**265**

Figure 7.3 - Weighted Evaluation of Supplier 2

In our examples in Figures 7.2 and 7.3 above, even though Suppliers 1 and 2 received raw scores of 1, 2, and 4, Supplier 2 received a higher total weighted score of 265, which was 30 points higher than Supplier 1's score of 230. This higher score was the result of Supplier 2 receiving a higher score in the KPI most important to the purchaser (right quantity delivered).

Supplier evaluation processes are very dependent on the product or service purchased. At one end of the spectrum, the only evaluation possible is the post- transaction supplier rating.

Chapter 7 Case Exercise

QuickBuilt Limited, Key Performance Indicators, and Supplier Selection

QuickBuilt Limited is a manufacturing company that uses a just in time system to support its manufacturing operations. QuickBuilt currently has two suppliers (Super Supplies and Greatest Goods) that provide it with all its needs. The company has decided to use a single source for its supplies and has set up a supplier evaluation system to help it decide whether Super Supplies or Greatest Goods best meets QuickBuilt's needs. QuickBuilt's purchasing manager will use the following key performance indicators (KPIs) to select a single supplier to provide its inputs:

- ▸ **KPI 1: Rejected parts score.** This KPI will receive a weighting of 50.
- ▸ **KPI 2: Delivery (within 15 minutes) score.** This KPI will receive a weighting of 30
- ▸ **KPI 3: Right quantity delivered score.** This KPI will receive a weighting of 20.

Super Supplier's raw scores are:

- KPI 1: Rejected parts score. 3 out of a possible 4
- KPI 2: Delivery (within 15 minutes) score. 1 out of a possible 4
- KPI 3: Right quantity delivered score. 4 out of a possible 4

Greatest Goods' raw scores are:

- KPI 1: Rejected parts score. 2 out of a possible 4
- KPI 2: Delivery (within 15 minutes) score. 4 out of a possible 4
- KPI 3: Right quantity delivered score. 4 out of a possible 4

INSTRUCTIONS:

You are the purchasing manager for QuickBuilt Limited. Upper management has asked you to prepare a visual presentation of each supplier's past performance and make a recommendation for which supplier should they use. Use the charts in Figures 7.2 and 7.3 in the "Evaluating the Current Supplier" section of this chapter as a guide to develop your presentation.

Chapter 8

Understanding Negotiation in the Purchasing Process

Dr. Francis Jeffries & Dr. Philip M. Price

Jack and Judy have just arrived for a three-day stay in Istanbul, Turkey onboard a cruise ship. They heard that leather goods were much cheaper in Turkey than in the U.S., so they decided to purchase Jack a leather jacket. Judy had looked for a leather jacket for Jack back home in Topeka, Kansas but was put off by the $200+ price tags.

During their first day in Istanbul, the happy couple passed through the main bazaar and saw a store with really nice leather jackets. When Judy asked the vendor the price of these jackets, she was pleasantly surprised to hear, "$125 dollars." This was a savings of at least $75 dollars on the Topeka, Kansas price! Jack and Judy immediately purchased the jacket and felt that they really had gotten a terrific bargain.

When they went back to the cruise ship, Jack and Judy, who were still quite pleased with their purchase, mentioned their fantastic bargain to their friends, John and Kate. Coincidentally, John and Kate had also visited the same leather goods vendor and purchased the same jacket, but they purchased theirs for only $65. John and Kate explained that the vendor also first asked for $125. Before they went into the bazaar, however, John and Kate did some research about costs and discovered that, in the bazaar, the first price is never the final price. Instead, it is both a tradition and an expectation to "haggle" with the vendor for a better deal. What Jack and Judy failed to do, in business talk, was to *negotiate*.

Negotiation is something we all do everyday without even giving it much thought. Any time we have a conversation with another person and conclude by making a decision or an agreement, we have conducted a negotiation. When we decide with our friends or family on which movie we will go to see at the theater, we have conducted a negotiation. In the context of purchasing and supply chain management, this process is critical to the successful conduct of business and moving material every day.

THE BASICS OF NEGOTIATION

Negotiation is the process of making a decision involving two or more parties that will affect all of those involved. The parties are interdependent; that is, each has something that the other desires and they will be better off if they can agree to some mutually acceptable terms. Negotiations take many forms, from simple decisions regarding where to have dinner to complex agreements between corporations or countries.

Negotiations are a voluntary process and all parties are involved by choice. However, there is always a conflict of needs and/or desires to resolve. Each party to the negotiation believes that his/her outcome will be better by negotiating than by accepting what the other will offer voluntarily. In a negotiation, we expect that there will be a process where there is give and take. Concessions will be made and concessions will be offered in return. Through this process, each side will modify their initial position, moving away from opening statements or demands to a position that is acceptable to the other side. The process of negotiation is chosen to decide issues because it is preferable to fighting, having a third party decide the issue, or having one side just give in to the other.

In theory, everything is negotiable unless the other party tells you it is not. Therefore, any time we feel that negotiating will help us minimize our costs of ownership or help us maximize our internal or external customers' satisfaction, we should negotiate. It might be in the best interest of a business to invest the time and costs involved in negotiation when:

- *the negotiation will commit the company to a long-term contract;*
- *considerable amounts of company resources will be committed;*
- *the contract is complex, involves a high degree of risk, and contains many sub areas;*
- *the items you are purchasing are critical inputs to your final product's production (If the quality, quantity, time and place of delivery are not met, it could have serious implications for your company's survival.);*
- *the items are first time purchases; or*
- *you want to develop a sound, continuing, trusting partnership to ensure all your future transactions will result in a win-win agreement.*

Despite its advantages, negotiation can be a very time consuming and expensive process. But as we saw in our example of Jack and Judy' foray into the Turkish market, these unfortunate purchasers could have saved a considerable amount of money if they had spent some time in preparing for the negotiation. In the business world, purchasing and supply management professionals can commit considerable company resources to prepare for strategically important negotiations. Though the costs can be high, so also can be the negotiated benefits. In our example of Wasilla Winter Wines way back in Chapter 2, we saw how the new purchasing manager negotiated a 15% reduction in the cost of materials, which increased Wasilla Winter Wines Profit by 30%.

In the context of purchasing and the supply chain, negotiation involves all the materials and services the company needs to meet their internal and external customers' wants. For example, in order for a manufacturer to be able to use a just-in-time process, everything about the incoming material must be negotiated and agreed to. Areas that should be negotiated include:

- *Quantity to be purchased*
- *Quality required*
- *Who performs incoming inspections and how they are to be done*
- *Unit price, price modifications, and the total costs of ownership*
- *Mode of shipping to be used and outsourcing details*
- *Delivery time and place*
- *When payment is due and how it should be made*
- *How to resolve issues that are not covered in the originally negotiated agreement*

The way we go about negotiating these agreements will have a lasting impact on the nature of the relationship between ourselves and other members of the supply chain. In essence, we are a group of business partners that depend on each other for success.

Should we become involved in a negotiation in the purchasing and supply chain management environment, it will be either a *distributive negotiation* or an *integrative negotiation*. **Distributive negotiation** can be best described as fighting over a cake. Each side attempts to maximize their share of the cake, even at the expense of their counterparts in the negotiation.

Integrative negotiation is present when the two parties to the negotiation view the process as one that can create value. The objective of an integrative negotiation is to collaborate in a win-win mode by increasing the size of the cake by finding solutions that create value to each side. Integrative negotiation works best when there are many issues to be negotiated and parties can trade off concessions based on how important each issue is to them.

For example, consider the situation in which a purchaser from Seattle, Washington orders goods from Anchorage, Alaska. The cost of getting goods from Alaska is a major concern for the Seattle purchaser. Because the negotiations are being conducted with an integrative approach with full sharing of information, however, the company in Alaska informs the Seattle purchaser that they can offer reduced shipping costs because they can combine the Seattle order with goods they are already shipping from Alaska. The reduced rate is of value to the Seattle purchaser but it is of lesser cost to the Alaska shipper as the space would otherwise not be used.

APPROACHES TO NEGOTIATION

There are several alternate approaches to negotiation that we can choose from. Five common approaches are: *competitive, avoidance, compromise, accommodating,* and *collaborative.*

THE COMPETITIVE APPROACH

When people think of negotiation, many times they think of situations where one desires to win at any cost or maximize his/her outcome at the other person's expense. This **competitive approach** is also called a **win-lose** or **distributive negotiation**. While there are situations that may call for this sort of approach, in reality they are rare occurrences. In order for distributive negotiation to work in the long run, the following conditions must be met:

- ✓ The parties must not have an on-going relationship that matters. If the relationship is important, a distributive approach will be a poor choice because it has great potential to damage the relationship.

- ✓ There must be only a single issue to negotiate, usually money. For a negotiation to be win-lose, everything you gain must be at your opponent's expense and vice-versa. If you gain a dollar, your opponent must lose a dollar.

- ✓ Finally, the respective parties' goals must be in direct conflict so it becomes one's goal to maximize one's own outcomes at the other's expense. The opening case of Jack, Judy and the Bazaar vendor is an example of a distributive negotiation.

THE AVOIDANCE APPROACH

The **avoidance approach**, also known as a **lose-lose negotiation**, is not used often but is appropriate in some situations. If the issue is not important enough to merit the investment of time or if you can satisfy your needs without negotiating, it may be the best choice. Also, if neither the relationship nor the outcome is important, the avoider may refuse to negotiate. This approach may have a negative effect on the relationship. Even if the outcome is not important, it is a good idea to consider the effect on the relationship and whether or not the potential damage to the relationship is acceptable before employing this approach.

THE COMPROMISE APPROACH or SPLIT THE DIFFERENCE

The **compromise approach**, also know as a **split-the-difference negotiation**, is sometimes considered a type of win-win approach, but it really is not. It is instead a satisficing strategy that is employed when the parties cannot make collaboration work or one party is not willing to do the work to create a collaborative solution. It is also employed when the parties are under time pressure and need to decide quickly because preserving the relationship or the issue are not of great enough value to warrant investment of the time and resources to create a collaborative solution to the negotiation.

THE ACCOMMODATING APPROACH or LOSE TO WIN

The ***accommodating approach***, also known as a ***lose-win negotiation***, is employed when the relationship is more important than the outcome of the negotiation. It may be that we are interested in strengthening the relationship or attempting to make the other person happy. Another reason to employ this approach is to facilitate gaining concessions in return in the future. A short- term loss is exchanged for a long-term gain.

THE COLLABORATIVE APPROACH or WIN-WIN

In the ***collaborative approach***, also known as a ***win-win*** or ***integrative negotiation***, the relationship will continue and is important. There are multiple issues to negotiate and there is potential for mutually beneficial trade-offs to be made benefiting all. In other words, it is possible to find ways to make concessions to the other that can be mutually beneficial. For example, when there are multiple issues, it is very unlikely that the respective parties place the same relative value on all of the issues. If the parties were negotiating for a house, the issues might include: a) *the price of the house*; b) *repairs to be made prior to closing*; c) *the length of the escrow period*; d) *whether or not the appliances stay with the house*; and e) *payment of the various fees for services at closing*.

In this case, the respective priorities for one negotiator may be a, e, d, b, c and a, c, b, d, e for the other negotiator. If this is the case, it becomes possible for one party to make a concession on an issue that is a lesser priority for than it is for their negotiation counterpart. In this way, the negotiators create more value in the negotiation because each gains more of what he or she wants by sacrificing little to get it. This creates a win-win situation and creates more value in the negotiation than if each issue was negotiated one at a time as if it were a set of five distributive negotiations.

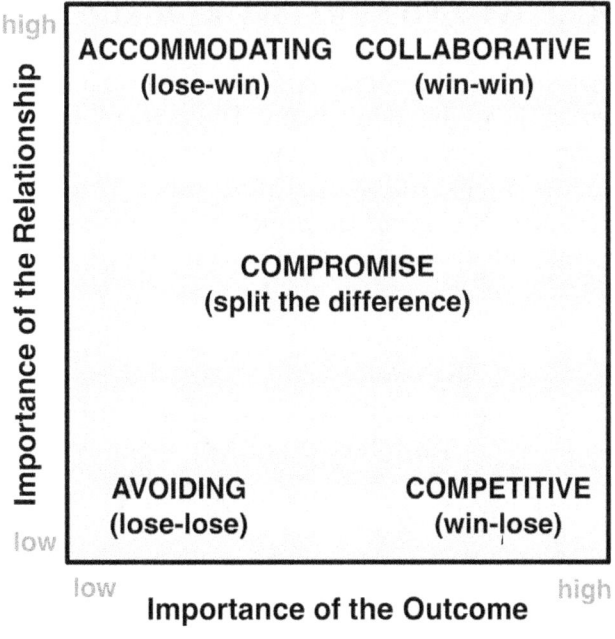

Figure 8.1 - Approaches to Negotiation

Let's now look at the example of the ugly orange. Two sisters were given one orange. Both sisters desired to have the orange and they needed to resolve the issue regarding how to divide it. If they were to use the common distributive approach, they would simply cut the orange in half and let each have one half of the orange. However, by using the integrative approach, each sister can get what she really wants. By inquiring what the respective sisters wanted to do with the orange, it is discovered that one wants to bake a cake and needs the zest (shredded rind) of the orange and the other wants to eat the fruit because she is hungry. The sisters agree to allow one to zest the orange and then give the remainder to the other. The first sister concedes the rind, which is of no value to her, to the other and the other concedes the fruit, which is of no value to her, and both get all of what they want.

In this case, the relationship in the negotiation is important because both parties are sisters. The issue looked to be distributive in that there was a single orange and it appeared that one could not get what she wanted without the other losing part of what she wanted. Instead, by finding out what each wanted to do with the orange, it was possible to find a better solution. In our example of Jack and Judy at the Turkish Bazaar, we presume that Jack and Judy will never meet the bazaar vendor again. It was a single transaction and the experienced bazaar vendor clearly won the day.

But what if it was a single issue and the same two sisters had to resolve it? Wouldn't it then be a distributive negotiation? It would not be because the negotiation takes place inside an on-going relationship. Therefore, one sister could make concessions today that could be reciprocated in a future negotiation to their mutual benefit, resulting in a win-win outcome overall. It is very important to consider the relationship between the parties involved and the future negotiations that may take place when deciding if a negotiation is truly win-lose or not. Alternatively, adopting a distributive approach to a negotiation in an ongoing relationship can cause problems down the road.

UNDERSTANDING POSITIVE AND NEGATIVE BARGAINING ZONES

Before we delve further into the world of negotiations, it is important to understand some of the basic terminology used within the negotiation process. The ***buyer's reservation price*** is the highest amount a buyer will pay before walking away. Conversely, the ***seller's reservation price*** is the lowest amount that a seller will accept before walking away. The ***buyer's aspiration point*** and the ***seller's aspiration point*** are the goals set by each party in the negotiation. Each is an estimate of the best potential outcome they could reasonably expect to get in the negotiation.

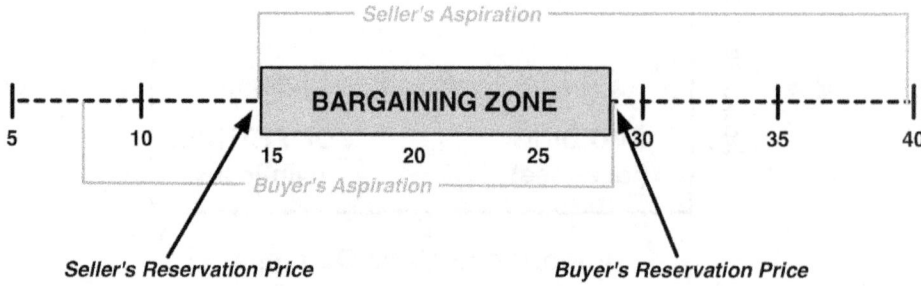

Figure 8.2 - The Bargaining Zone

Finally, the ***bargaining zone***, as shown in Figure 8.2, is the overlap between the minimum one negotiator will accept and the maximum his/her opponent will pay. If there is overlap between the purchaser's maximum and the seller's minimum, there is a ***positive bargaining zone*** or ***zone of potential agreement***. If there is no overlap, then there is a ***negative bargaining zone*** and ***no zone of potential agreement***.

PHASES IN A NEGOTIATION

Effective negotiations occur in three phases: the *pre-negotiation planning phase*, the *actual negotiation*, and the *post-negotiation phase*.

PHASE 1: PRE-NEGOTIATION PLANNING STAGE

Often the difference between success and failure in negotiation comes from whether or not the negotiator planned effectively. At the very minimum, one should determine a goal for the negotiation, the limit to what he or she is willing to give, what his/her *BATNA* is so that a realistic limit can be set, and what the opening offer will be.

A ***BATNA***, or ***best alternative to a negotiated agreement***, is the option/choice available if an agreement cannot be reached. One's BATNA may be very good (you have a good job and can be neutral about accepting a new job unless it is a big step up) or it can be poor (your car is broken down in a blizzard and the only towing service wants a fortune to move it so your alternative is to abandon the car). Failure to determine one's BATNA and set a realistic limit is a primary cause for accepting deals that are not beneficial.

Setting Goals

Setting goals requires that one consider not just his/her own position and needs, but those of his/her opponent as well. There are limits to what your goals can be and they are linked to the other's goals. For a goal to be effective, it must be very specific, not a range or a fuzzy general statement. Whether or not you expect to negotiate with your opponent in the future affects your goals as well. If this is a one-shot deal, your goals can be much more aggressive. If the relationship is important and you expect to negotiate again in the future, your goals will need to be less aggressive.

Planning for negotiation should be done systematically to be most effective. First, ***define the issues***. Analyze the conflict or problem and determine what needs to be discussed and decided. Name the issues and be certain to limit the number of issues that will be discussed. The risk of not limiting the number of issues and agreeing on them at the start of the negotiation is that it leaves the negotiation open to being dragged out indefinitely by an opponent who wishes to gain an advantage by putting time pressure on you or by chipping away slowly and gaining a few concessions at your expense on small issues.

Second, ***prioritize the issues*** from your point of view and then do the same from the other's point of view. At this stage you may not be sure of their priorities, but it is important to guess.

You are making assumptions that will become the basis of questions you will need to ask to validate your assumptions during the negotiation.

Third, once the issues are identified, it is time to ***identify your interests***. Interests are the "why" behind the issues. These include why you desire the particular outcome you are seeking, how the negotiation process should be conducted, and what the relationship outcomes are that you desire after the negotiation is concluded. The interests in the substantive issues, the essence of what it is that you each seek, are usually straightforward. In planning for an initial negotiation, it is also important to think carefully about how you desire for the negotiation to proceed since this initial negotiation will set the pattern for future negotiations. If you desire to create a pattern or norm of cooperation and information exchange, it is vital to plan for that and behave in a manner consistent with your goal.

Finally, it is critical to ***develop supporting arguments*** in support of your desired outcome. There are two critical points to remember in this process. First, no one will support your proposal to resolve the negotiation if, when asked by the other party, you are not able to answer, "WIIFM?" (*What's in it for me?*) Negotiation is pursued as a way to reach an agreement because you and your opponent are mutually interdependent. Both of you will be better off if you cooperate and come to an agreement than if you take your respective BATNAs.

Another point to remember developing supporting arguments is that you must use objective sources of information to support your position. For example, if you were negotiating the purchase price of a car, you would be wise to research the NADA or Blue Book values for the vehicle to use as a way of establishing its market value. Being familiar with the recent asking prices in the local car advertisements would be helpful as well. If you were buying a house, it would be good to know the sale prices of comparable properties in the area. The sources of the information supporting your position will be more powerful and useful if your opponent sees them as credible.

In presenting your argument, it is important to think carefully about the other party's point of view and to anticipate any arguments or objections. Plan your choice of responses to the anticipated objections and, if the negotiation is of sufficient importance, role-play the negotiation during the planning stage in preparation for the real negotiation. While this may seem silly, it will prepare you to negotiate and to think on your feet as no other method will. Taking the time to practice the negotiation will be time well spent. The *Planning for Negotiation* forms at the end of this chapter will give you a systematic method for planning for negotiation. As you become proficient, you may desire to modify them to better fit your style and needs.

Tactics

To conduct negotiations efficiently and to avoid being taken advantage of, it is good to understand both *distributive* and *integrative tactics*. In the world of negotiations, ***tactics*** are behaviors that you engage in to achieve your goals in the negotiation. Even in an integrative negotiation, there is a time for creating value and a time for claiming value. This creates a mixed-motive situation in which one has an incentive to cooperate to enlarge the pie and one also has an incentive to claim as much of the expanded pie as possible while preserving the relationship. The primary difference between *distributive negotiation* and *integrative negotiation* when claiming value is that in ***integrative negotiation***, it is critical to avoid being predatory and to keep fairness in mind while dividing the value created. Failure to do this will surely impact the relationship in a negative manner and make it harder to be open and trusting in future negotiations.

The object of the game in ***distributive negotiation*** is to push your opponent to his/her limit or point of resistance in order to gain the most out of the negotiation. To do this, it is helpful to begin with an extreme opening offer. If you are a buyer, the opening offer should be the lowest one that the seller would consider without walking away. This will allow you to set an ***anchor***, or the first offer that is taken seriously by the respective negotiators. You then make small concessions from there, capturing most of the positive bargaining range.

When in a distributive negotiation, many people resort to what are called ***hardball tactics***, such as:

- *Good Guy/Bad Guy:* Having one negotiator pretending to take your side while the accomplice acts hard-nosed.
- *Highball/Lowball:* Making an extremely low or high offer to force you to your limit.
- *The Nibble:* Asking for small concessions after the deal is decided.
- *Chicken:* Refusing to agree if time is a factor in order to force you to accept a less favorable agreement than you might ordinarily accept.
- *Intimidation:* Being a bully by using anger, a loud aggressive style, and threats.

Constructive ways to counter these tactics are to ignore them, name them, discuss them with your opponent, or co-opt/befriend your opponent. You may be tempted to respond in kind, but this is not advisable because it is likely to lead to an escalation of the behavior. For example, if your opponent begins bargaining by making an extremely high opening offer, you can counter by: a) making an extremely low opening offer (*not advisable*), b) laughing and saying "oh, so I see we are going to play high ball, low ball" (*good*), or c) just acting as if you did not hear the offer at all and make a reasonable opening offer (*good*).

To create ***integrative solutions*** that capitalize on creating more value in the negotiation, it is important to create a free exchange of information. Just as in the stories about the ugly orange and the Seattle purchaser, if we can learn *why* our negotiation partners want what they want, it becomes possible to find ways to help them get what is desired and create more value for both sides at the same time. To do this, we must discuss the issues openly and completely, share information, and ask questions so that we fully understand both what our partners want and why they want it. It is important to emphasize commonalities and minimize differences so that we do not take an adversarial position with respect to each other. If you think and act like members of the same team with a conflict to resolve, it will create an environment conducive to open communication that is necessary for negotiating mutually beneficial solutions to the issues at hand.

Finally, it is critical to search for alternatives that will meet the needs of both sides of the negotiation. While creating these options, it is important for both sides to be firm but flexible. For example, be firm on meeting your respective needs and fulfilling your interests, but, at the same time, be flexible and open to new ideas and approaches to meeting those needs and interests.

Only when you adopt the mindset that you can achieve your own objectives while also assisting others to achieve theirs can integrative negotiation reach its full potential.

Concessions

In any negotiation, it is expected that concessions will be made and reciprocated. ***Concessions*** are things of value that you agree to give your opponent in order to move closer to an agreement to gain what you are seeking. It is also expected that the concessions on both sides will be of similar value to the respective parties engaged in the negotiation. ***Boulwarism***, or making a take it or leave it offer, is usually not a good idea. People feel better about the process and outcome of the negotiation if concessions are made and reciprocated. Concessions do involve risk taking, however. There is no assurance that if you make a concession it will be reciprocated. If you desire to establish trust in the relationship, taking a risk and trusting the other to reciprocate is one good way to start the process.

The beauty of integrative negotiation is that it is possible to find concessions that can be made at relatively little expense to one person in exchange for a concession from the other that has greater value. This involves ***logrolling*** in which you exchange one concession for a concession from the other side. Issues are combined to make mutually beneficial tradeoffs. Using logrolling, value can be created rather than treating each issue as a distributive negotiation independent of the other issues. In the story of the ugly orange, one sister gave up the rind, which was of no use to her, in exchange for the entire inside of the fruit, which was of much greater value. The relative value to the sisters of what they received was the same. The value of what each gave up was the same. The joint value created as a result of making the small concessions was twice what either would have received if they had not each made a concession.

Initial concessions made in a negotiation send a clear message to the other party. If the concession is small, it sends a message that the person is firm on his/her position. Often, this approach will capture most of the bargaining range. This may also annoy one's opponent, however, and turn the negotiation competitive. If you are flexible on concessions, it will communicate that you are willing to work toward a settlement.

Later in the negotiation, concession size can send signals to your fellow negotiator. If you begin to make smaller and smaller concessions, it can signal that you are approaching your resistance point. If you make several concessions of about the same size, it will signal that you are willing to continue to work the issue and have sufficient room to move before hitting your limit. Making one last large concession and announcing that it is as far as you can go will signal that you are at your limit. It is important not to do this unless you really mean it. If you are not really at your limit, you may need to either accept a BATNA that is not as good as the deal you could have had if you kept negotiating or you will keep negotiating and show your partner that you were bluffing. Either way, you lose. You will lose value or you will lose face and credibility.

In a negotiation when buying a house, there are multiple issues to decide and concessions play a major role in reaching an agreement. For example, the buyer may want the appliances left in the house and the seller may desire to have the buyer pay for the home inspection. They could agree to each make a concession to gain what they respectively desire. The buyer could make a concession by agreeing to pay for the home inspection and, in exchange, the seller could make a concession by agreeing to leave the appliances in the house.

Power

Power is the ability to influence others to do what you would like to have done. In negotiation, it is better to persuade than to coerce another since the results are generally more favorable and the commitment to fulfilling the agreement is greater. There are many types of power one may wield in a negotiation. **Legitimate power** is derived from one's position in the organization or one's office, rank, or social position. It depends on having the consent of those governed and can be enhanced by having a positive image in the organization and performing at a high level of competence.

Resources are another source of power. To have resource power, you must have something the other wants and be willing to trade the resources for compliance or cooperation of some form. If the resources are available from other sources, your power is diminished. **Attractiveness** or **friendliness** is another source of power. Friendliness and the ability to develop personal relationships through showing warmth, caring, and empathy create power.
It has been shown that those who others find attractive (friendly and approachable) both gain larger concessions and are asked for lower concessions than those who are not seen as being as attractive to the other. This is one situation where being nice really pays off!

Finally, **integrity** creates power as well. Having a reputation for character, solid values, and ethical behavior creates the basis for trust and the belief that one will not be taken advantage of. It is easier to develop persuasive arguments if you have integrity in the eyes of your opponent. They are more likely to believe you and trust your arguments. While it is possible to gain what one wants by using pressure and coercion in negotiation, most negotiations are of the integrative nature and less aggressive tactics will yield more positive results. Agreements reached relying on persuasion and rational appeals are more likely to have the commitment of the parties involved to follow through and honor the agreements.

PHASE 2: CONDUCTING A WIN-WIN NEGOTIATION

As shown in Figure 8.3, to conduct a win-win negotiation, both parties must engage in a series of six steps.

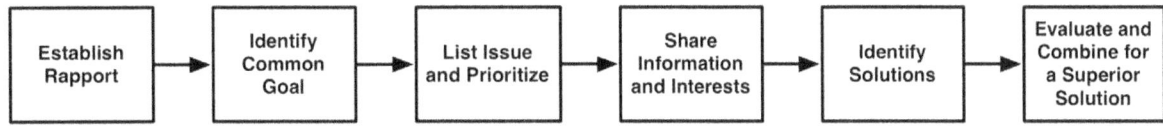

Figure 8.3 - Steps for a Win-Win Negotiation

Step 1: Establish Rapport

First establish rapport with the other negotiator. When people are negotiating with someone they find agreeable or attractive, they are more likely to cooperate and to work toward mutually beneficial solutions than if they see the other person as an adversary. Taking the time to become acquainted and establish a base level of trust is well worth the time it takes at the beginning of a negotiation.

Step 2: Identify a Common Goal

The next step is to decide on a common goal both sides can agree to. In the supply chain, all members are dependent on each other, so if one does well, the others will too. The ultimate customer is impacted by the agreements made between all of the members of the supply chain because the price paid by the end user is a result of the efficiencies (or inefficiencies) from the beginning to the end of the supply chain. If all parties focus on making efficient deals that make a fair profit and keep costs low at the same time, all parties benefit from the initial supplier to the end user. If that is the case, it makes sense to state a common goal for the parties involved because both will profit from a continuing relationship that serves the others in the supply chain well and the end user in particular. This goal may be: *Working together to maintain a close working relationship that is mutually profitable and efficient at keeping costs low.* This goal keeps both parties in business, is something both can agree to, and will be helpful in refocusing efforts to find integrative agreements when the negotiations get strained.

Step 3: List the Issues to Be Negotiated & Prioritize from Each Side

Once the common goal is identified and agreed to, it is time to identify all of the issues that will be negotiated. It is very helpful to have both the goal and the issues in view of both parties to the negotiation. It becomes easy to lose sight of the common goal and it is difficult to keep too many things in one's short-term memory at once. If the issues are named and each side then shares the relative priority of each of the issues, it becomes easier to see potential for logrolling and creating greater value in the negotiation.

Step 4: Share Information and Interests

Once the common goal is agreed and issues are identified, you are ready to begin the negotiation. Sharing information is critical to conducting a successful integrative negotiation. A common misunderstanding is that by offering information, one compromises his/her position. This is not the case. In fact, by offering information, one provides the other necessary information to use in order to make mutually beneficial trade-offs. In the example of the sisters and the orange, each got half of what they wanted until they were willing to talk about what they wanted to do with the orange. It was then that both realized each could benefit by making a concession to the other that cost essentially nothing and gained all of what they really wanted. In the same way, if you will share information about not only what you want, but also why you want it, your opponent can potentially see new ways to make concessions that will get you closer to your goal and at the same time get closer to his/her goal as well. At this stage of the process, it is important to remember to be firm but flexible. You need to attend to your interests but not at the expense of the relationship. In your search for acceptable solutions, it is important to remember the other party's goals and to search for solutions that will satisfy both your goals and theirs.

Step 5: Identify Acceptable Alternative Solutions

In every negotiation, the search for possible solutions is where the value is created. Rather than stopping at the first acceptable solution that is the minimum acceptable outcome, like the sisters sharing half an orange, search for a variety of possible solutions and keep all of the options open. In this way, it is possible to explore a range of options and take the best parts of all to create a solution that will be superior to any of the others. Negotiation is problem solving. If you generate a larger number of possible solutions, it is more likely that you will arrive at a superior solution, creating more value for all involved.

Step 6: Evaluate Solutions and Combine Good Ideas to Create a Superior Solution

Once the potential solutions have been generated, evaluate them for acceptability and rank them. It is important to explain why you prefer one alternative to another in terms that others in a negotiation can understand and appreciate. This helps them to better understand your needs and gives them the ability to better see how they can make concessions that will benefit you and at the same time help themselves. During this stage of the process, there are times communication can be difficult and emotions can get intense. If you or your opponents begin to get tense and the conversation becomes a bit heated, take a break and cool off. When you get back together, refocus on the common goal and recommit to working toward achieving the common goal to each other's benefit. Staying engaged when things get tense will not benefit either side. If it becomes clear that a break is needed, take the initiative and call for one rather than let the negotiation dissolve into a win-lose mindset.

PHASE 3: POST-NEGOTIATION

Once the negotiation is concluded and you have an acceptable agreement for both sides, it must be documented. This is one step that must be well executed regardless of the relationship between the parties. Failing to write out the agreement is a primary cause for misunderstandings after the fact. In Chapter 9, "The Legal Side of Purchasing," we will look at the legal consequences of contracts that are breached by either the purchaser or the seller. When contracting for services or products, there will be a purchase contract that should specify all of the terms that were discussed and agreed to by both parties. It is also helpful to include dispute resolution procedures for larger contracts to reduce the chance for conflict should an issue arise. Once the execution of the agreement is underway, it is important to monitor progress and provide feedback to the other party on performance. If they are doing a great job, let them know. If there are errors or other issues that need to be addressed, let them know and work with them to address the issue in a mutually agreeable way.

ETHICS IN NEGOTIATION

One of the challenges in any negotiation is the ***dilemma of trust***, or how much to trust the other person. Can you really believe what the person is telling you? Another dilemma is how much to reveal to the other person. If you trust him/her, it is easier to take the risk of divulging information. If you don't trust other parties in your negotiations, the risk of giving them an advantage may be too great. This is of great importance when discussing integrative negotiation because creating value in negotiation requires the exchange of information and being able to believe that what you are being told is true. This creates an obligation on your part to tell the truth as well. In the context of a personal or business relationship, it would appear that mutual respect for telling the truth would be a very good thing.

In negotiations, however, it is common to bluff. ***Bluffing*** is a deliberate act of deception and is intended to give one party (the bluffer) an advantage at the expense of the other (the person being deceived). Jack and Judy's friends, John and Kate, were able to get their leather jacket for only $65 in the Turkish bazaar because, after lengthy haggling, they told the vendor that they had only $65 left when, in fact, they had $525 on them at the time.

Some contend that it is acceptable to bluff in negotiation because it is a common practice and everyone does it. Others say that if your partner bluffs, it is acceptable to bluff in retaliation. Those who condone the use of bluffing never come right out and say that it is a moral and ethical practice, but rather contend that it lies in a vague ethical area and that it is a rational behavior because others do it. The weakness in this approach is that if bluffing is a deliberate attempt to deceive the other to one's own advantage, the best argument offered is that two wrongs make a right, which is no moral justification at all.

In the context of a distributive negotiation, there may be an argument that bluffing is rational (as opposed to ethical) behavior since the situation is a one- time negotiation and the relationship is not considered important. In this situation, it is a win-lose negotiation and one is not concerned with the other's outcome. However, if the negotiation is taking place with the expectation that it will be a long-term relationship, bluffing becomes less rational. In integrative negotiations, the way to create value is to exchange information and discover mutually beneficial trade-offs. However, the respective parties take risks and share sensitive information that potentially could be used to place them at a disadvantage.

If you suspect that the other party in a negotiation is going to be opportunistic at your expense, there is no real incentive to take a risk and attempt to create value by sharing information. This will restrict communication and mutual information-sharing, resulting in defensive behaviors that limit the potential for creating value in the negotiation. The net result will be agreements that, while minimally acceptable, are not nearly as profitable for either side as they could be if there was an open, trusting exchange of information in the negotiation. In the example of the orange and the sisters, it was only after they shared information that each got what she really wanted. If information is exchanged, value can be created that is not going to be found if the information is not exchanged.

If integrative negotiation is going to work well, both parties need to be committed to telling the truth and avoiding bluffing and other forms of misrepresentation of their positions and interests. In the context of an ongoing relationship, it is imperative to establish trust in order to be able to take the risk involved with sharing information and seeking mutually beneficial trade-offs. In order to maximize the potential to develop this necessary trust, it is critical that the respective parties avoid deception, even when it will provide a momentary advantage over the other. Once the practice of deception is introduced into an integrative negotiation within a long-term relationship between a buyer and supplier, it will hinder both parties' ability to create value and will make both less competitive because the most efficient solution will not be found.

In negotiations, a concern that often arises is, "What do I say if I am asked what is the least I will accept? If I am honest, it will be to my disadvantage and if I bluff, I am lying." Your best recourse may be not to answer at all! If you choose not to supply the information, that is not a breach of trust and, in this case, it is common sense not to reveal your limit and the other person knows it.

However, if you bluff and name a figure that you represent as your limit, most likely it will be over your real limit and you may find yourself caught in a dilemma later in the negotiation. You could be faced with a choice of either admitting you lied by accepting a lower offer or walking away and taking your BATNA that is worse than the deal you have to pass up to cover your lie. Either way, bluffing will have created a no-win situation for you.

When deciding whether you want to bluff or tell the truth, you should consider:

- *Does the relationship matter?* If yes, tell the truth.

- *Can I morally justify my actions?* If yes, let your conscience be your guide.

- *What are the likely consequences if I am found out?* If the consequences are negative, don't do it.

- *How will I feel about my decision after I see how it impacts my negotiation partner?* If it will not be good, don't do it.

- *Is what I am thinking of doing something I want done to me?* If the answer is no, don't do it.

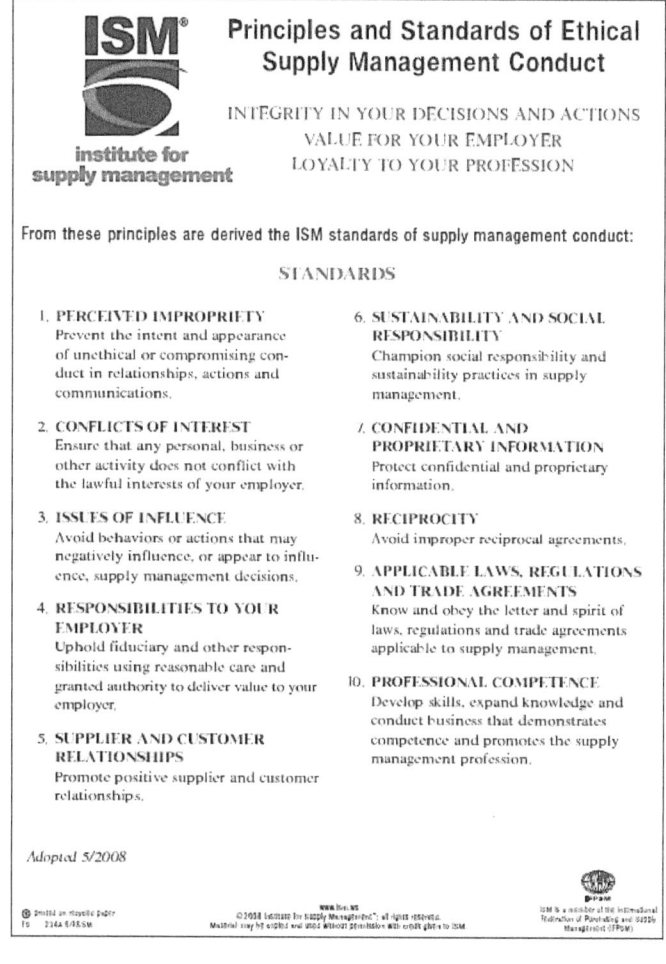

Many large organizations have formal codes of ethical conduct that all employees, including purchasing professionals, are expected to follow. Professional associations, such as the Institute for Supply Management (ISM), also provide a wealth of resources for purchasing professionals regarding ethical standards in purchasing. For example, the chart above includes the ISM *Principles and Standards of Supply Management Conduct*.

BECOMING A SKILLED NEGOTIATOR

Negotiation is a skill that improves with practice. Anyone can become more proficient at negotiation, but it will not happen by accident. To become more proficient and to get more out of the negotiations you complete, you need to practice ***effective negotiation behaviors***. Some areas to develop include:

- *Become comfortable establishing rapport in the beginning of the negotiation.* Rather than just jumping in, take the time to establish common ground. Ask other parties in a negotiation what they do for fun or ask them about their family or hobbies. Chances are, you will discover that you have common interests or experiences that will become the basis for a conversation that is neutral with regard to the negotiation and you will get to know each other a bit. Remember, it is easier to make concessions to someone that you like or find friendly and nice.

- *Learn to use open-ended questions.* An open-ended question is one where you ask for information that requires a response beyond a yes or a no. For example you could ask, "What information did you use to determine the asking price of this car?" It cannot be answered with a one-word answer. Exchange of information is critical to creating integrative agreements and creating value. Also, be willing to offer information to get the ball rolling. Talk about what you want and why you want it.

- *Watch the other person as you are speaking, making offers, and making concessions.* Other people will show you a lot about how they feel about your proposal or concession through their body language. If you are not getting the response you expected, ask a question to find out why. This way, you can move toward a better understanding of what they are looking for and create a better agreement.

- *Build trust in the negotiation.* If you offer information first and commit to tell the truth, you will lay the foundation for building trust. It is common to discuss the ground rules before starting negotiations. If you both commit to tell the truth and avoid the use of bluffing before you even start, it makes it easier to exchange information and work cooperatively toward a deal that creates value for both sides.

- *Plan for the negotiation and debrief after the negotiation.* Planning will ensure that you are ready to engage the other and it will help keep you focused on gaining what you need out of the negotiation. Debriefing after the negotiation is a process in which you think through the negotiation and identify what went well and what didn't from both your perspective and the perspective of the other party. The object is to learn from the experience and use the lessons learned to further hone your skills for future negotiations.

- *Take notes and use them.* Too many negotiators try to manage too much information in their head often forgetting important information and losing track of what has been said. If the negotiation requires several meetings to conclude and there is a time lag between meetings, good notes are the best way to keep track of the progress made and what you have learned about the other side.

Negotiation is a skill that can be developed with practice. It is also one skill that pays off well the more you develop it. If you take the time to plan well before and debrief after negotiations, identify areas where you can learn to do a better job, and practice the skills and behaviors that you need develop, you will see your skills and your outcomes both improve dramatically.

CHAPTER 8 REVIEW QUESTIONS

1. Describe one everyday *social negotiation* that you have experienced recently. In a purchasing decision, what is negotiable? When might you not want to negotiate?

2. *Integrative negotiation* sounds ideal, but would it be the appropriate style of negotiation for an expensive, one-off cash purchase, such as the purchase of an expensive sports car? Explain your answer.

3. Considering the *five approaches to negotiation*, which approach do you tend to use most when negotiating with friends and family? (Please be honest!) Would this be the best approach to use for business negotiations when trying to develop a long-term relationship with a supplier? Please explain your answer.

4. In the story of the two sisters with the ugly orange, was their negotiation *distributive* or *integrative*? Which of the five approaches to negotiation did they use? Was it successful? Why?

5. During a negotiation, why is the *pre-negotiation planning phase* important?

6. If you were a purchasing manager for a greeting card company, would you use *boulwarism* or *logrolling* during negotiations when trying to build a long-term relationship with a paper supplier? Why or why not?

7. When attempting to conduct a win-win negotiation, which should you do first when sitting down with the other party: a) *establish rapport* or b) *list issues and prioritize*? Why is it important to do this first?

8. What is your opinion on *bluffing* during a negotiation? Is it a good idea or bad idea? Why?

9. Conduct an online search to find a *purchasing code of ethics* for two businesses, educational institutions, or nonprofit organizations. What principles or practices are shared by both organizations?

10. When looking at the areas to develop to become a skilled negotiator, which one might be the most difficult for you? Why?

CHAPTER 8 CASE EXERCISE

Planning for Negotiations

Before entering into any negotiation, it is critical to be prepared. Think about a current or potential negotiation you have encountered or might encounter in your work or home life. Complete the worksheet below to prepare for your negotiation.

Planning for Negotiation - Worksheet

The Issue: *What is it that needs to be resolved and why?*

The Other Party:
What do I know about the other person? What have I heard about him/her?

Positions:
the desired solution to the issue prior to beginning to negotiate
Mine:

His/Hers/Theirs:

Interests:
Why do the negotiators want what is in their position? Any other concerns?
Mine:

His/Hers/Theirs:

BATNA:
What alternatives are available that will be used if no deal can be reached?
Mine:

His/hers/theirs:

Target:
What is the most desirable outcome?
Mine:

His/hers/theirs:

Resistance Point:
the point at which no further concessions will be made
Mine:

His/hers/theirs:

Criteria:
What standards can be used to support the appropriateness of offers in the negotiation?

Options:
What are the possible solutions to the negotiation that create value and satisfy both parties' interests?

Possible Options?	Impact on the Other Side?	What Is the Worst Response Likely to This Option?	What Can I Say in Response to the Worst Likely Response?

Chapter 9

Purchasing, Contracts, & the Law

Dr. Philip M. Price

Purchasing professionals need to understand the basics of contracts and the laws that govern them. This is true even though most large organizations have legal departments and smaller organizations have access to legal advice when it is needed.

Unlike many people within an organization, purchasing professionals deal with the law on a daily basis. They sign contracts, often for significant financial amounts, and can legally commit the company to responsibilities that can have a very negative effect on its financial security and future. Of course when an organization is entering into very large, long-term commitments, it is important to have professional legal advisors, but a basic understanding of the law governing contracts will help purchasing professionals conclude the majority of day-to-day buying activates without problems. Most contracts work out as intended because both parties fulfill their promises. The importance of following correct procedures when contracting only becomes important when something goes wrong and one party is attempting to enforce or dissolve the contract. The real objective of contracts is to make business dealings more predictable.

LAW DEFINED

What is law?

Law can be defined as a body of conduct prescribed by a controlling authority and having binding legal force.

How much of the law purchasing professionals need to know will depend on their job roles, but what is quite clear is that most purchasing officers will not need a detailed knowledge of the law. What is needed is a sound basic grounding in the principles of law so that potential legal problems can be identified when they arise and handled correctly at the outset, both confidently and accurately, before they escalate into serious issues. Before we delve into the world of Contracts, Consideration and Uniform Commercial Codes, let us understand that for a purchasing professional, litigation (going to court) should always be the last resort. The best way to deal with potential disputes and continue a good working relationship with our suppliers is to negotiate a settlement. Having a grasp of the principles of contract law helps avoid litigation.

When a problem arises with a supplier, follow the steps below before pursuing litigation:

1. **Communicate:** Talk to them.

2. **Negotiate:** Seek an agreed solution.

3. **Arbitrate:** Get someone to help reach an agreeable solution

4. If and when all the above fail, you may have to **Litigate:** Go to court.

WHAT IS A CONTRACT?

A *contract* is an agreement or exchange of promises between two or more persons or entities. The promises can be between individuals, businesses, organizations, or government agencies. Basically, a contract in the business sense is a promise to do, or to refrain from doing, a particular thing in exchange for something of value. Contracts can be written, using formal or informal terms, or they can be entirely verbal. When one side to the exchange of promises fails to live up to their part of the bargain, there's a ***breach*** and certain remedies for solving the differences are available. The terms of the contract - the who, what, where, when, and how of the agreement - define the binding promises of each party to the contract.

Most terms and condition contained in contracts are the result of negotiations between the purchaser and the seller of the goods. The contract is the formal agreement of what was decided at these negotiations and, once signed, has legal responsibilities attached. Often new contracts are based on previous contracts or certain parts of previous contracts. This ***boiler plate*** style of contracting can save a lot of time, but it is always a good idea to get some legal advice before you sign long-term or complicated contracts.

All purchase contracts, formal and informal, should include at least the following set of elements:

- *The names of the parties involved.*

- *Date the contract will come into effect.*

- *The total costs of the goods or service and the payment process.*

- *Where, when, and how the goods will be delivered.*

- *The required quality and quantity of goods, and how they will be inspected. It can also provide provisions detailing what to do if the goods are rejected.*

- *If disagreements arise, who will be the final arbitrator.*

International purchase contracts should include all of the elements above, but many also contain some of the following additional clauses:

- *If a dispute happens under which legal jurisdiction will the case be heard?*

- *What language will be used to write the contract? This can be important, as many critical performance elements of the contract could be lost in translation.*

- *Which currency will be used in the final payment and at what exchange rate?*

Force majeure is another clause commonly found in contracts, which can free both parties from liability or obligations imposed by the terms and conditions in the contract. Force majeure becomes applicable when a contract cannot be performed because of an event that prevents its discharge, which is beyond the control of the parties. These events can include: wars, labor strikes, riots, crime, or events that are called **acts of God**, such as flooding, earthquakes, and volcanic eruption.

Figure 9.1 - Force Majeure Applies to Acts of God, Damage from Including Natural Disasters

The Law of Contracts

The laws involved in business are there for two principal purposes: 1) *to protect the seller of goods* and 2) *to protect the purchaser of goods*. The law not only protects businesses from other businesses, but it also protects the final consumer of their products or services. Through issuing warranties, it also provides consumers with the means to get compensation, or our money back, if they receive a product or quality of service different than originally promised.

Throughout the English-speaking world, a **contract** is defined as a formal, legally enforceable exchange of promises. However, not all promises are legally binding. For example, courts would decline to hear a dispute arising from a domestic agreement between spouses over housekeeping money.

In essence, a contract is a deal. It is an **enforceable** promise. In business, every aspect of buying, selling, or transporting goods and every aspect of engaging services for remuneration depend on competently conceived contracts. Some lay people might mistake a statement of intent or a "mere promise" as a contract, but if it lacks the remaining elements of a contract listed previously, it is not a contract. The law of contracts decides which promises can be enforced, whether promises agreed have been performed, and what remedies are applicable when the contract has been breached. The object is to ensure the person wronged in the breach is compensated or, in certain cases, they can ensure compliance of the contract.

THE CASE OF THE CAREFUL CAR COMPANY

John Lewis had, at long last, saved up enough down payment cash to trade in his old car and purchase a newer second hand car. He went to the Careful Car Company and met with their sales representative Louis Lyes. Louis tested John's old car and valued it at $2,000 if traded in. Louis showed John various cars on the parking lot. After much looking and thinking, John finally decided on a 5-year-old Ford Explorer that was within his price range. The sticker on the car read: $15,000. John offered Louis $12,500. Louis counter-offered with $14,250. After much offering and counter offering Lewis agreed to accept an offer of $12,750, plus Johns' old car. During the negotiation, Louis explained that there was a two-year limited warranty on the car. Louis also agreed to replace the two front tires that were nearing the end of their useful life. As part of the deal, John also agreed to give Louis his four, one-year-old winter tires valued at $100. Just three hours after John entered the sales lot, he signed the final contract, paid his money, and drove the car away. While they were working on the paperwork, the garage staff at Careful Car's mounted the new tires. Two days later John dropped off the winter tires to Louis.

The Careful Car Company case is one of millions of normal transactions that happen daily and have legal consequences. Purchasers and sellers can be either individuals or representatives of companies. The final agreements that are signed into contracts represent from small amounts to millions of dollars. The Laws covering contracts are in place to protect both the buyer and seller. In our Careful Cars Company case, Louis held up his end of the bargain by fitting the new tires. If John had refused to hand over the winter tires, Louis could have sought legal recourse.

In the case of John and Louis and the Careful Car Company, all parties involved followed the law of contracts, but where did this law come from? There are two sources that have formed contract law today, the Uniform Commercial Code and Common Law.

THE FIRST SOURCE OF CONTRACT LAW: UNIFORM COMMERCIAL CODE

Before 1952, each U.S state had its own commercial laws. In 1952, the **Uniform Commercial Code (UCC)** was published. The objective of the UCC was to unify the national marketplace by developing some form of legal uniformity and predictability, i.e., establish a uniform set of rules to govern commercial transactions, particularly when a purchaser is buying goods out of state. The UCC was developed as a joint project between the National Conference of Commissioners on Uniform State Laws (NCCUSL) and the American Law Institute (ALI). Both NCCUSL and ALI are private organizations and, for the UCC to have any legal authority, it had to be adopted by each individual state.

During adoption, each state had the option to accept or replace certain parts of the UCC. This last sentence is very important, as even though the UCC has achieved a high level of conformity, not all of the states have accepted the UCC and its many revisions in total. It is important for purchasing professionals to understand that there are still some interstate differences in the approach to contract enforcement and rejection. For example, Louisiana has enacted most of the provisions of the UCC with the exception of Article 2, which deals with the sale of goods. They prefer to maintain their own unique French heritage and use their own civil law tradition (code law, as opposed to a common law system) for controlling the sale of goods.

The UCC is not actually the law of commercial contracts. Once contracts are properly constructed, parties can agree on any terms and conditions they wish. The UCC comes into play when they have left out something that has now become important. For example, if I am a purchaser and the sales representative forgets to state in our contract form when payment is due, I might want to delay payment. However, the seller can insist on their payment upon delivery, quoting the provision under UCC Article 2, which reads that "Unless stated otherwise payment for goods received is due at the time of delivery."

There are nine articles in the complete UCC, but purchasing professionals are principally concerned with Article 2 for protection when dealing interstate (between states). Protection under the UCC Article 2 only covers the sale of goods (tangible things that people buy and sell). Tangible goods are things that can be both identifiable and are moveable at the time of the sale. For example, coats are goods, as are railroad cars, bottles of wine, cars, and computers.

Article 2 does not cover transactions involving service contracts. These contracts are governed by common law or other parts of the UCC. For example, the sale of a building or a membership in a health club or a contract between you and a snow remover would not be covered. The sale of your house would also not be covered. A house certainly is a good, but the sale of a house involves the sale of land. Article 9 of the code covers transactions involving the transfer of land. However, land sales are replete with state-by-state differences in both written statutes and common law, which one must look to instead of relying on UCC Article 9. Also, if you lease a car at the airport, this would not be covered by UCC as it does not involve a permanent change in ownership.

When purchasing interstate, purchasing professionals should be aware of problems that may arise due to different interpretations of the UCC. The UCC has moved a long way in achieving its goal of making interstate commerce more predictable and less parochial, but is still not yet fully uniform.

THE SECOND SOURCE OF CONTRACT LAW: COMMON LAW

Common law is, in modern times, a system of decisional or precedential law, which influences much of the non-English speaking world as well. It is sometimes referred to as "case law" in that past decisions in cases made by courts provide the basis for present day decisions. When the highest court in a given jurisdiction rules on a certain set of facts in a dispute, the lower courts in that jurisdiction must rule in the same way the highest court did in identical or substantially similar cases. This principle of common law is based on the old legal tradition of ***stare decisis***, Latin for let the decision stand. It is the legal principle by which judges are obliged to obey the precedents established by prior decisions. In other words, under common law, the precedent set by the higher court is binding on a lower court. All contract disputes not covered by the UCC are covered by common law.

Figure 9.2 - Worldwide Influence of Common Law by Country (from the Free Software Foundation)

Two examples of contracts not covered under the UCC and would instead be covered under common law are *service contracts* and *contracts with minors*. For example, if you hire a contractor to paint your house, this is a ***service contract*** because you have entered into a contract with another party to perform a service. Let's assume that the painter does a really poor job. This case would fall within local statutory law and common law, not the UCC. In contract law, there are cases with past decisions that deal with services that were not performed correctly.

Let's consider another example in which a ***minor*** (person under 18 years old) enters into a contract to purchase a new motorcycle. After two months, the minor decides that she does not want the motorcycle and returns it to the dealer for full reimbursement. Because the UCC does not apply to contracts with minors, the judge will look for **precedents**, or older cases that have dealt with the same issue. He will find that a contract generally cannot be enforced against a minor. This past ruling has set a precedent that is binding on such cases and the minor can rescind the contract and expect to have her money refunded in full. However, as is the case in many legal situations, there can be exceptions to the rule.

If the minor enters into a contract that is plainly for his/her benefit, the contract cannot be **rescinded**, or removed by a higher party and the situation restored to its previous status as if there had been no contract. This exception to the rule comes under the heading of **necessaries**. Necessaries are goods or services that are deemed necessary to the party receiving them and include obvious purchases such as food and clothing. Necessaries also include services or goods which are in furtherance of education or apprenticeship. Therefore, in our example of the minor purchasing the motorcycle, if she made the purchase for the sole purpose of getting to school or work, this may legally viewed as a necessary. Therefore, the contract could not be rescinded and the minor would be expected to uphold her end of the contract with the motorcycle seller.

The objective of all lawmakers, whether they are operating under the common law on contracts or the U.C.C., is to try to level the playing field to ensure that businesses, purchasing professionals, and individuals can know that the deals they make are valid and enforceable contracts.

BINDING CONTRACTS

A contract is valid, or **binding**, when it meets all of the requirements for the formation of a contract. Binding contracts occur when the parties involved have what is considered a *meeting of the minds* in which all parties fully understand the agreement and are certain that no misunderstandings or mistakes exist. All parties enter into the contract freely.

For a contract to be binding, it must fulfill the following requirements:

- *Offer and Acceptance:* A valid offer by one party and a valid acceptance by the other

- *Consideration:* Bargaining that leads to an exchange of value between the parties involved.

- *Intention to Enter into a Legally Binding Relationship*.

- *Legal Capacity*: Both the parties involved in the contract must be at least 18 years old and mentally competent.

- *Legality of Contract*: The contract must be for a lawful purpose.

OFFER AND ACCEPTANCE: OFFERS

Contracts should be as clear and unambiguous as possible. All offers, be they offers to buy or sell goods for a given price or offers to perform services for money, are considered to be a party's definite promise to be bound on certain specified terms. The person making the offer is called the

offeror and the person to whom it is made is called the ***offeree***. An offer can be made to one person, a group of people, or to the public at large, such as in an advertisement. An offer, once made, creates a power of acceptance or rejection in an offeree to ***lock in*** to the terms of the offer, which is tantamount to creating a contract. The offer is intended to create a legal relationship once the offer is accepted. For a communication to be an offer, it must clearly express a promise, commitment, or undertaking to enter into a contract with certainty and definiteness and it must be communicated. Ambiguities will defeat the creation of an enforceable contract.

If, for example, instead of saying "I promise" or I offer," someone states, "I am asking $5,000.00" or "I would consider selling for 'X'," such phrases would be regarded by nearly all counts as preliminary negotiations or exploration of a potential market, NOT an offer which could be locked in by an offeree. In our Careful Car Company case, John makes the first offer but Louis made a counter offer. John was first the offeror but when Louis made the counter offer, John became the offeree. For practical purposes, a counter offer operates as a rejection of the first offer and gives the original offeror the options of an offeree: to *accept* or *reject* the new offer (i.e., the counter offer) or to make a *counter-counter offer*.

The law makes two important distinctions about what can be an offer. *A request for a mere supply of information is never an offer* nor is what is referred to as an **invitation to treat**.

Request for Mere Supply of Information

A request for information (RFI) or a request for quotation (RFQ) is not an offer. If you request information from a supplier as to the availability of goods in their published catalogue and they merely indicate that they have stock at standard advertised rates, this is a mere supply of information and not an offer. Most courts would not consider this as an offer to supply you at a fixed price. They are merely confirming that they still stock the items at the catalogue prices. This will often be described as a quotation.

If, on the other hand, you request the same information but also request them to indicate if they were willing to supply you with the goods on a certain date, their response is likely to be more than merely supplying information. Their response may well be that they have the goods in stock at the advertised price in the quantities requested and that their quote price remains goods for a fixed period of time, such as 30 days. This more detailed response is also a quotation, but it is also effectively an offer to supply, for it is sufficiently detailed and indicates their willingness to supply the goods to you on specific terms.

Invitation to Treat

The expression ***invitation to treat*** is used to describe that part of a transaction where goods are displayed, or advertised with a price. This applies in retail situations in advertisements for sale, catalogues, price lists, and circulars. Here the law quite clearly states that there is no offer to sell by the retailer or advertiser and that they are in fact, inviting potential purchasers to make an offer. This offer can be accepted or rejected by the seller. Therefore, if a retailer or a product restricted by law were approached by a person not entitled by law to purchase that item, then the retailer could legitimately refuse to sell, for in law, the purchaser is making an offer to buy and the retailer is rejecting such an offer that he or she is perfectly entitled to do. In our case of the Careful Car Company, even if John offered the sticker price, Louis is still entitled to reject the offer, as the sticker price is only an *invitation to treat*.

After the supply of information or invitation to treat, the offeror may want to make an offer, but what constitutes an offer? An offer must be a proposal which is sufficiently precise in terms of its requirements and sufficiently clear that a supplier need only agree in the simplest terms and both parties would be clear that a contract existed and the terms of that agreement. A purchase order form from a purchasing professional will most often meet these requirements.

In the ***tendering process***, the offer and acceptance works differently. The purchaser invites the seller to tender. Tenders, when received are the same as the more detailed quotation referred to above. They are sufficiently detailed to amount to an offer. In this case, therefore, the purchaser is in the position of accepting the supplier's offer. The purchase order form when placed now by the buyer is not an offer but an acceptance.

OFFER AND ACCEPTANCE: ACCEPTANCE

The first important rule is to note that acceptance must be complete and unequivocal. Any attempt to change the terms of the original offer or alter any aspects of the offer will not be an acceptance, but a counter offer. A counter offer revokes the original offer and replaces it with a new offer. This can give rise to a *battle of the forms*, as we will see below.

The kind of communication the offeree uses to accept the offer can be of any kind that someone in the offeror's position would consider consent. Forms of acceptance can be either oral or written, unless the person who made the offer said the acceptance had to be in a specific form, any reasonable form of acceptance will make a contract. For example, at auctions the auctioneer makes an offer and you can accept by nodding your head or by raising your hand.

Acceptance is effective as soon as the message leaves the possession of the offeree. An example of this is the ***mailbox rule***: unless an offer requires a different form of acceptance, as soon as the letter of acceptance is put in the mail, the offeree's acceptance is effective. Because of a steady erosion of the mailbox rule's continuing influence, it is increasingly good practice to send critical documents by certified mail with *return receipt requested*. This also helps provide proof that an offer was in fact received and when it was received. Acceptance is effective as soon as it leaves the position of the offeree.

What about electronic contracts and signatures?

In today's increasingly electronic world, more contracts are initiated and accepted electronically. In 1999, the **Uniform Electronic Transactions Act (UETA)** was created by the National Conference of Commissioners on Uniform State Laws to provide a legal framework for U.S. states and territories governing the use and legality of electronic records and signatures for business and government transactions. Since its creation, forty seven states and Puerto Rico and the Virgin Islands have adopted the UETA. Only Washington, Illinois, and New York have not, but these states have their own laws governing electronic records and signatures.

Most offers have a time limit, within which you must decide whether to accept or reject. Some offers specify a set time or date at which the offer will expire. If you do not accept before this date or time, the offer will terminate. However, even if the offer does not have a specific time or date, it will terminate at the end of a reasonable time.

Using our case of the Careful Car Company, we will now look at reasons why offers terminate:

- **Revocation:** The person who makes the offer decides he wants to take it back. Either Louis or John can cancel the offer as long as neither has accepted.

- **Rejection:** If either John or Louis rejects each other's offers, there is no deal.

- **Counteroffer:** Both John and Louis made counter offers. When each counter is offered, this rejected the other's first offer. If at some stage, a counteroffer was rejected and no new offer made, the negotiations would stop.

- **Intervening illegality:** This happens if the subject matter of the offer becomes illegal before it is accepted. For example, if the car John was making the offers on had an engine fitted to enhance speed, the offer would terminate because the engine was declared illegal in their state.

- **Destruction of the item:** If the car were destroyed by fire before the contract was signed, this would terminate the offer.

- **Death or insanity of either party:** If John dies before the contract is signed, there is no deal. However, as Louis was acting as an agent of the car company and not a principal, the deal can still go through if Louis died.

It is important to note that although silence alone cannot amount to acceptance of a contractual offer, conduct can indicate acceptance. Therefore, a supplier or purchaser may indicate acceptance by actually working to the terms of the new agreement or by not objecting to the goods or services being provided within a reasonable time. Silence accompanied by sufficient conduct implying assent is clearly going to suffice as acceptance.

For example, the ABC Company orders specifically manufactured goods from the XYZ Manufacturing Company. XYZ, recognizing that time is of the essence, begins to manufacture the goods. This constitutes an acceptance of the ABC Company's order and creates an implied promise that the XYZ Manufacturing Company will complete manufacture of the ordered goods. It also obligates ABC to fulfill its contracted obligation by paying XYZ. Notification within a commercially reasonable time is a critical condition to the duty of the ABC Company to pay once the specified goods are completed.

In business transactions, who ultimately becomes the offeror and offeree can be very important. The person who accepts the offer is, by his action, accepting the terms and conditions set out by the person who made the offer. This has caused many problems within business situations and is often referred to as the ***battle of the forms***.

Most organizations have a standard purchasing contract form, which contains, often on the reverse side, their standard terms and conditions of business. Standard terms protect the interest of the organization that uses them. Therefore, for example, a buyer will want the longest payment time and the seller the shortest. The buyer will want the greatest protection against defects and the seller the least. As can be expected, it is highly unlikely that the terms and conditions on both the purchaser's and seller's purchasing forms are exactly the same.

When an offer is placed on a standard purchasing contract form, it is often responded to with a seller's standard form of acknowledgement. As the terms on the reverse will not match, this cannot be an acceptance. However, if the details and specifications on the front of the acceptance do match, it will not be a rejection. It must then be viewed as a counter offer and, if accepted by the purchaser, the contract is concluded on the seller's terms.

BATTLE OF THE FORMS		
DOCUMENTATION/FORM	STATUS	CONTRACT CONDITION
Catalog or Price List	Invitation to Treat	Terms Irrelavent
Order Form	Offer by Purchaser	On Purchaser's Terms
Acknowledgement from Supplier or Written Confirmation	Counter Offer Containing Supplier's Terms	On Supplier's Terms

Figure 9.3 - Battle of the Forms

CONSIDERATION

For a contract to be enforceable, it also requires more than just an agreement. It requires that the agreement must be supported by valuable *consideration*. This means that the agreement must be supported by mutual obligations or promises by each party, which have some real legal value. Therefore, if the parties to the contract agree that something is of value, that will be enough. It does not have to be of equal value. The ***Peppercorn Theory of Consideration*** states that something as insignificant as a little peppercorn can suffice as consideration when given in exchange for a promise. The courts will decide on whether consideration was given, not based on the value of the consideration. The court will not cancel a contract based on the fact that you feel afterwards that you made a bad deal. For example, Louis could sell the car to John for as little as a peppercorn or a penny. A nominal consideration may be sufficient to cement an agreement into a legally binding contract. Consideration is, more often than not, money, exchanged for goods or services.

However, under the concept of ***legal detriment***, rather than money, a person can give up an existing right or accept a new duty. Each party must give up something for what they are going to receive from the other party. A gift is not a legally binding contract as it lacks the necessary valuable consideration passing from the recipient of the gift to the giver.

Consideration is basically something of value given immediately or a promise to do something of value in the future. If I agree to cut my neighbors lawn next week in return for tickets to a football game, there is consideration as both the service and the tickets have value. Therefore, there is a contract when we exchange considerations. It is also important to remember that without consideration from both sides, there is no contract. In our Careful Car Company case, John gives Louis money and Louis gives John the car.

Let's now consider an example where there is a **lack of consideration**. John, knowing that Mary is shopping for a new car and guessing she might also need to sell her old car, says, "You know, I'm starting to look for a safe used car for my teenage son." Mary, sensing a convenient opportunity, tells John, "I'll sell you mine for $5,000.00." John tells her he'll withdraw funds from his bank and stop by her office the next day to exchange $5,000 for the keys and title to Mary's old car. The next day, John shows up with the money. Mary, who had visited a couple of internet sites the evening before and realized her old car was worth a great deal more than she had thought, refuses to sell John the car.

Can John successfully sue Mary to enforce their deal? Probably not. That potential deal lacked consideration at the time it was made to make it enforceable. Mary's offer to sell John the car was a *mere promise*. The laws governing contracts will not enforce a mere promise. If John had paid Mary when they first spoke, their agreement would have been an enforceable contract, even if Mary tried to give back the money and get back her car. In this revised version of the facts, consideration was exchanged: John's $5,000. In one form or another, money is the most common form of consideration.

Below are further examples that constitute a lack of consideration:

- *Promise of a gift without consideration:* A promise of a gift is an unenforceable agreement if there is no consideration. If you promise to give someone something but get no promise in return, then the promise you made is unenforceable. For example, parents promise their son a car for his birthday. The parents later decide that they will not give the car but take the son on a holiday instead. The son cannot sue for breach of promise. The car was to be a gift they were going to give their son without expecting anything in return.

- *Pre-existing duty:* If you have made a promise to do something you already have a duty to do, your promise is not a consideration. It is instead a pre-existing duty. You are not giving anything new. There is no consideration because one is not giving up an existing right or accepting a new duty.

- *Past consideration:* If an act has already been performed, it is not possible to bargain for something that has already happened. For example, you paint your neighbors' house while they are away on vacation as a surprise. When they arrive home, they promise you that they will pay for the paint. However, they later decide that they are not going to pay you. You cannot sue them as there was no promise on the neighbor's part and the act has already been performed.

Although consideration in required for a contract to be enforceable, there are exceptions to this rule. There are two alternative theories for enforcing contracts that do not require consideration. They are:

- **Quasi Contract:** This occurs when someone unjustly benefits from the actions of another without the other person receiving fair compensation. For example, you receive a package of DVDs from the History Channel Store in the mail by mistake. You know that you did not order the DVDs but you decide to keep them anyway. The History Channel Store can demand payment, even though you had no contract with them. The doctrine of Quasi Contract will imply that you promised to pay for it and will enforce your implied promise under Quasi Contract. Quasi Contract is sometimes referred to as unjust enrichment.

- **Promissory Estoppel:** A promissory estoppel occurs when someone promises you something that is not part of a valid contract. Detrimental reliance means you will be at a loss if the other person does not come through for you with what they promised. The courts can enforce the contract in order to avoid an injustice. For example, Bill has a wealthy uncle who tells him that he will pay all his college fees if he ever decides to quit his job and go back to college full time. Bill quits his job but the uncle refuses to pay. In Bill's case, there was no contract so he cannot sue for breach. Bill can sue for performance, however, under the doctrine of Promissory Estoppel if:

    ✓ *Bill can prove the person who made the promise knew or should have known he would rely on it.*

    ✓ *Bill can prove he relied on the promise to his detriment.*

INTENTION TO CREATE A LEGAL RELATIONSHIP

In all business transactions where an offer is made by one person and it is accepted by another, it is generally implied that there is an intention to create a legally binding relationship with a legally binding contract. However, both parties can expressly state that they do not want to be bound. In most domestic and social agreements, the majority of times there is not an intention to make the promise legally binding.

Case Example: Balfour v Balfour, 1919

Balfour and his wife lived in Ceylon. Balfour worked as a civil engineer with the British Government. In 1915, they both traveled back to England. Mrs. Balfour got ill and was advised by a doctor to remain in England. Balfour promised his wife 30 pounds sterling per month until she returned to Ceylon. During the absence, they drifted apart. The wife sued for the continuation of the monthly allowance but the Judge ruled that this was merely a domestic arrangement and the promise could not be enforced.

The case can be compared to the facts found in *Merritt v Merritt* [1970]. Here the court distinguished the case from *Balfour v Balfour* on the fact that Mr. and Mrs. Merritt, although still married, were estranged at the time the agreement was made and therefore any agreement between them was made with the intention to create legal relations.

LEGAL CAPACITY

Legal capacity is the ability to enter into a contract. A person 18 years of age and of sound mind may enter into any contract. If all the elements of the contract are present, they will be forced to complete the agreement or pay restitution. Certain classifications of people may, within certain circumstances, disaffirm or rescind the contract. They include:

A. **Minors**: A minor is someone under the age of 18 years. Most contracts entered into by minors are voidable. If a minor enters into a contract to buy a car but decides later on that he does not like the car, he can return the car and demand his money back. (One exception to this rule is in case of *necessaries*, as covered earlier in this chapter.)

B. **Mentally Impaired Person:** In law, a person suffering a mental impairment creates only a contract that is voidable. Whoever seeks to terminate the contract must show that the person could not understand the consequences of their conduct.

C. **Intoxication:** A contract is voidable by the person intoxicated if they can show that they could not have understood the nature and consequences of the transaction.

In our example of the Careful Car Company, if John was a minor, mentally impaired, or intoxicated when Louis sold him the car, John could, at his leisure, return the car and demand his money back.

ILLEGALITY OF CONTRACT

Any contract that has an illegal purpose or object cannot be enforceable. For example, if I make a contract with you to rob the local food store and you do not hold up your end of the bargain, I cannot successfully sue you as the original contract was for an illegal act.

Contracts can become *valid, void, voidable,* or *unenforceable* if a valid defense is made by one of the parties.

- **Valid**: Contracts are considered valid when two or more people with capacity make an agreement involving valid consideration to do or refrain from some lawful act.

- **Void Contract**: Where there never was a valid contract, it cannot be enforced by either party.

- **Voidable Contract**: This is a valid contract that can be voided if it can be rejected on legal grounds by one of the parties to it. In the Careful Car Company case, let us presume that John was only 16 years of age. As John would still be a minor, he could not legally enter into a contract and therefore there was no contract. Put another way, John could not be bound by the contract.

- **Unenforceable Contracts**: An unenforceable contract happens when the parties intended to have a binding agreement but a court declares that some rule of law prevents enforcing it.

In the case of the Careful Car Company, let us presume that John will not have the full deposit necessary to purchase the car until 18 months from now. Louis, the salesman, *verbally* agrees that he will wait until then to conclude the contract. Unfortunately for John, two weeks later Bob makes Louis an offer he cannot refuse. Louis sells the car to Bob. John cannot sue Louis, as under the Statute of Frauds, all contracts over 12 months must be in writing, as must all contracts for sale of real property (land).

BREACH OF CONTRACT

A ***breach of contract*** is a failure to do something that is required in the contract. Three types of breach of contract are:

- **Substantial Performance Breach:** This is a slight breach of the promise that occurs when the performance of the promisor falls slightly below the expectations of the promisee. The party to the agreement performed, but they did not do a very good job. Their performance was substantial but not complete. However, no contract can require perfection, just performance. With a performance breach, the promisee must pay for the contract but can deduct a sum to compensate for the promisor's poor performance. The promisor can also negotiate to make up for the slight breach. Cases of performance breach often wind up in court, which is generally a bad idea for both parties. It is rarely cost effective to seek a court ruling in such disputes.

- ***Material Breach of Contract:*** When the promisor's performance is far below the reasonable expectations of the promisee, a material breach of contract occurs. In this case, the promisor did so little that they are not entitled to get anything. It is a breach of much greater degree than the substantial breach. ***Material*** is treated in the law as a subject so important to the case that, without the term's fulfillment, there would likely have been no contract formation at all.

- ***Anticipatory Breach:*** This is a breach that happens before the performance of the duties, services, or payments are outlined by the contract. In this case, the promisor informs the promisee before the time of the contract that they will not be able to perform their end of the contract. The promisee can sue immediately if they are unable to negotiate a compromise to define their liquid damages.

Sometimes it is not in one of the parties' best interest to fulfill their end of the contract. When the defaulting party fails to perform and cannot reach a settlement with the other party, they are in breach of contract. There are seven defenses that the defaulter may use to minimize their damages. Please note in passing that common law in most English speaking jurisdictions requires a suing party to take reasonable steps to mitigate his damages. He can't simply sit back and let his damages accumulate to absurd amounts.

When defaulting on a contract, eight possible defenses are:

1. **Lack of Capacity (Voidable).** This occurs when one of the parties entering the contract had neither the ***capacity*** nor the legal ability to make a contract. In other

words, they are unable to understand the implications of making contractual obligations. Parties that meet this criterion include minors, the mentally incapacitated, and intoxicated people. In the case of the Careful Car Company sale, let's say that John was intoxicated at the time of the sale and did not understand what he was signing. Louis knew this and took advantage of the situation. In this situation, the contract is voidable by John. However, John would have the burden of proof to show he was incapacitated due to heavy alcohol consumption.

2. **Fraud (Voidable)**. This occurs when one party deliberately misrepresented the facts and you relied on these facts, i.e., there was intent to deceive. In the case of the Careful Car Company, let's say that Louis knows that John is looking for a car that will give him over 40 miles to the gallon. Louis states (knowing it to be untrue) that John's choice of car will give him 50 miles per gallon. This is fraud and the contract is voidable by John.

3. **Duress (Voidable)**. *Duress* is considered present when any threat of harm or actual physical harm deprives a person of freedom of will to choose and decide. This can also include emotional or economic harm. In the case of the Careful Car Company, duress would be present if Louis threatened to set the car lot's two Rottweiler dogs on John if he did not sign the contract.

4. **Undue Influence (Voidable)**. This occurs when there is wrongful and unfair persuasion, often by a fiduciary or other trusted individual, which deprived the victim of freedom of will in making the contract. It can also be described as the manipulation of the plaintiff to enter into a contract that was not to their benefit by someone they trusted. They were unduly influenced. In the case of the Careful Car Company, let's imagine that John did not really like the car and initially decided not to buy it. Louis, the salesman, knew that John was a very religious person, so he contacted John's pastor. Louis and the (unbeknownst to John) shady pastor agreed between them that Louis would give the pastor a percentage of his commission if he could persuade/influence John to buy the car. The shady pastor called John and assured him that the car was a good deal and he would be disappointed with John if he did not buy it. Not wanting to upset his religious advisor and relying on his pastor's assurance that the car was a good deal, John decided to forget his initial doubts and buy the car. When the clunker of a car broke down soon after the sale, John was able to void the contract by proving his pastor had unduly influenced him to enter into the contract.

5. **Illegality (Voidable)**. This occurs when the substance of the contract is illegal. In the case of the Careful Car Company, let's say that Louis, in a moment of desperation to get the car sale, tells John he will fit an illegal speed trap warning device in the car free of charge. This device is illegal in the state where John is buying the car. If Louis does not fit the device, John cannot sue Louis, as the substance of the agreement to fit the detector was illegal.

6. **Unconscionable (Voidable)**. Being unconscionable is another reason why contracts can be declared illegal. This occurs when, even though a contract is valid, the insistence of its performance would be grossly unfair to one person and the courts would be creating an unjust result by enforcing it. In the case of the Careful Car Company, let's say

that Louis arranges additional finance of $400 so John can fit a new stereo CD player in the car. Louis does not tell John that the financing charge for the $400 borrowed is $800. This is a total cost of $1200 for a $400 dollar loan. In all probability, the courts would not enforce John to pay the exorbitant financing fee.

7. **Impossibility for a Reasonable Person to Perform (Unenforceable).** This occurs when something unexpected or uncontrollable happens that prevents the contract from being completed. If one party cannot complete their end of the contract, the other party is also relieved of the responsibility to perform. This can result from destruction of subject matter or death of one of the parties. In the case of the Careful Car Company, if the car is destroyed by fire before the contract is signed, neither party can perform the contract. Put another way, the seller bears the risk of loss until the contract is signed. Similarly, in most but not all U.S. states, a buyer of real property can rescind (get out of) a contract if the structure or land burns up before the deal is closed.

8. **Statute of Frauds (Unenforceable).** To be valid, some contracts must be in the form prescribed by law. Valid contracts can be either written or oral, but there are four situations under the statute of frauds in which contracts must have a signed, written document. Under this statute, if the contracts are not written and signed, they will be unenforceable. The four situations requiring a signed, written contract are:

   A. *Any contract involved in the sale of land or any interest in the sale of land.* Most states also require a lease of more than one year to be in writing.

   B. *Collateral promises.* These are secondary or underlying contracts when one person promises to pay the debts or duties of another.

   C. A *contract for the sale of tangible goods.* Contracts under the UCC sale of goods for $500 dollars or more must be in writing.

   D. *Any contract that cannot be completely performed within one year from the date of agreement.* These contracts must be in writing. The same contract may be valid even if it is only oral if it is performed in less than one year.

When a contract is defaulted on by one of the parties, there is a breach in the contract. The other party can then seek a remedy to the breach of contract. The purpose of a remedy is to compensate the person who was harmed by the breach of contract. The courts attempt to rectify wrongs and to enforce rights. Typically, the remedy for breach of contract is an award of money damages. Two types of monetary award for breach of contract are *compensatory damages* and *consequential damages*.

Compensatory damages are an amount awarded to make good or replace the actual loss suffered by a parties as a result of a breach in contract. The amount in money awarded is equivalent to the actual loss suffered by the plaintiff.

Consequential damages are an amount of money awarded to make good or replace indirect but foreseeable damages. Let's consider consequential damages in the purchase of faulty goods. In this case, you buy a new printer that is faulty. Unfortunately, not only does your printer not work properly when you plug it into the electricity mains, but it also blows out the main circuit board in your computer. Under the consequential damage rule, you can also seek compensation for the damaged computer.

Although the most common remedy for breach of contract is an award of money damages, when dealing with unique subject matter, *specific performance* of the contract may be ordered. **Specific performance** means forcing the breaching party to fulfill the terms of the contract. In cases of specific performance, the courts rule that the original contract must be fulfilled. This occurs in circumstances where monetary damages will not be sufficient. Often this is the case when unique items are offered for sale. In our example of the Careful Car Company, let's presume the car John is buying is not a Ford explorer but a vintage model-T Ford. Non-performance by Louis to deliver this unique item cannot be compensated by money. The courts will rule that Louis must deliver the car as promised.

WARRANTIES

A **warranty** is a contractual promise that goods or services will meet certain standards. It can also be called a **guarantee** that certain goods or services are being sold as stated or implied by the seller. Whenever the manufacturer or the seller offers warranties, it is making a promise to stand behind the quality of its product. The warranty will often state a specific remedy, such as repair or replacement in the event the article or service fails to meet the warranty. The warranty or promise is breached when the good or service is defective or does not meet the standards expected by a reasonable buyer. **Product liability** is the area of law in which manufacturers, distributors, suppliers, retailers, and others who make products available to the public are held responsible for the injuries those products cause.

Breach of warranty-based product liability claims usually focus on one of three types: 1) *breach of an express warranty*, 2) *breach of an implied warranty of merchantability*, and 3) *breach of an implied warranty of fitness for a particular purpose*.

An **express warranty** is one that the seller creates with her own words or actions. Express warranty claims focus on express statements by the manufacturer or the seller concerning the product. Often the advertising surrounding a product is full of expressed warranties. These may often function as a limitation on damages a consumer may seek: if your old fashioned film fails to capture your wedding images, you're only entitled to the cost of the defective film, not the much larger, consequential damages of not having wedding photos. In the case of the Careful Car Company, if Louis tells John that the engine in the car will run for 250,000 miles before it will need to be replaced, this is an express warranty.

An **implied warranty** is one that arises from the nature of the transaction and the inherent understanding by the buyer, rather than from any statements made by the seller. The various implied warranties cover those expectations common to all products unless specifically disclaimed by the manufacturer or the seller. It basically means that goods must be of a merchantable quality, that they conform to a reasonable person's expectation, and that they are what they say they are. In the case of the Careful Car Company, the car John is purchasing from Louis has an implied warranty that the car complies with all the state's road safety requirements necessary to allow John to legally drive it on the highway.

A ***warranty of fitness*** for a particular purpose arises when the purchaser states the intended use of the desired product and then buys a product based on the seller's selection or advice. In the case of the Careful Car Company, let's say that John explains to Louis that he wants a car that can carry six normal sized adults comfortably to his Grandma's bingo night. If Louis selects a two door Volkswagen Beatle and John purchases the small car based on Louis' selection, John can sue later when he finds out that six normal-sized adults will not fit comfortably into the two-door Volkswagen.

As we discussed earlier, purchasing professionals should have at least a fundamental understanding of the law surrounding contracts, their formation, drafting, modification, enforcement, or avoidance. Understanding existing contracts, order forms, bills of lading, sales agreements, and whatever specialized contracts your business is using can be quite helpful to the purchasing professional, but if a form makes no sense or seems inadequate or wrong in some respect, **get legal advice**. A few hundred dollars spent today to draft a good contract tailored to your business needs or to review a contract you've been presented with is far cheaper than defending a lawsuit brought on by a defective or inappropriate contract later. Similarly, having counsel, who is then, by law, *on your side*, review a contract which has been tendered to you (formally presented or offered) can save your company many thousands or even tens of thousands of dollars in a suit for damages (usually, monetary) or rescission (i.e., undoing a contract) growing out of a faulty contract.

CHAPTER 9 REVIEW QUESTIONS

1. Why might a purchasing professional need an understanding of *contracts* and the laws that govern them? Imagine you are the purchasing manager for a large winery and your new cork supplier didn't didn't deliver your order on time but sill charged you full price. Should you sue your supplier for damages and take them to court? Why or why not?

2. If you are a purchasing manager and your supplier cannot get a much needed item to your company on time because of a tornado, is the supplier liable for this delay? Why or why not?

3. In your own words, what is the *Uniform Commercial Code*? In which U.S. states does it apply? Does it cover the sale of land? Why or why not?

4. What role does *precedent* play in commercial law?

5. List three *necessaries* you need for your education and describe why each could be labelled a necessary.

6. If you enter into a contract with someone to slash the tires of your former spouse because they have been harassing you, would this contract be valid and enforceable? Why or why not?

7. You read a grocery store ad in the Sunday newspaper online advertising organic apples for sale at $0.50 per pound. When you get to the store, you are dismayed to find out that they have sold out of their organic apples. Because of the ad in the Sunday paper online, is the store contractually obligated to get more organic apples in and sell them for $0.50 per pound? Why or why not?

8. In many states across the U.S., if you are selling your home and wish to include non-permanent appliances with the sale, such as a refrigerator or washer and dryer, you must draw up a separate contract of sale for these items, even if the amount to be paid is only $1. In legal terms, why might this practice be required?

9. If you are the manager of a coffee shop and your coffee supplier sends you an additional 300 pounds of very expensive coffee you didn't pay for, what should you do? Why? What does this have to do with contracts and the law?

10. Provide an example of a time when you experienced a *breach of contract* from another party. What type of breach of contract was it? What did you do about it?

Chapter 9 Case Exercise

Defenses for Defaulting on a Contract

Please read about the eight possible defenses for defaulting on a contract in the "Breach of Contract" section in this chapter. Next, read each of the scenarios below and decide which of the eight possible defenses could be used for each. Explain your answers for each scenario with at least one to two paragraphs. Warning - some scenarios may have more than one possible defense!

Scenario #1

Big Bad Bob, a local dealer of narcotic substances and machine guns, has decided to sue Innocent Irma for defaulting on the initial payment of her verbal contract to purchase 15 cases of fully automatic machine guns and 5 pounds of heroin. What defense does Irma have for defaulting on the contract?

Scenario #2

Betty Mae Morrison works for Shyster Sam's Sub Shop. She is dependent on her paycheck to take care of her ailing mother and her baby son. She needed to buy a car to get to work on time. Her boss, "Shyster" Sam Simon, tells Betty Mae that his wife owns a used car dealership and forcefully adds that Betty Mae should buy her car there "if she knows what's good for her." Betty Mae bought the car from Sam's wife's dealership at a cost of $2000 more than other dealerships offer for the same car. A week later, Betty Mae decided that she didn't make the right decision and wants to return the car and default on her sales contract. What defense does Betty Mae have for defaulting on the contract?

Scenario #3

During a drinking session at Paddy's Irish Pub, Joe Jones told Bob Barker about a nearby parcel of land he was selling. Bob verbally agreed to buy Joe's land for $50,000. The two agreed to meet two days later at the site so that Bob could pay Joe for the land. Two days later, Bob showed up with his $50,000 but Joe did not show up because he changed his mind. Bob decides to sue Joe for defaulting on the contract. What defense does Joe have for defaulting on the contract?

Chapter 10

Purchasing on the Global Stage

Dr. Philip M. Price & Natalie J. Harrison, M.Ed.

Right now, go to your closet and look at the labels of at least twenty items of clothing to see where they were made. Chances are, they weren't all made in the country in which you live. Instead, your closet is likely to look like a United Nations of contemporary fashion – dress shoes from Italy, sports shoes from China, t-shirt from India, dress pants from Jordan, jeans from Mexico, wool socks from the United States, a winter coat from Bulgaria, and a hand knit scarf from Ireland.

Since World War II, markets have expanded on a global scale as the volume of world trade increased. No longer can each country rely on its national prestige to maintain its economy. Interdependence between countries has become more prevalent. The United States and the United Kingdom are not the economic powerhouses they once were. Much of what is consumed in these countries now comes from abroad as local industry has declined over the past five decades due to recessions and cheaper goods available from elsewhere.

Today's marketplace is an increasingly global one. Companies not only have to worry about competitors from other countries with potentially cheaper prices for their goods. They also have to consider that purchasing the right quality of goods for the right price could mean exploring suppliers from other countries. Finally,

Figure 10.1 - Our Closets Are Now a United Nations of Fashion

companies have to consider expanding their markets to include overseas customers, often just to stay afloat and keep track with their competitors!

As we continue to explore purchasing on the global stage throughout the rest of this chapter, let's consider the case of the American cola wars. Both Coca Cola and Pepsi have waged bitter wars for market share since the inception of both companies in the United States in the late nineteenth century. Coca Cola had more of the initial market share in the early twentieth century because the company decided to expand its sales and operations into other countries, including the Philippines, France, Australia, Austria, Norway, and South Africa. Pepsi kept its operations within the US but ended up going bankrupt in 1923 because it couldn't obtain enough sugar due to World War I sugar rationing. Pepsi was then sold and, as World War II approached, the company decided to play it smart and use global sourcing strategies by obtaining its sugar from Cuba to avoid potential wartime sugar rationing.

Pepsi fully rebounded from its bankruptcy and became a fierce competitor for Coca Cola by expanding into the global market and selling its products to customers in more than 100 countries by the mid 1950s. Coke countered by ensuring that it had bottling operations in more than 100 countries by the late 1950s. Both companies knew that they could not remain within the U.S. to stay competitive and continued to duke it out on the global stage, searching for international suppliers, global customers, and overseas locations for operations. Today the two companies are investing heavily in the rapidly growing economies of China and Brazil to stay competitive.

No matter which side of the purchaser-supplier spectrum they are on and how big or small their company may be, today's purchasers and suppliers have a lot to consider in our increasingly global marketplace.

GLOBALIZATION AND MARKET ENTRY STRATEGIES

The trend of business taking place across national boundaries, or ***globalization***, is increasingly important for organizations as they buy more goods and services from overseas suppliers. The following four factors are the primary reasons an organization considers doing business across national boundaries:

- **market:** Lifestyles and tastes are converging across the world. Customers today are less concerned with where a product is made. They are instead concerned with the nature of the product itself, its quality, and its price.

- **cost:** As organizations have grown and buy products from suppliers in larger quantities, they now look to the global market for those that can give the best volume discounts. Because some overseas suppliers can offer reduced prices low enough and volumes discounts large enough to offset higher shipping costs, organizations are now looking to overseas suppliers to reduce operational and production costs.

- **government:** Over the past 30 years, many governments have removed non-tariff trade barriers and set up trade agreement to facilitate commerce between countries. (We will explore some of these later in the chapter.)

- **competitive factors:** When companies look across borders for their purchasing needs, their number of potential suppliers for each product increases dramatically. As a result of this dramatically increased global competition, suppliers must make themselves stand out by reducing their prices, improving their product line, or increasing their service.

When a company decides to sell its goods in a new foreign market, it selects a ***market entry strategy***, the mode of ownership and operations in this new market. A company's market entry strategy may vary according to the politics, culture, market size, location, geography, and transportation infrastructure of that country. As the company continues to operate in the market, it develops its ***market operating strategy***, a modified mode of ownership and operations in this market. A company may use the same market entry and operating strategies or, after entering the market with one strategy, it may find than a different strategy is more beneficial to continue operation in that market. A few examples of market entry and operating strategies used by companies include:

- ***Indirect exporting***. This strategy occurs when a company uses an independent intermediary to export its product. A representative of the company may actually never even set foot in the target country! Compared to the next four strategies, this market entry strategy requires the least cost and risk for the company, but also typically produces the lowest levels of profit overall. Companies use this strategy to "test the waters" to see how whether or not they want to locate more assets and operations in that country.

- ***Direct exporting***. When a company decides to export its products on its own to the desired foreign market, it engages in the somewhat riskier and potentially more profitable market entry strategy of direct exporting. When engaging in direct exporting, a company may use: a domestic- based export division, an overseas sales branch or subsidiary, traveling export sales representatives, or foreign-based distributors or agents. Companies with large, expensive products often use direct exporting for smaller and newer markets. In these situations, a company might find it too expensive to set up extensive production or distribution operations but would benefit from having highly knowledgeable sales reps to market and represent the company's products in these markets.

- ***Joint venture***. A joint venture occurs when two or more otherwise independent companies join together to form a new company, sharing knowledge, cost, risk, and profits. Joint ventures with local partners often ease a company's entry into foreign markets, providing political advantage and access to local market knowledge. Partnering with a local enterprise for a joint venture helps the entering company defray cost, minimize risk, and get immediate knowledge of the local market.

- ***Wholly owned subsidiary***. If a company sets up an operation in a foreign country and owns 100% of the stock, it is a wholly owned subsidiary. The company may set up a new operation or it may purchase an existing operation to produce and/or promote its product. With wholly owned subsidiaries, companies have complete control over strategy, marketing, and manufacturing. Although the wholly owned subsidiary strategy presents a company with the highest cost and greatest risk of all market entry and operating strategies, it also provides the potential to reap the greatest profits.

It is important for purchasing professionals to understand these market entry and operating strategies for two reasons. First, purchasing professionals who are procuring goods from overseas suppliers may not necessarily have to deal with the suppliers' overseas offices. Instead, the overseas supplier may have entered the purchasing company's domestic market using one of the market entry strategies above. For example, Comforting Confections and Candies, a U.S. candy retail chain, may purchase its German chocolates from a German company that has set up a direct exporting office in Fargo, North Dakota.

Second, the purchasing professional's organization may already be selling its goods overseas in a variety of markets using some or all of the market entry strategies above. In this case, if the purchasing department is looking to procure goods from a particular unfamiliar foreign market, such as outer Mongolia, the purchasing department can piggyback on the marketing department's recent efforts to enter the Mongolian market. The marketing department can share valuable market information with its purchasing department about the country's business conditions, business norms, and its political, legal, economic, social, and cultural environment.

PURCHASING AND GLOBAL SOURCING

The impact of globalization on purchasing has resulted in organizations not simply purchasing goods from overseas suppliers but instead coordinating and integrating global operations between purchasers and suppliers. In many business and academic forums, this has led to the distinction between the terms *international purchasing* and *global purchasing* (or *global sourcing*). **International purchasing** suggests that firms are buying goods from foreign suppliers. Typically, there is a lack of coordination of requirements between business units both within and across companies. As an example, let's say that Brown's Bouncing Balls, Inc. has production plants in both Germany and the U.S. Both of the production plants purchase goods needed for the manufacturing process from Australia. If each plant purchases these goods independently from Australia, each can be classed as using *international purchasing*.

Global purchasing, however, is the integration and coordination of procurement requirements across the worldwide business units of companies, looking at common products, processes, technologies, and suppliers. It is clearly strategic in nature and must be implemented as part of the corporate plan. To exemplify, let's now say that Brown's Bouncing Balls, Inc. decides to coordinate all of its purchasing worldwide for all of its production plants through an International Purchasing Office (IPO) centralized in the U.S. In this case, Brown's is now using global purchasing.

Global purchasing, also called **global sourcing**, involves the integration and coordination in: 1) *the internationalization of purchasing activities* and 2) t*he adoption of a strategic orientation for all inbound production inputs*. Thus, the goal of global purchasing is to leverage the power of purchasing on a worldwide level. Global purchasing and the competition it brings are indeed powerful because, as mentioned earlier, they offer lower costs through economies of scale, strategic cooperation between partners to improve quality standards, and improved strategic relationships across global supply chains.

Although it may take considerable integration and coordination between an organization's many production facilities worldwide, global sourcing offers many advantages. A few reasons why organizations source globally include:

- *Cost benefits.* Purchasing from an overseas supplier rather than a domestic one can give the purchaser considerable cost benefits, including low cost skilled labor and raw materials. This allows an organization to reduce its selling price or increase revenues by achieving a higher profit margin. In the case of Luxury Lamps, their suppliers decided to reduce their price by 40%.

- *Best/only option.* Sometimes the global supplier is the only source available or it is the world leader in new technology development.

- *Higher quality.* When we think of quality, we often think of countries such as Japan and Germany. Japan, through the influence of W. Edwards Deming, introduced quality never before seen in the motor industry. Through activities such as production quality control techniques and quality circles, the Japanese motor industry today signifies quality. Procuring quality inputs for the production line is an important element in the quality of a company's finished product.

- *Counter trade agreements.* Organizations exporting to developing nations often agree to accept goods rather than money for their products. Purchasing professionals are responsible for dealing with this counter trade. For example, the Boeing (aircraft) Company has a policy of purchasing inputs from countries where they intend to do business.

- *Improved domestic market environment.* Purchasing a portion of its inputs from an overseas supplier will help an organization stimulate competition among its suppliers at home. This is especially true when the domestic supply market is an oligopoly. Local suppliers often use practices that are less efficient and effective from a purchaser's viewpoint, simply because of the lack of competition. When competition from foreign suppliers has been introduced into the local U.S. market, domestic suppliers have traditionally found it in their best interests to change in order to match their global competitors' offerings.

Despite its many advantages, the disadvantages that accompany global sourcing include: the amount of import documentation needed, cultural differences, political differences, legal differences, different business practices, different attitudes towards foreign trade by governments, lack of knowledge of the local language, financial risks, longer supply chains with increased risk of late deliveries, port shutdowns, and different understandings of quality.

FROM DOMESTIC TO GLOBAL PURCHASING

As a company moves from domestic buying only to developing an integrated global procurement strategy, it typically passes through the following five stages:

- **Stage 1:** A company assigns purchasers within one of its locations or business units to engage in limited, as-needed international purchasing.

- **Stage 2:** When purchasers within a given business unit must increase their international purchasing, they turn to their company's subsidiaries or other business units, such as the marketing department as previously mentioned, for international sourcing assistance. At this stage, this information and expertise is invaluable because subsidiaries and other business units may be located closer to foreign suppliers or have a better understanding of foreign suppliers and their business practices.

- **Stage 3:** As the need for global goods increases, a company sets up international purchasing offices (IPOs) throughout the world. These offices offer a variety of invaluable services as a company moves from international purchasing to global sourcing. These services include: identifying foreign suppliers, expediting and tracing shipments, negotiating supply contracts, ensuring that the purchaser and seller understand all communications, obtaining product samples, managing technical samples, and acting as a sole representative of the firm to its suppliers in that country.

- **Stage 4:** At this stage, a company begins to think strategically at a global level as it assigns design, manufacture, and sourcing responsibility to a specific business unit somewhere in the world. This strategy recognizes that, within the firm, one unit or location may have a comparative advantage over another in technology, manufacturing, distribution, service, or cost. By exploiting such advantage, a company can begin to attain superior results. For example, the procurement strategy for Ford Motor Company involved centralizing the development of a car or component wherever Ford has the greatest worldwide experience.

- **Stage 5:** At this final stage, a company moves into integration and coordination of a worldwide global sourcing strategy. The main objective of this stage is to maximize the company's buying leverage on a global basis. Business units must be committed to using common worldwide sources of supply to achieve maximum procurement benefits. Companies at stages 4 and 5 will experience maximum benefits in terms of cost and performance improvements, but they must be prepared to commit significant resources to benefit from their increased levels of global sourcing.

Perhaps one of the best examples of a company at stage 5 is Xerox. The worldwide photocopy and printer manufacturer introduced centralized commodity management, which involved identifying geographical areas of excellence where groups of products would be competitively priced while remaining at world-class quality levels. Each commodity manager was made responsible for the coordination of the company's material requirements purchased for manufacturing operations regardless of supplier location.

Global sourcing is becoming a prerequisite for competing in today's global marketplace. Lower costs are no longer the only benefit of global sourcing. Many firms are finding that the payoff increasingly comes from improved availability, uniqueness, and quality. Global sourcing offers the potential for a lasting advantage in market supremacy, penetration of growth markets, and high-speed responsiveness. A firm must continuously develop its organizational structure, information systems, and global sourcing expertise to facilitate global performance just as Xerox has done.

Companies in stages 3, 4, and 5 in developing a global purchasing strategy have some degree of operations in the country of their supplier. Although global purchasing can seem a daunting task for the inexperienced purchasing professional, help is often near at hand. As we discussed earlier, many organizations in the U.S. already have a finished goods presence in the global world through their marketing departments. A company's purchasing department can often piggyback on the global experiences of its marketing department.

SELECTING GLOBAL SUPPLIERS

THE ROLE OF THE PURCHASER

In the practice of global purchasing, purchasers must be able to: locate an overseas source in a given country for materials available in that country; display an awareness of the special circumstances to be taken into account when dealing with a foreign source; apply recognized supplier rating methods; and understand the preliminary stages and documentation of an import transaction, all of which we will explain later in this chapter.

In a specific global purchasing situation, the purchaser of overseas goods should have some knowledge of: the supplier's country; the language and basic culture of the supplier for effective communication; the unit of currency and its rate of exchange; contractual obligations, legal liabilities, and financial workings related to the supplier's country; and the specifications, quality, and standards of the product within the country in question. Effective global purchasers need more than education and experience in procurement practices. They also need a deep understanding of the business environment and culture of the country of their supplier.

SELECTING THE SUPPLIER

When purchasers are seeking overseas suppliers, they first establish a list of potential sources based on information from local government agencies, trade associations, and the Internet. Purchasers next issue an enquiry that clearly and unambiguously states what goods or services are required, such as an **RFI** *(request for information)*, an **RFP** *(request for proposal)*, or an **RFQ** *(request for quotation)*. This enquiry is sent to potential suppliers as an invitation to submit a bid for a contract to provide the needed goods or services. Although this is the same process used when procuring goods from domestic suppliers, there are frequently major differences in the way purchasers state requirements to foreign companies.

Some of the following additional considerations must be stated in the initial enquiry when seeking foreign suppliers:

- *Which currency will be used in the transaction, such as the purchaser's currency or the supplier's currency? Most foreign companies prefer payment in their local currency or U.S. dollars. Because of drastically fluctuating exchange rates, some suppliers will deal in a different currency if a fixed rate of exchange is offered for the life of the contract.*

- *What method of transportation will be used to deliver goods, such as rail, road, sea, air, or intermodal?*

- *What are the terms of trading, such as Ex Works or Delivery Duty Paid?*

- *Is the delivery address different from the ordering and billing address?*

- *What is the unit of measure for the order, such as pounds or kilograms?*

- *Is all correspondence translated clearly and unambiguously into the languages of both the purchaser and supplier? Specific technical and commercial terms can be especially confusing and problematic in translation. Even drawings for technical specifications may have different interpretations in different languages.*

When selecting foreign suppliers, purchasers must also consider the location and accessibility of the supplier, which will impact the cost of travel to foreign countries to negotiate with suppliers. Depending on the product, its importance, and the size of the order, several visits may be required before placing an order with the potential supplier. Further consideration must be made of the cost of communication, especially long distance phone calls, between both parties.

The opinions of others can also be useful in selecting foreign suppliers. If a proposed supplier is already providing goods or services to a friend of the purchaser or even to another section of the purchaser's company, much valuable information can be gained about the proposed supplier with just a quick phone call. Also, a summary of the supplier's performance can be obtained by the purchaser's contact that recommended the supplier in the first place.

Most major companies also operate some form of **vendor rating** scheme, wherein they assess suppliers' capabilities in providing **the five Rs**: the right quantity, the right quality, at the right place, at the right time, and at the right price. Both federal and state government offices also typically have vendor rating schemes. Vendor ratings could include assessment of suppliers' capability, capacity, systems and procedures, quality standards, financial stability, and management structure.

OTHER PLAYERS IN THE GLOBAL PURCHASER-SUPPLIER RELATIONSHIP

In establishing an initial relationship with a foreign supplier, a purchaser must understand the roles of other parties that may influence the global purchaser-supplier relationship, including: *trading companies, buying agencies, import brokers, freight forwarders, representatives,* and *distributors*.

Trading companies trade on behalf of others on an import/export basis, often buying and selling commodities and finished goods to domestic and international customers. They act on behalf of smaller companies whose budgets do not allow them to engage in vast amounts of overseas trading and whose operations are too small to achieve economies of scale by themselves.

Buying agencies serve importers that either have very little knowledge of overseas markets or do not have the financial resources to visit abroad to search for overseas suppliers. A buying agency specializes in obtaining suppliers for particular clients. It also takes care of all import transactions on behalf of the importer, acting as an intermediary between purchaser and seller, taking responsibility for buying the goods from overseas and passing them on to the purchaser, and charging a fixed fee or percentage commission for work accomplished.

An ***import broker*** acts as a representative for the purchaser in clearing all imported goods through Customs on the purchaser's behalf. It also deals with all associated documentation needed to import goods into the country.

A ***freight forwarder*** acts as an agent for exporters and importers alike, arranging for export shipments of goods to their destinations and clearing imported goods through Customs. A freight forwarder also arranges for handling goods in both ports and airports, often storing the goods prior to shipment or dispatch to the customer. In addition, freight forwarders consolidate goods, grouping smaller quantities of goods together for a larger shipment. In the case of imported consolidations, the freight forwarder breaks down goods into their respective consignments, conducts all Customs clearance procedures, and makes the goods ready for dispatch to the importer. A freight forwarder is also known as an **NVOCC**, or **non-vessel operating common carrier**, because the forwarder does not own a ship or aircraft but will conduct all other activities for the consolidation and shipment of goods.

Representatives and distributors are appointed by exporters and importers to take care of running their operations elsewhere, particularly when the exporter or importer does not have a presence in a given country or geographic location. A ***representative*** acts on behalf of the importer or exporter on a contractual basis, agreeing to represent the company in the sale or purchase of goods. The ***distributor*** is a type of representative that distributes importer's goods to its customers in that country or geographic region. A distributor also has the ability to generate business for the company he represents and charges commission on all sales made, usually as a result of gaining the goods from the supplier at a discounted price and then adding a mark-up percentage to the end user's price.

GLOBAL BUSINESS CONSIDERATIONS

When companies engage in global sourcing, there are a variety of factors that must be considered that aren't encountered when purchasing domestically. First, the political, economic, and social environment of the supplier's country can influence business operations such as purchasing. Next, international trade agreements must be considered when dealing with foreign suppliers. Finally, a variety of business factors, such as currency management, must be considered for companies engage in global trade.

COUNTRY CONSIDERATIONS

When a company's supplier is in another country, it faces many new challenges, including country-to-country differences in: culture and language; politics, economics, and currencies; business practices and norms (bribery may be the norm!); time zones and attitudes toward time; required documentation and contracts; and security and types of legal recourse when infractions occur. Even between two countries that have relatively similar cultures and who speak the same language, words, demeanor, tone of voice, and body language can send confusing and conflicting messages. For example, English-speaking logistics managers in both the United States and England sometimes use very different words to describe the same thing, as in the case of "18-wheeled tractor-trailer" (US) versus "articulated lorry" (UK).

Before working with a foreign supplier, it is important to learn as much as you can about the country in which its operations are located. It is then important to consider the ways in which its location might impact the purchaser-supplier relationship based on the following supplier country factors: *political/legal*; *economic*; and *social/cultural*.

Examples of ***political/legal factors*** that might influence purchasing relationships include a country's:

- **Political climate.** When a country is in political turmoil, this wreaks obvious havoc on supply chains. After the dissolution of the Soviet Union in 1991, for example, many Russian-foreign joint ventures quickly formed and folded because of the difficulty of getting goods to customers largely because the foreign partners did not understand the nature and location of political power within Russia at the time.

- **Attitude toward foreign trade.** Countries with more positive attitudes toward foreign trade are generally much easier on global purchasers because these countries have considerable economic support, often from the IMF (International Monetary Fund) and other economic communities. Countries with less positive attitudes don't have this economic support and often impose restrictions on foreign companies, including license requirements, tariffs, taxes, quotas, complicated customs procedures, and discriminatory government and private procurement policies, all of which make business relationships within these countries far more expensive and challenging to operate.

- **Government stability.** The stability and reliability of a country's election process and the consistency and predictability of its policies and practices (e.g., regarding taxes, profits, and ownership rights) can also influence international business relationships. For example, in a 1996 study of the domestic and international operations of Hungarian businesses published in the *International Journal of Physical Distribution and Logistics Management*, Atilla Chikan found that Hungary's embargo against Yugoslavia cost the nation $50 million (US) in distribution channel and supply chain management costs.

- **Legal system.** A country's legal factors that can influence global purchasing include: legal understanding and accountability, protection of patents and trademarks, freedom in market competition, recourse for dispute adjudication, and adherence to international laws. One of the most commonly cited legal factors affecting international business in many emerging and less-developed economies around the world is corruption and the lack of legal recourse of companies to counteract it.

Examples of ***economic factors*** that might influence global purchasing relationships include a country's:

- **Economic orientation.** Often, the degree to which a country embraces a capitalist economic orientation has a significant influence on business relationships with companies in that country. People in many of the world's developing, transitioning, and less-developed economies are more worried about product availability and less accustomed to streamlined global business practices, such as Just-In-Time. As a result, companies in these countries sometimes use hoarding as a means of assuring their supply, resulting in production delays in other companies due to material shortages (i.e., the materials the original company hoarded), which can then mean longer lead times and late deliveries.

- **Geography.** A country's physical barriers and geographic distances can also influence a global purchaser-supplier relationship. For example, getting goods from suppliers in landlocked countries without large seaports may be far costlier than getting them from supplier located near ocean ports.

- **Infrastructure.** A country's energy, communications, and transportation systems form its infrastructure, the backbone that allows businesses and individuals to operate as quickly, conveniently, and easily as they do. Global purchaser-supplier relationships are largely at the mercy of the infrastructures of the countries in which they operate. Countries that have poor or outdated telecommunications networks, road systems in disrepair, and frequent power outages all experience significant delays and increased costs.

Finally, examples of *social/cultural factors* that might influence global purchasing relationships include a country's:

- **Language differences.** Language difference is one of the most obvious external influences on international business. For example, there are three different languages spoken within the North American Free Trade Agreement's (NAFTA's) three countries. These language differences along with NAFTA's labeling requirements have posed many challenges to the purchasing relationships of North American companies, from effective communication to ensuring that all product labeling is correct in all three languages and NAFTA-compliant.

- **Values and customs.** Differences between the values and customs of purchasers' and suppliers' home countries often pose complex problems for effective purchasing relationships. Even something as simple as a business card can confound purchasing managers when working abroad. For example, an American purchasing manager, who typically travels with approximately 20 business cards in his/her wallet, may unknowingly insult Chinese suppliers when accepting their business cards in the normal American fashion (grasping the center or center edge of the business card between the thumb and edge of the forefinger) instead of the customary Chinese fashion (grasping each of the two bottom corners of the business card using the tips of the thumb and forefinger).

INTERNATIONAL TRADE AGREEMENTS

The formal and informal relationship between a purchaser and supplier's countries can have a significant impact on the purchasing relationship between these companies. Formal relationships between these counties are often spelled out in terms of international agreements. In order to promote and protect international commercial trade, countries set up trade agreements with other countries around the world. A *trade agreement* is a contractual agreement concerning the trade relationship between nations. Trade agreements may be *bilateral*, i.e., between two nations, or *multilateral*, i.e., between more than two nations.

Bilateral and multilateral trade agreements often establish areas of trade covered under the agreement. A *free trade area (FTA)* is a set group of countries that have agreed to eliminate or minimize tariffs (such as customs duties), product quotas, and other restriction for goods traveling across the FTA countries' borders. NAFTA and the European Union are examples of FTAs. A

trade bloc is a large free trade area that is formed by formal trade, tariff, and tax agreements between its countries. Again, NAFTA and the EU are examples of trade blocs.

A ***regional trade agreement (RTA)*** is a term used by the World Trade Organization (WTO) when two or more of its members enter into a regional trade arrangement presenting more favorable trade conditions (such as minimization or elimination of tariffs, quotas, and other restrictions) to each other than to other WTO members. The sea of politics and economics gets a bit murky here because the terms *free trade area*, *trade bloc*, and *regional trade agreement* often mean the same thing or apply to the same relationships. It all really depends on the agreement and whom you ask!

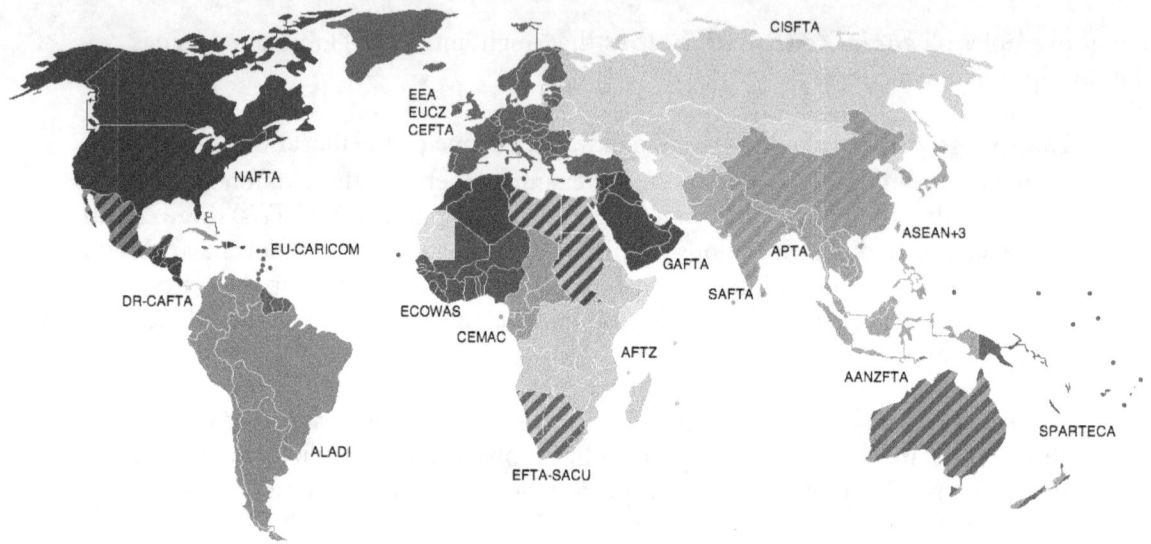

Figure 10.2 - Regional Trade Agreements Around the World

According to its website, www.wto.itn, the ***World Trade Organization (WTO)*** is: "the only international organization dealing with the global rules of trade between nations. Its main function is to ensure that trade flows as smoothly, predictably and freely as possible." At the time of this book's publication, the WTO reported more than 379 RTAs officially operating around the world and more than 200 planned or under negotiation. Some of the more widely known RTAs include:

- ***the European Union (EU)***, whose member states include Austria, Belgium, Bulgaria, Cyprus, the Czech Republic, Denmark, Estonia, Finland, France, Germany, Greece, Hungary, Ireland, Italy, Latvia, Lithuania, Luxembourg, Malta, Poland, Portugal, Romania, Slovakia, Slovenia, Spain, Sweden, The Netherlands, and the United Kingdom;

- ***the North American Free Trade Agreement (NAFTA)***, whose members include Canada, Mexico, and the United States;

- ***the Southern Common Market (MERCOSUR)***, whose members include Argentina, Brazil, Paraguay, and Uruguay;

- ***the Association of Southeast Asian Nations (ASEAN)***, whose members include Brunei, Darussalam, Cambodia, Indonesia, Laos, Malaysia, Myanmar, the Philippines, Singapore, Thailand, and Vietnam; and

- ***the Common Market of Eastern and Southern Africa (COMESA)***, whose members include Angola, Burundi, Comoros, the Democratic Republic of Congo, Djibouti, Egypt, Eritrea, Ethiopia, Kenya, Madagascar, Malawi, Mauritius, Namibia, Rwanda, Seychelles, Sudan, Swaziland, Uganda, Zambia, and Zimbabwe.

The ***North American Free Trade Agreement (NAFTA)*** between the United States, Canada, and Mexico, which came into effect on January 1, 1994, has definite implications for global purchasing. NAFTA's goal is to remove trade barriers, allowing companies to easily conduct cross-border business. It is phasing out trade tariffs between its members, allowing for less costly purchaser-supplier relationships among its members.

Another international trade factor with implications for purchasing in the U.S. are the growth of maquiladoras in Mexico and, more recently, other parts of Latin America. A ***maquiladora*** is a foreign factory in Mexico that imports materials and equipment (duty-free and tariff-free), assembles or manufactures goods, and then exports them, typically back to the company's home country. Most Mexican maquiladora factories are owned by U.S companies representing a wide variety of industries, including transportation, electronics, textiles, and machinery. Maquiladoras may be 100% foreign-owned, but they may also be a joint venture between both foreign and local companies.

Finally, in addition to the RTA and the maquiladoras is the ***free trade zone (FTZ)***, also called an ***export processing zone (EPZ)***. A free trade zone is an area within a country in which tariffs, quotas, and bureaucratic requirements have been eliminated or minimized in order to attract foreign companies by providing incentives for doing business there. While the concept of free trade zones began in Latin America in the first half of the twentieth century, there are now more than 3000 FTZs in more than 100 countries worldwide. Examples of FTZs are areas within Waigaoqiao FTZ in Shanghai, China and the Colón FTZ in Panama at the Atlantic gateway to the Panama Canal. Such free trade zones allow for easier and less costly global purchasing relationships.

BUSINESS FACTORS AFFECTING INTERNATIONAL TRADE

In addition to country-specific environmental factors of the supplier's country and international trade agreements, there are many additional factors that have a significant impact on international trade and global purchasing. A few of these factors include *currency management*, *duties*, *exemptions*, and *non-tariff barriers*.

There are currently 180 official currencies operating in the world market, all of which fluctuate in value relative to one another on a minute-by-minute basis. When the purchasers and suppliers involved in global purchasing come from countries with different currencies, they place themselves at financial risk because the price they are paying or receiving for goods can go up or down, depending on currency fluctuations. Therefore, one major factor for consideration in global purchasing is ***currency management***, or making sure that the foreign supplier is protected against currency fluctuations. One common method of currency management is called ***hedging***, in which a company minimizes its risk from participation in the world market by simultaneously buying and selling currency contracts in two markets so any losses in one market will balance out with gains in another.

Another factor for consideration in global purchasing are ***import duties***, which are financial charges imposed by a country on foreign businesses wishing to do business in or with that country. Although they can sometimes be a deterrent to international business, import duties are often a needed source of revenue for a country's national economy. Countries can also pose ***exemptions*** regarding the imposition of duties on imported goods. For example, a country might decide that an importer doesn't have to pay import duties when importing medical supplies, instruments to be used for scientific research, or goods for industrial research.

In addition to the financial considerations of currency management and import duties, there are also ***non-tariff barriers*** that must be considered in global purchaser-supplier relationships. Although they do no experience immediate financial gain from them, countries impose non-tariff barriers on foreign businesses for a variety of political and economic reasons. Examples of non-tariff barriers include *quotas*, *boycotts*, *embargoes*, and *sanctions*.

To control imports of some commodities, governments may establish ***quotas*** instead of tariffs. With a quota imposed, a seller is allowed to import a limited number of a specified type of good within a specific timeframe. For example, the U.S. government maintains quotas on the import of sugar from the Philippines, Dominican Republic, and other sugar-producing nations. In Europe, the Multi- Fibre Agreement (MFA) poses a quota on the import of textile fabrics from India, Bangladesh, and the Far East. Once the quota is exhausted (often just three or four days into the new year), import duty must be paid at a full rate on all future imports.

A ***trade boycott*** is organized by a government to eliminate the import of either a specific commodity or all imports from a specific country. An ***embargo*** is a government-posed restriction from conducting business transactions with businesses within a specific country. An embargo may be enforced either on a specific category of goods, such as strategic materials, or on the total range of goods that private businesses normally send to the country against which the embargo has been imposed.

A ***sanction*** is a measure of economic pressure that is used by one or more governments to express displeasure or dissatisfaction with the policies of another country, particularly in the case of human rights violations and oppressive political regimes. Examples of sanctions include the United States' sanctions against North Korea since the Korean War and the European Union's sanctions against Burma (now Myanmar) for human rights violations and democracy infringements. The nature of sanctions usually includes freezing the target country's financial assets held abroad and banning all trade with that country.

A Look at International Documentation

As global purchasing has grown to span across more countries around the world, the amount of corresponding paperwork required has also grown. In the world of international trade, such documentation is a necessity. Without accurate and timely paperwork, companies would not be permitted to trade outside their own countries. Exporters, importers, shipping companies, freight forwarders, banks, insurance companies, the regulating authorities of the countries both importing and exporting the goods, consular offices, chambers of commerce, and a massive battery of attorneys are all involved in ensuring that global purchasing's complex network of documentation is completed.

While there are thousands of different trade documentation forms that vary from country to country and from company to company, there are six primary categories of trade documentation. The amount of documentation required may vary according to the nature of the goods and the regulations of the countries importing and exporting the goods. In addition, some forms of documentation are multi-functional and can be found in multiple categories of trade documentation.

The six categories of ***international trade documentation*** are:

1. ***Transaction documents***. Also found in domestic trade, transaction documents are those documents exchanged between a purchaser and a seller as part of the agreement to sell and/or purchase goods. Unlike domestic trade, in global purchasing situations, both parties must be very careful about providing these documents in the languages of both the purchaser and supplier. Examples of transaction documents include: RFPs (request for proposal), proposals, purchase orders, sales contracts, and commercial invoices.

2. ***Export documents***. Documents required by the export authority of a country are called export documents. When completed and approved, these documents allow goods to leave a country. Export documentation varies according to the country of export and the goods involved. Examples of export documents include: export licenses and permits; export declaration and inspection certificates; Bill of Lading; and Certificate of Origin. A ***bill of lading (also referred to as BOL or B/L)*** is a document issued by a carrier, which acknowledges that specific, listed goods have been received as cargo for conveyance to a specific, listed place for delivery to an identified consignee. A ***certificate of origin*** is a document that certifies the country of origin of a shipment. For example, a NAFTA certificate of origin is used by Canada, Mexico, and the United States to determine if imported goods receive reduced or eliminated duty as specified by the North American Free Trade Agreement.

3. ***Carrier documents***. Carrier documents are those documents issued and used by a carrier or transportation provider such as a barge or shipping line, a railroad, an airline, an international trucking company, a freight forwarder, or a 3PLP. Examples of carrier documents include: bill of lading and insurance and inspection certificates.

4. ***Import documents***. Those documents required by the import authorities of a country are called import documents. When completed and approved, these documents allow goods to enter a country. Import documentation varies according to the country of import and the goods involved. Examples of import documents include: import licenses and permits, commercial invoices, bill of lading, certificate of origin, import declaration, and inspection certificates.

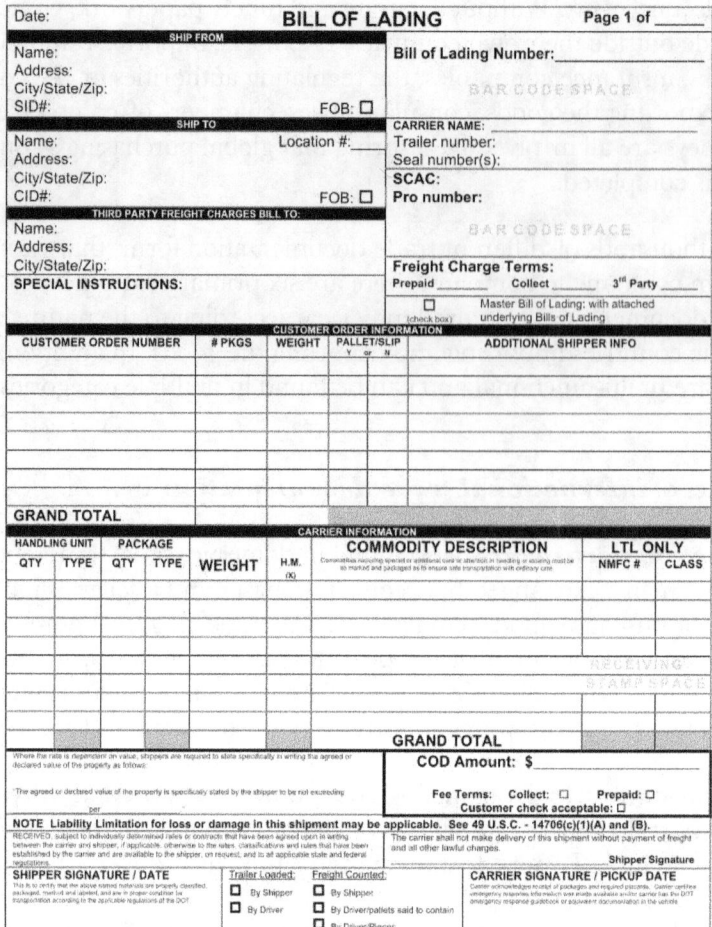

Figure 10.3 - Example of a Bill of Lading Form

5. ***Banking documents.*** Banking documents are those documents required by the banks participating in international transactions. The types and degree of banking documentation required is influenced by the regulations and banking practices of the importing and exporting countries involved. Examples of banking documents include all documents associated with company credit issues. Of particular interest to global purchasers are letters of credit. A ***confirmed irrevocable letter of credit*** is used when an importer and exporter who don't know each other very well enter into a direct transaction without a third-party broker. The letter is issued by the importer's bank, is addressed to the exporter, and states that the importer indeed has credit with the bank. It is an important part of global purchasing because it serves as a satisfactory way of ensuring payment before the exporter surrenders the control of goods.

6. ***Goods-specific documents***. Finally, goods-specific documents are those documents required for import and/or export based on special requirements for the nature of the items being trades. Goods-specific documents are typically required for international

trade of goods including: arms and ammunition, radioactive materials, animals, and food products.

In exploring the world of international trade documentation, we must also discuss ***INCOTERMS (International Commercial Terms)***, the standardized international trade terms that describe the obligations of both the purchasers and the sellers under the contract of sale. Specifically, INCOTERMS are a set of eleven terms created and published by the International Chamber of Commerce (ICC) that clearly outline and allocate the costs, risk, customs, and insurance responsibilities of each the purchaser and the seller in the international transaction. The most recent update to these terms was in 2010.

Each of the eleven INCOTERMS is referred to by a three-letter abbreviation. The complete list of all eleven terms, with a brief explanation of each, is:

- **EXW or Ex Works**. The exporter must make the goods available for collection from his premises by the importer or the importer's agent. The goods are generally packed ready for shipment.

- **FCA or FREE CARRIER**. The exporter will transport the goods to an Inland Clearance Depot (ICD), where they will be consolidated into a larger consignment ready for shipment by an intermodal carrier.

- **FAS or FREE ALONGSIDE SHIP** (waterway transport only). The exporter delivers the goods alongside the ship that will carry the goods overseas. This is where the responsibility of the exporter ends. The purchaser bears all costs and risks from this point on.

- **FOB or FREE ON BOARD** (waterway transport only). The goods are delivered by the exporter to the port of export, where they then become the responsibility of the importer as soon as they are loaded over the ship' side rail. The purchaser bears the loss if the goods should fall and become damaged just after being loaded onto the ship.

- **CFR or COST AND FREIGHT** (waterway transport only). The seller must pay the costs and freight as far as the port of destination, but the risk passes to the purchaser as the goods cross the ship's rail in the port of shipment.

- **CIF or COST, INSURANCE AND FREIGHT** (waterway transport only). The seller is in the same position as in CFR but must also provide marine insurance during the carriage. The risk passes to the purchaser as the goods cross the ship's rails, but the insurance policy covers the purchaser's risk.

- **CPT or CARRIAGE PAID TO**. The seller pays the freight and the risk passes to the purchaser once the goods are delivered to the first carrier, regardless of the type of transportation used.

- **CIP or CARRIAGE AND INSURANCE PAID TO**. The terms are the same as in CPT, but the seller also has to insure the goods for all modes of transportation to the purchaser's destination. The risk transfers to the purchaser when the goods are given into the custody of the first carrier, after which point the risk is covered by the insurance policy.

- **DAT or DELIVERED AT TERMINAL.** The seller pays for delivery to the terminal, not including import clearance costs, and also assumes all risk until the goods are unloaded at the terminal.

- **DAP or DELIVERED AT PLACE.** The seller pays for delivery to the named place or destination, not including import clearance costs, and also assumes all risk until the goods are ready to be unloaded by the buyer.

- **DDP or DELIVERED DUTY PAID.** This represents a maximum commitment from the seller and a minimum one from the purchaser. The seller delivers to the purchaser after paying the import duty to the country of destination.

As the world moves towards more and more integration, the ability of purchasing professionals to secure their production's inputs on a global stage will play an important role in their organization's future success. Skills and knowledge that were sufficient for purchasing in a domestic market will not be enough for operating in this global world. New skills and new knowledge, such as the topics covered in this chapter, will provide a good foundation but just as important will be the purchasing professional's attitude and ability to be flexible when sourcing in this wide, global world.

CHAPTER 10 REVIEW QUESTIONS

1. Look around your kitchen. Which items of food in your kitchen came from abroad? Now look in your clothes closet. What percentage of your clothes came from abroad? Which countries were represented the most? Did you have a larger percentage of imported items in your kitchen or closet? Why might this be?

2. Pretend that you are the CEO of a famous American bubble gum company. You are thinking of entering the global market as a bubble gum manufacturer. Describe some things you should consider before entering the global market.

3. What is *global sourcing*? List three companies that you know of that use a global sourcing strategy. What benefits do these companies likely reap from this strategy?

4. What role does *currency* play as a consideration when selecting foreign suppliers?

5. What is a *freight forwarder* and who might use one? As the CEO of a bubble gum company, how might you use a freight forwarder to your advantage for global operations?

6. If a Mongolian company wanted to do business with suppliers in the United States, what specifically American country considerations might they have to think about?

7. What is *NAFTA*? What impact might it have on an organization's purchasing decisions?

8. What are four *non-tariff barriers*? Do a bit of searching online and provide current examples for each of the four barriers.

9. What is the difference between a *bill of lading* and a *certificate of origin*?

10. What are *CPT* and *CIP*? What is the difference between the two? If the cost to the purchaser is the same for both, which would be more advantageous for the purchaser? Why?

Chapter 10 Case Exercises

Global Purchasing at Luxury Lamps Ltd.

Luxury Lamps Ltd. has been very successful over the years. They have offered their customers high quality lamps at a competitive price. The competition within the luxury lamp industry has always been tight. In all, there are five competitors that have consistently competed for the major share of the high value market. The pricing structures and retail prices of all have been very similar in the past. Each company had relied on original design to appeal to customers so that their lamps would be selected over those of their competitors. Because each company had similar pricing structures and retail prices in the past, design had always been the deciding factor. This has worked well for Luxury Lamps Ltd. over the past few years and all the organizations have managed to maintain good sales and profit margins. However, two of the competitors have recently introduced a new design of equal quality lamps at a retail price that is 40% less than the Luxury Lamps standard price.

On examination of their competitors, Luxury Lamps has found that competing luxury lamp sellers are importing most of their production inputs from China at substantially lower costs. The lower costs from China have allowed Luxury Lamps' competitors a huge price advantage. Billie Bates is the Purchasing Manager for Luxury Lamps Ltd. and has been assigned the task of gathering information for the company's senior management team on the opportunities and challenges of doing business in China.

Billie, who has not previously purchased from an international supplier, needs to give some serious thought to the issues and challenges Luxury Lamps will face if importing items from China. For operations in China, Billie will need to consider the transportation system used to import the items such a distance and the country-to-country legal issues. She will need to consider the documentation required to accomplish this in a timely and efficient manner. Billie will also need to consider the culture and customs of her local suppliers while simultaneously keeping an eye on the fluctuating currency rate and its effect on supply costs.

Billie and Luxury Lamps Ltd. will certainly have a lot to consider as they explore purchasing and sourcing on a global stage!

Instructions:

Based on what you have learned from Chapter 10, discuss the issues that Billie will need to consider in her report. If you were a consultant, what advice would you give Billie based on the information in Chapter 10?

And now it's time for a SECOND case exercise!

INCOTERMS and the Dunbar Company

The Purchasing Officer for the Dunbar Company in North Dakota must purchase a part for the company's assembly process that is only available from Paris, France. The unit price of the item is $100,000. The transportation cost to the French port is 5% of the item's unit price, the French export customs duty is 5% of the item's unit price, and handling and loading onto the ship costs 10% of the item's unit price. When the item arrives into the U.S., the following costs apply: U.S. customs import duty is 5% of the unit price and the U.S. customs clearance cost is 20% of the unit price. In addition, the cost for unloading the item at the U.S. port is 10% of the unit price and delivery to Dunbar's North Dakota plant is 15% of the unit price.

INSTRUCTIONS:

Using the information above, please complete the following:

1. What would the total cost, including the unit price, be to the Dunbar company if the goods are purchased under the Ex Works INCOTERM from its foreign supplier?

2. What would the total cost, including the unit price, be to the Dunbar company if the goods are purchased under the DDP INCOTERM from its foreign supplier?

3. What would the total cost, including the unit price in Dollars, be to the the Dunbar Company if the goods are purchased under the FOB INCOTERM from its foreign supplier?

4. What would the total cost, excluding the unit price in Dollars, be to the French company if the goods are purchased under the FOB INCOTERM?

5. Under the terms of the Ex Works INCOTERM, the unit price, the costs of transport to the French port, the French export customs duty, and the handling and loading onto the ship at the French port must be paid for in Euro (Europe's currency). Working with any online currency converter, determine the total amount of Euro the Dunbar company will need to pay these costs.

Chapter 11

The People Side of Purchasing

Natalie J. Harrison, M.Ed.

When we picture the purchasing process, we typically imagine physical products, prices, deliveries, and information systems managing it all. We know we need to purchase a high definition, widescreen television, so we picture the television. If we think about it a bit longer, we may even picture the delivery and set-up of the television or even wonder about how it was made in the factory. What most of us do not picture are the tens, hundreds, or even thousands of ***people*** that are involved in this simple act of getting the television from a concept to the reality of a 54" machine hanging on our living room wall. Not only are there many people who participated in designing and manufacturing this television, but there also are many other people working for multiple companies involved in this process, including a wide range of buyers and sellers. Every television has multiple component parts, each of which is obtained for the manufacturer by a *procurement professional* making purchases from the sales agents of a variety of suppliers.

Sadly, we often forget about the many buyers and sellers, or *people*, engaged in the process. Like much of supply chain management, purchasing involves interpersonal relationships between the people engaged in the process. Each of these people have unique ways of communicating, taking in information, making decisions, and structuring their life and work. In this chapter, we will explore the interpersonal relationships within the wonderful world of purchasing and the knowledge and skills buyers and suppliers can leverage to enhance the procurement process, including an understanding of emotional intelligence, personality types, and communications techniques.

PURCHASING AND INTERPERSONAL RELATIONSHIPS

Throughout this book, the only people or roles we mention with any frequency are the purchasers and the suppliers. You might even think that the purchasing process involves just a single buyer purchasing something from a single supplier. Au contraire! The world of purchasing is filled with people. On a daily basis, purchasing professionals interact with many types of people. Throughout the purchasing process, they form a variety of relationships with others both internal and external to the company they represent. They engage in a variety of both *vertical* and *horizontal* relationships.

In the purchasing organization, **vertical relationships** are those that flow up and down a vertical chain of command, such as the relationship between you and your boss or you and your staff. **Horizontal relationships** are those between peers across and organization, such as the relationship between a purchasing manager and a manufacturing manager.

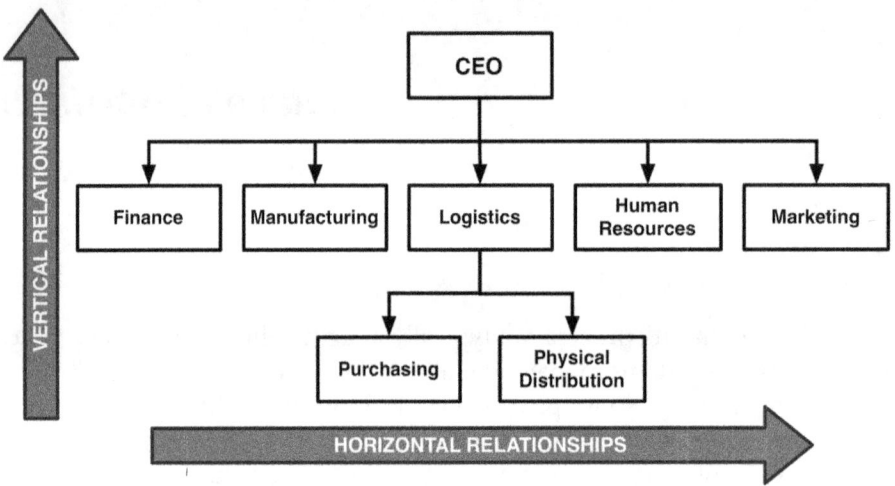

Figure 11.1 - Vertical and Horizontal Relationships in the Purchasing Organization

When we think of supply chains, we often think of a physical flow of goods, initiated by a user's need, purchased from the supplier by the user, and then moving seamlessly from materials' suppliers to factories, warehouses, distribution centers, and, eventually, to the retailer and end user. Often overlooked are the people involved in theses processes and the importance of their

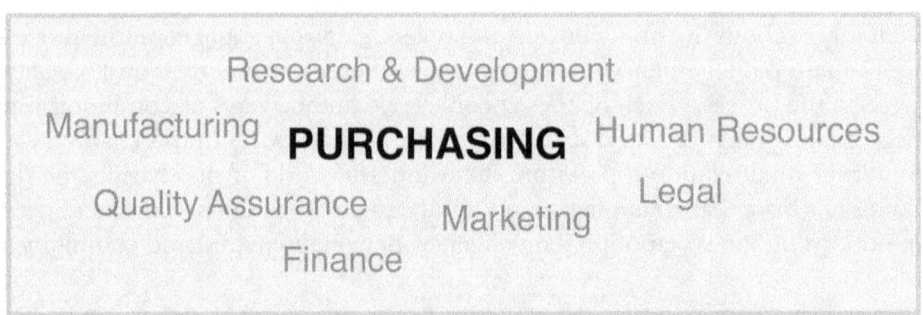

Figure 11.2 - The Purchasing Department's Horizontal Relationships

interpersonal relationships. People and their relationships are the essential solder of the purchasing processes links within the supply chain. As shown in Figure 11.2, there are many horizontal relationships across a variety of departments within an organization.

All of the relationships shown in Figures 11.1 and 11.2 above are relationships between members of the purchasing department and others within the same company. These are all examples of **internal relationships**. Purchasing professionals also have many relationships with people from other companies, such as the suppliers' sales agents. These relationships with others from other companies are called **external relationships**. The chart in Figure 11.3 below highlights the locations of people and their external relationships in a simple supply chain.

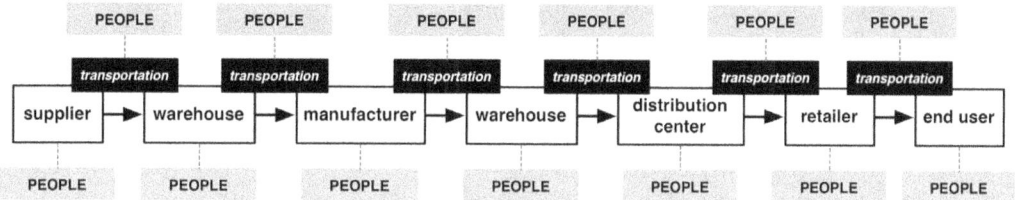

Figure 11.3 - People and External Relationships in the Simple Supply Chain

Purchasing professionals have to manage all of these internal and external interpersonal relationships for procurement success. **Interpersonal relationships** are social associations, connections, or affiliations between two or more people. They vary in different levels of intimacy and sharing, implying the discovery or establishment of common ground. Typically, they are centered around something shared or in common.

For interpersonal relationships within the purchasing world, those involved may work for the same company, have similar work methods and personalities, and be working toward identical goals. They often share much in common and often form easy, immediate, and successful interpersonal relationships. There are also interpersonal relationships within the purchasing world where the members of the relationship have far less in common, however, often with the need for the purchasing transaction being their only common bond. Most participants in supply chain and purchasing relationships will have a variety of differences, including the companies or departments for whom they work, their work methods and goals, or even their perception of the relationship and work to be done.

Successful relationships, in both purchasing and the world at large, often depend on our ability to understand others and build relationships. Before we begin to explore *how* to build improve purchasing relationships, let's consider *why* successful interpersonal relationships are important for purchasing success. When purchasing professionals have open, supportive, and long-term buyer-supplier relationships, they can reap a range of benefits, including:

- *valuable input from suppliers during product design stage,*
- *commitment from suppliers to manage and improve the quality of goods and services supplied, and*
- *commitment from suppliers to examine cost reduction.*

Suppliers also reap many benefits when they engage in effective buyer-supplier relationships, including:

- *long-term business and economic security,*
- *ethical and satisfying business relationships,*
- *prompt payments,*
- *opportunities for business expansion,*
- *an enhanced reputation, and*
- *an openness in sorting out misunderstandings before they escalate.*

Relationships through Emotional Intelligence

When you are a procurement professional, you understand your role as the buyer and your vendor's role as the supplier. Is that enough knowledge to master the human side of the Buyer-supplier interaction? Not by a long shot! In any human interaction, including those in the world of purchasing and supply management, in order to communicate effectively, you must understand yourself and the person with whom you are speaking. You need to develop a type of intelligence that helps you understand the spoken and unspoken messages of communication through understanding the context in which both you and your suppliers are operating, exploring why you say what you say and how you say it, and empathizing with your suppliers so they are encouraged to communicate more openly. The type of intelligence needed is known as *emotional intelligence*.

Throughout our first eighteen years or more, most of us are measured in terms of academic success and our IQ. How well we perform in elementary school determines our course placement in secondary school. How well we perform in our secondary school courses and on our college placement tests then impacts which colleges or universities will accept us as students. Finally, the reputation of the college we attend and our academic performance there have an enormous impact on which companies will hire us and how much they will pay us. Although this focus on academic performance and IQ has been the predominant model in the United States and other countries for many years, companies are now finding that a person's emotional intelligence (or *EQ*), not IQ, is a better predictor of employment, management, and customer service success.

Before we explore the notion of emotional intelligence and EQ, let's take a quick look at the human brain. When our body experiences something through one of the five senses, information about this sensation (such as the pain experienced when we hit ourselves on the thumb with a hammer or the wonderful smell of fresh bread baking) travels to our brain by way of our nerves, up the spinal column, to the **brainstem** the base of the brain. The brainstem is the brain's intermediary, which receives and sends messages to the rest of the body. Information travels immediately from the brain stem through the brain's **limbic system**, the region in which we experience our emotions. Only after traveling through this emotional center does the information finally reach the outer layers of the brain, including the **frontal lobes** of the cerebral cortex, which assists in our rational thinking by evaluating whether our potential actions and reactions may be good or bad and perceived by others as socially acceptable or unacceptable.

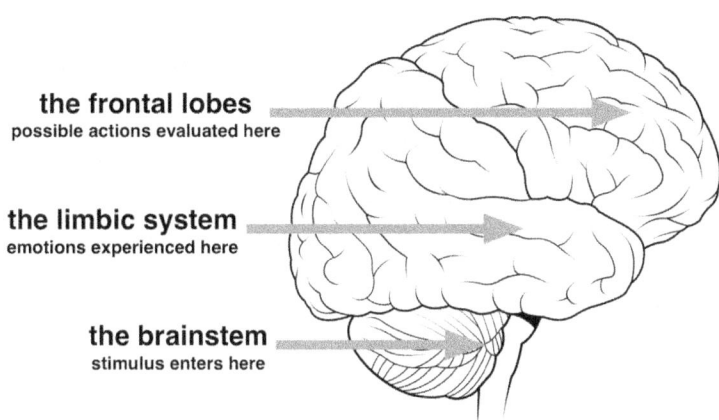

Figure 11.4 - The Human Brain

Therefore, when we hit our thumb with a hammer, we first experience the emotion of extreme, blinding pain before we experience the rational thought that, although we might want to scream in pain non-stop for thirty minutes, we must instead go to the hospital because our thumb looks broken. In a more pleasurable experience, when we smell fresh bread baking, we first have happy feelings and experience pangs of hunger before we experience that rational thought that, although we want to rip the bread from the oven and eat the entire loaf immediately, we just ate and are actually not hungry and the bread must be saved for dinner to be shared among the entire family. But what does all of this brain anatomy have to do with success in the purchasing process? Everything!

During the past twenty years, computers have increasingly been doing much of the grunt work of the cognitive thinking process for us. (Think about how different filing your taxes is now, thanks to software programs like TurboTax.) The human population and the average workplace, however, have grown increasingly full of people. Therefore, much of the time in our day must now be devoted to getting along with the people with whom we must interact. Where we could once sit quietly in our closed-door offices performing our small, insular tasks, we now must sit in cubicles, side-by-side with our coworkers, with whom we must frequently interact to solicit information and opinions in order to get our jobs done. The purchasing professionals among us engaged in interactions with others, such as internal co-workers with procurement needs and external suppliers, face the added pressure of these additional critically- important social interactions.

Therefore, we must now have good *people skills*, which puts our frontal lobes into overdrive as we try to regulate our emotions so that we don't yell at our coworkers and suppliers or run screaming from the building when things go wrong. For many employers, our ability to regulate our emotions in order to get along and work with others is becoming a more highly valued commodity than pure intelligence alone. In contrast to IQ, this ability is called our ***EQ*** or our ***emotional intelligence***.

Although the concept of emotional intelligence has been around since the mid-1980s, it has been popularized more recently in the works of author Daniel Goleman. In his book *Emotional Intelligence*, Goleman describes our emotional intelligence as the combination of our personal competence (how self-aware we are and how well we manage ourselves) and our social competence (how socially aware we are and how well we manage relationships with others).

In order to develop greater emotional intelligence, we must first look inward to become aware of who we are, what we are, and the decisions we make that affect our own lives. To look inward in developing our emotional intelligence, we can explore the personalities of ourselves and others, focusing on how different personality types can work together in the purchasing environment. Once we have looked inward, we must then look outward to become aware of social dynamics and the decisions we make and actions we take in our interpersonal interactions. To take greater ownership of our interpersonal interactions in the purchasing environment, we can begin to focus on developing enhanced communication skills.

PERSONALITY IN THE PURCHASING PROCESS

At the beginning of this chapter, we said that the solder of a supply chain's links are people and their ***interpersonal relationships***, the social associations, connections, or affiliations between two or more people. Interpersonal relationships vary in different levels of intimacy and sharing and they are typically centered around something shared or in common. As previously discussed, those in interpersonal relationships within the purchasing environment, such as the relationships between buyers and suppliers, may sometimes have nothing in common other than the need for the transaction. Buyers and suppliers in supply chain relationships will have a variety of differences, including the companies or departments for whom they work, their work methods and goals, or even their perception of the relationship and work to be done.

Successful relationships, in both purchasing interactions and the world at large, often depend on our perceptions of reality, or *paradigms*. A ***paradigm*** is the set of experiences, beliefs, and values that affect the way an individual perceives reality and responds to these perceptions. It is the way we see the world, not literally and visually, but within the realm of perception, understanding, and interpretation.

In the best-selling management guide *The Seven Habits of Highly Effective People*, author Stephen Covey asserts that our paradigms are a powerful influence in our lives and in our ability to be effective individuals. He describes paradigms as the maps in our heads of "the way things are" (our realities) and "the way things should be" (our values). Covey states that we assume that the way we "see" things is the way that they are or should be, i.e., we see the world not as it is, but as we are conditioned to see it. He further adds that, "our paradigms, correct or incorrect, are the source of our attitudes and behaviors, and ultimately, our relationships with others."

Conventional wisdom and the idea of *conditioning* might lead us to believe that the maps in our heads, our paradigms, are based on our past experiences. (The paradigm of Pavlov's dog, for example, is that every time a bell rings, I get a treat.) Contemporary personality theory research, however, reveals that paradigms are also related to our innate personality types. Therefore, how we see the world depends partially on the personality we were born with.

As used by psychology, management, and education professionals, ***personality type*** refers to a personality preference typology first outlined in psychologist Carl Jung's *Psychological Types* (1921) and later developed further by mother and daughter personality researchers, Katherine Briggs and Isabel Briggs Myers. According to personality type theory, we are capable of acting according to any of the personality characteristics outlined, but we have an innate preference for specific characteristics and most often behave according to those preferences. Just as we can use both of our hands but are born with a preference for our right or left hand, we can use all of the personality types but are born with specific preferences.

In 1942, Briggs Myers and Briggs developed a psychological personality inventory, the **Myers Briggs Type Indicator (MBTI)**, to help individuals sort their preferences and determine their unique personality type. In the MBTI, there are four categories in which you are sorted into one of two preferences. Each of these preferences is designated by a single letter. After you have been sorted according to all four categories, you will have been assigned four separate letters. These four letters combined will reveal your personality type. There are sixteen different combinations of letters and, correspondingly, sixteen different distinct personality types.

The first of the four preference categories sorts people according to how they gain energy. If you become more energized from the outside world, you have a preference for **Extraversion** and are given the letter **E** as the first letter of your four-letter personality type. If you become more energized from your own inner resources, you have a preference for **Introversion** and are given the letter **I** as the first letter of your four-letter personality type. For example, if you prefer to spend more of your free time with people or "out and about," you may have a preference for Extraversion. If, however, you prefer to spend your free time alone or working on independent pursuits, you may have a preference for Introversion.

The second of the four preference categories sorts people according to how they take in information. If you prefer to deal with individual, specific facts, you have a preference for **Sensing** and are given the letter **S** as the second letter of your four-letter personality type. If you prefer to deal with the "big picture," you have a preference for **Intuition** and are given the letter **N** as the second letter of your four-letter personality type. Intuition is given N instead of I to avoid confusion because I has already been assigned to Introversion.) For example, in the crime and mystery genre of popular television shows, the detail-oriented forensic researchers on CSI demonstrate a preference for Sensing while the guesswork and intuitive reasoning of Columbo demonstrate a preference for Intuition.

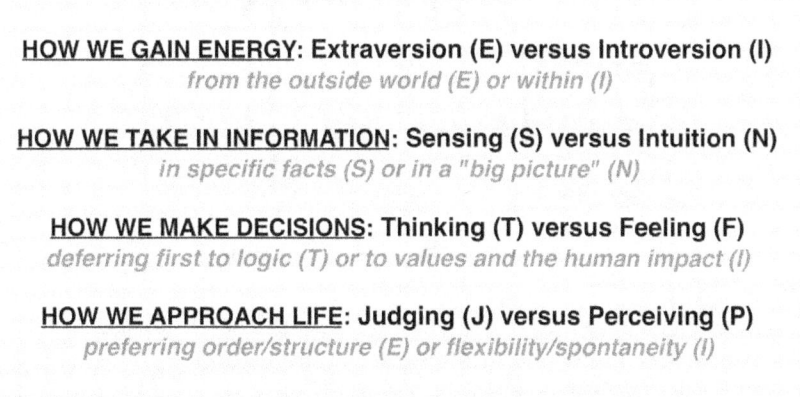

Figure 11.5 - The Four Categories of the MBTI

The third of the four preference categories sorts people according to how they make decisions. If you more often make decisions using logic and critical analysis, you have a preference for **Thinking** and are given the letter *T* as the third letter of your four-letter personality type. If you more often make decisions based on your values and by taking other people into account, you have a preference for **Feeling** and are given the letter *F* as the third letter of your four- letter personality type. Often, those with a preference for Thinking would prefer others to view them as right or competent while those with a preference for Feeling would prefer for others to like or care about them.

The fourth and final of the four preference categories sorts people according to how they approach life. If you prefer order and structure, you have a preference for **Judging** and are given the letter *J* as the final letter of your four-letter personality type. If you prefer flexibility and spontaneity, you have a preference for **Perceiving** and are given the letter *P* as the final letter of your four-letter personality type. For example, if you enjoy making "to do" lists, you may have a preference for Judging. If you prefer instead to "go with the flow," you may have a preference for Perceiving.

After you have been sorted in each of the four preference categories, as shown in Figure 11.5 above, you will be left with four letters. When written together, these four letters represent your MBTI personality type. As show in Figure 11.6, there are sixteen possible MBTI types. Each of these sixteen types is unique and has unique means of communicating, learning, handling conflict, working with others, and relaxing. Typically, people of one given type will have an easier time communicating with and understanding people of the same or similar types and a more difficult time with those of very different types.

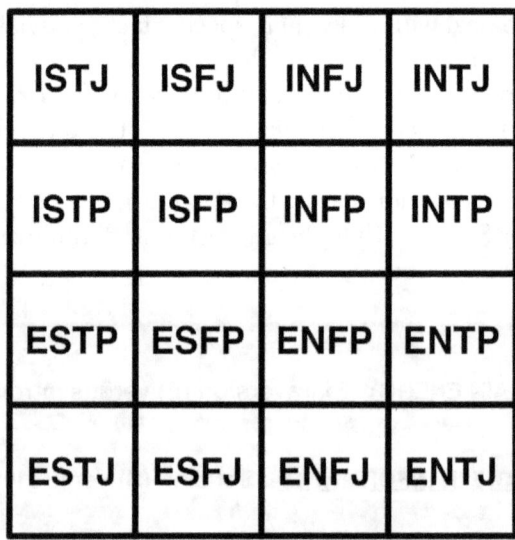

Figure 11.6 - The MBTI Type Table

According to personality type theory, we cannot change our innate personality preferences to match those of others with whom we interact, such as our customers. By learning about the personality type preferences of ourselves and others, however, we can adjust our behavior to improve communication and enhance understanding. Although you may not be able to change the personality type you are born with, you can adjust your paradigm (remember - the map in your head) to better understand and communicate with others. Knowing about personality type theory allows you to better understand your own paradigm, the paradigms of others, and how these maps in our heads influence our actions.

At companies like Southwest Airlines, the MBTI is used in leadership and employee training so that employees can understand each other's differences, enabling them to understand why their coworkers approach the same challenge from a completely different perspective. In a corporate setting, knowing the "why" behind coworkers' and suppliers' behaviors can you help build trust and empathy with each other, which are critical factors in close buyer-supplier relationships.

In the world of purchasing, there appears to be a link between career choice and personality type. When comparing career choice tables for those involved in the supplier-purchaser relationship, the results of studies in Macdaid et al's 2005 compilation *Atlas of Type Tables* show that Purchasing Agents, Sales Representatives, and Marketing Personnel have very different personality type distributions.

PERSONALITY PREFERENCE	PURCHASING AGENTS	MARKETING PERSONNEL	SALES REPRESENTATIVES
E	56.25%	74.70%	67.04%
I	43.75%	25.30%	32.96%
S	77.50%	39.76%	62.01%
N	22.50%	60.24%	37.99%
T	75.00%	61.45%	58.98%
F	25.00%	38.55%	43.02%
J	76.25%	55.42%	63.69%
P	23.75%	44.58%	36.31%

Figure 11.7 - **Personality Type Distribution in the Purchasing Environment**

As seen in Figure 11.7 above, Purchasing Agents appear to display a greater preference for Introversion than their more Extraversion-oriented Marketing and Sales counterparts. Purchasing Agents also display greater preferences for Sensing, Thinking, and Judging. More than 52% of all Purchasing Agents are reported as ISTJ or ESTJ, only two of the sixteen MBTI personality types.

In the purchasing process, purchasing professionals and supplier's salespeople work closely together. Not only do they have a professional, transactional relationship, but they have an interpersonal one as well that influences the purchasing process. Human psychology reveals that there is a natural tendency for people to spend time with people that they like more and that are more like them, i.e., have the same or similar personality types. Purchasers are more likely to have higher levels of interpersonal satisfaction and spend more time with salespeople who are similar to or complement their own personalities. In order to make the best decisions for the companies they represent, purchasing professionals should know how to recognize personality types to prevent confusing satisfying interpersonal relationships with the best purchasing deal or the salesperson's willingness to go above and beyond standard levels of service. Thus, personality type may have a direct influence on the purchasing process and people involved within this process can have an advantage when they understand the role of personality type within it.

Developing Communication Skills for Purchasing

Today's purchasing world can be stressful. Purchasing professionals feel pressure from their companies to find the highest quality goods at the lowest costs. One purchasing misstep could result in a low quality product that won't sell or a product too costly for consumers to buy. Suppliers must communicate openly with purchasers while still trying to achieve sales prices high enough to keep their company profitable. With all of this purchasing-based stress welling up inside of us, it can sometimes unintentionally spill out onto our loved ones and workplace colleagues. Because there is so much on our minds, we may say things we don't mean or unknowingly use an angry tone of voice. Our friends and colleagues, who are also feeling the stress of the workplace, may be super-sensitive and take offense at things we say when no offense was meant.

To form and sustain solid and open interpersonal business relationships, we must use emotional intelligence when communicating with others, especially during times of stress. We must be empathetic to the emotional state of others and we must be aware of our own state of mind. A good goal to keep in mind is to create more positive and open interactions with others, especially when you or the person you are communicating have an important, long-term business relationship that is worth preserving.

To create open and positive communication with suppliers, a few simple communication techniques can go a long way. These techniques, which focus on being careful of your word choices and respecting others' emotions and personality differences, include:

UNDERSTANDING & ADDRESSING BODY LANGUAGE

Sometimes you know when people (including purchasers and suppliers) will be difficult to communicate with before they even open their mouths just by reading their body language. For example, when people frown and stand with their arms crossed, you can take this as a clear signal that something is wrong. When they tap their feet and repeatedly look at their watch, you can tell that they are in a hurry and may not have time to talk to you. When they yawn and look at you with an expressionless face, you can guess that they are taking the time to speak with you but don't see the purpose or value of the conversation.

When you observe a person's body language or tone of voice and notice that they are upset or may not be open to communication, it is best if you acknowledge it and address it immediately. For example, to the person with the frown and crossed arms, you might say, "I've noticed that you seem a bit upset. Is anything wrong?"

Addressing negative body language provides an invitation for people to explain what might be bothering them. Once they have explained the problem, you can rectify or address it and get back to the business at hand. The problem may not even be about you. They might be upset about something else and not even be aware of their own body language or agitated state of mind. Expressing your concern or allowing them to vent shows that the interaction is important to you and that you value their opinion.

MAKING "I" STATEMENTS

When dealing with overly sensitive, demanding, and angry people, a particular turn-of-phrase can unintentionally appear insensitive or aggressive, providing a spark to ignite conflict with these powder-keg communicators. This dangerous language is the "You" statement. When you are speaking with difficult people (and everyone else, too), avoid starting possibly contentious statements with the word "you," which sounds accusatory and sets you up for an immediate conflict. Instead, take ownership of your statements by starting them with the word "I" and expressing what you have felt or noticed.

For example, if a coworker is complaining but does not know that they are wrong, it would be counterproductive to make them angrier by pointing out their mistake with a "You" statement, such as, "You've got it all wrong. Look at these figures here." A less combative way to make the same statement would be to use an "I" statement, such as, "I noticed that the figures in our paperwork are different from the ones you mentioned."

USING ANTICIPATORY STATEMENTS

When you want to make a suggestion to someone to which you suspect they might react negatively, using anticipatory statements is a useful technique that steers clear of conflict and even gets the person to consider your suggestion. With this technique, you anticipate a person's negative reaction to your suggestion and incorporate it into your statement to them.

An example of this would be, "I know that you had planned for me to bring cookies to the office party, but I'd like to suggest bringing a vegetable tray instead because I love vegetables and would prefer to bring a beautiful assortment of fresh vegetables instead of store-bought cookies." If you anticipate and mention the person's concerns yourself before making the suggestion, the customer might be open to listening to you suggestion because you have demonstrated that you have considered their concerns and point of view in your suggestion.

LISTENING & PARAPHRASING

In purchasing interactions, a final technique useful in dealing with stressed and non-stressed people alike is careful listening and paraphrasing. When people know that you have taken the time to fully understand their point of view, their stress, anger, or frustration is more likely to be diffused.

To listen effectively, you lean in, maintain eye contact, and nod periodically to show that you are interested in what the other person is saying. You do not interrupt, but instead let them finish what they have to say. You then check to ensure that you have fully understood them by paraphrasing their main points. To paraphrase effectively, you restate their main ideas in your own words, using a neutral tone of voice that conveys neither approval nor disapproval of their message. The purpose of paraphrasing is to make sure that you have understood the other person because the tension between the two of you could be the result of a simple misunderstanding.

While it is difficult to keep these techniques at the forefront of your mind, especially when stressed, it can be achieved by focusing on one technique at a time until it becomes a natural and automatic part of your communication behavior. We can't change overnight, but we can keep the *Platinum Rule* in mind. We are all familiar with the Golden Rule: *Do unto others as you would have them do unto you*. Therefore, if I like to receive hugs from business acquaintances, should I give them great big bear hugs whenever I see them? Unless all of your business acquaintances are similarly physically demonstrative, most will avoid you when they see you coming for the fear of your bone-crushingly close bear hugs. When dealing with purchasers and suppliers (and friends and family, too), a better rule to keep in mind is the empathetic, personality-conscious, and more emotionally intelligent **Platinum Rule**: *Do unto others as they would like to have done unto them*. Keeping this in mind is a great first step toward developing and improving communication skills in the wonderful world of purchasing.

Chapter 11 Review Questions

1. Are the relationships in the purchasing world *internal* or *external*? Why?

2. Do you think it is ore important for a purchasing manager to have a high IQ or a high EQ? Explain your answer.

3. Do you have the exact same *paradigm* as the other people in your life? Why or why not?

4. Describe a time in which your paradigm was very different from the paradigm of a coworker. What happened? What was the end result?

5. Looking at the E-I differences described in this chapter, are you more of an **Extravert** or an **Introvert**? Please explain your answer.

6. Looking at the S-N differences described in this chapter, are you more of a **Sensing** or an **Intuitive** type? Please explain your answer.

7. Looking at the T-F differences described in this chapter, are you more of a **Thinking** or a **Feeling** type? Please explain your answer.

8. Looking at the J-P differences described in this chapter, are you more of a **Judging** or a **Perceiving** type? Please explain your answer.

9. Imagine that you are a purchasing manager for your local school district. You noticed that your textbook order from a supplier was 100 books short. When you called your supplier to tell them about it, should your first statement to them be: "You shortchanged us by 100 books." Why or why not?

10. What is an *anticipatory statement*? Give an example of an anticipatory statement a purchaser might make to a supplier.

Chapter 11 Case Exercise

Rating Your Emotional Intelligence

This chapter provided an introduction to emotional intelligence and the works of Daniel Goleman. Part of improving your emotional intelligence is developing greater self awareness. The worksheet below is based on the competences of emotional intelligence as covered in Daniel Goleman's book, *Working with Emotional Intelligence*. Use the worksheet to rate your emotional intelligence. Then get a second opinion by having someone who know you well rate you, too.

Emotional Intelligence Self-Evaluation

Rate yourself on each of the areas of emotional competence. When you have finished, get a second opinion from someone who knows you well. Get that person to rate you and provide additional input.

RATING SCALE: 1 = very poor, 10 = exceptionally good
(Think about how often you exhibit these behaviors. If you do them 50% of the time when you could, write "5.")

Area of Competence	Self Rating	2nd Opinion	Notes from 2nd Opinion
SELF-AWARENESS			
emotional self-awareness I am aware of my feelings. I can accurately describe them and I understand how they affect me and my behavior.			
accurate self-assessment I am in touch with my strengths and weaknesses. I focus on self improvement.			
self confidence I am comfortable with myself and my decisions. I present myself to others in an assured manner.			
SELF-MANAGEMENT			
emotional self-control In stressful or emotionally charged situations, I remain calm and think clearly.			
transparency I do not hide my motive or intent from others. I admit my mistakes.			
adaptability I am comfortable with change. I like being flexible and adapting to new challenges.			
achievement orientation I work hard to meet my goals. I focus on continuous improvement.			
initiative I take the reins when opportunities arise. I am not afraid of starting a new challenge.			
optimism I look at the positive side of people and situations.			

Name of Person Offering 2nd Opinion & Their Relationship to You:

Area of Competence	Self Rating	2nd Opinion	Notes from 2nd Opinion
SOCIAL AWARENESS			
empathy I understand and sympathize with the feelings of others.			
organizational awareness I have a clear understanding of the informal leaders and unwritten rules in the workplace.			
service orientation I am interested in my internal and external customers' needs, not just because it's my job but because I genuinely care.			
RELATIONSHIP AWARENESS			
developing others I actively try to help and mentor others. I give of my free time to do so.			
inspirational leadership I take action to inspire others to follow me. I nurture and support my followers.			
change catalyst I lead the charge when change happens. I am often a champion for change initiatives.			
influence I am able to build buy-in with others. I develop personal networks to help increase the reach of my influence.			
conflict management I am good at understanding all sides in interpersonal conflict. I remain impartial and help all parties with a peaceful resolution.			
teamwork & collaboration I believe that teamwork and collaboration often yields the richest results. I work to bring others together into collaborative teams.			

Name of Person Offering 2nd Opinion & Their Relationship to You:

Chapter 12

Business Strategy and Purchasing

Dr. George Geistauts

Purchasing, like all other activities in the organization, must contribute positively to the organization's efforts to be successful. The organization's grand concept of what defines success and its overall path to achieving this success can be called ***strategy***. In this chapter, we will look at some basic strategic concepts and how purchasing relates to these. The significance of purchasing for strategy can range all the way from virtually none (purchasing is a trivial supportive activity for the organization) to effective purchasing being at the very core of the strategy.

This chapter focuses on ***strategically significant purchasing***. Purchasing is likely to be a strategically significant activity when one or more of the following is true:

- *The cost of materials, components, and equipment is a high percentage of total costs.*

- *The continued availability of a particular material, component, or piece of equipment is critical for your firm's product line and operations.*

- *The prices of key supplies, materials, or components are highly volatile.*

- *There is a developing scarcity of some critical input material or component.*

- *High product quality and reliability are key elements of your competitive strategy, and the quality of materials and components you purchase determines your product quality.*

- *Technology is changing rapidly, and access to the latest technology is crucial for maintaining competitiveness.*

Customers often make judgments about your firm's social responsibility and ethics based on your sourcing practices.

COMPETITION AND CONFLICT

Virtually all organizations exist in an external environment filled with competition and conflict. For the business organization, the major competition is for market share—that is, for more customers. Companies that attract more customers gain market share from their competitors and become winners! Their **market** or **competitive strategy** is successful. (There is also competition between firms for investor capital, but this capital tends to flow toward firms with effective competitive strategies.)

In modern economies, scarcity of goods and services is rare, and customers almost always have choices. For example, a customer can choose from many brands and/or models of TV sets, cell phones, laptops, refrigerators, automobiles, toys, coffee, beer, and soda pop. Different customers will use different criteria in making these choices. They look at such characteristics as product features, quality, price, warranties, follow-up service, and customer support. But these characteristics of products are, to a great extent, a result of the producer's choices of inputs and the ability to obtain the chosen inputs reliably at reasonable prices – i.e., effective purchasing.

Customers also consider the overall buying experience as part of their decision process. Thus, in the customer's mind, companies can **differentiate** themselves from others by offering differences in the product and differences in the buying experience.

In addition to the conflict between firms that is the inherent nature of competition, firms often encounter additional categories of conflict. These conflicts arise because businesses have many *stakeholders* beyond just customers, and some customers also apply their larger *stakeholder values* set to the buying decision. To succeed strategically, the business must not just be an effective competitor but also an effective manager of *stakeholder relationships*.

A **stakeholder** is anyone who is directly or indirectly impacted by the business or at least thinks that such an impact exists. Business investors, managers, employees, and customers are obvious

---

A specific case illustrates conflict between business goals and stakeholders values:

The development of a major new gold mine in Alaska is facing opposition because its possible negative environmental effects may threaten a rich salmon fishery and, in turn, threaten the lifestyle of the native peoples who depend on these salmon for both food and income.

One consequence is that a major U.S. jewelry chain has declared that it will not purchase any gold from that mine or any items made from that gold.

In this case, both **environmental stakeholders** and **cultural stakeholders** are combining to threaten the mining company's development strategy. However, *the jewelry chain, through its purchasing policy, is positioning itself as "the good guys."*

stakeholders. Less obvious stakeholders are suppliers, citizens in general, unions, environmentalists, ethnic groups, cultural groups, religious groups, and government agencies.

For example, environmentalists (and, increasingly, citizens in general) want the environment protected and products to be made from inputs and with processes that minimize environmental harm. In other words, they want **green products**, made as much as possible from *green inputs* and produced with *green processes*. These green-focused stakeholders exert influence on the business both through their personal buying decisions and through public advocacy and action.

As shown in Figure 12.1 below, the interface or intersection between the business and its external environment is the area where strategy takes place. Here is where a business encounters its competitors and other external forces. Here is where it will live or die strategically!

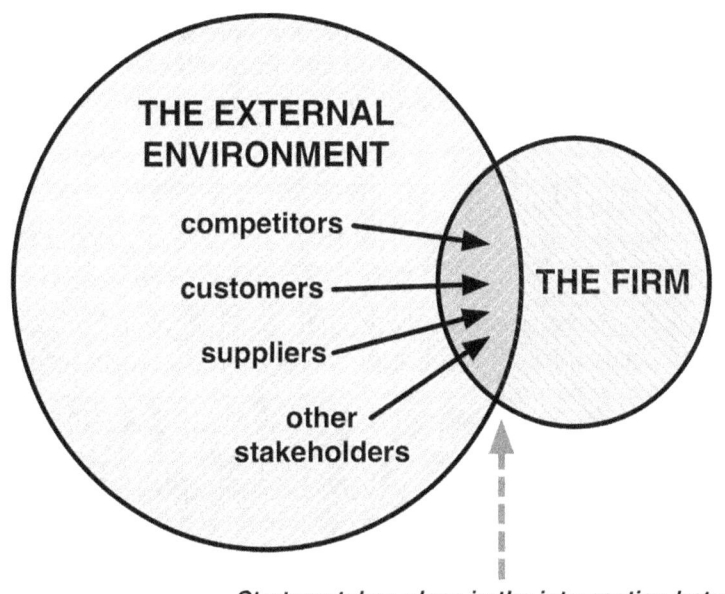

Figure 12.1 - The Area of Business Strategy

THE NATURE OF STRATEGY

Strategy focuses on achieving success in a business environment filled with competition and conflict. In order to explore the relationship between strategy and purchasing, we first need to develop a more complete understanding of what strategy is, how it is developed, and how it is implemented. Some key aspects of strategy include:

- Strategy is the *highest level of thinking* in an organization and the responsibility of top management.

- Concepts of strategy were *first developed in warfare*, and the word "strategy" originally meant "the art of generalship," or how the general was going to win the war.

- The equivalent of *the general in business is the Chief Executive Officer (or CEO)*, and it is the CEO's responsibility to develop and direct the implementation of the firm's strategy.

- *Strategic stakes are very high.* In war, you live or die depending on strategic success. In business, you must be among the winners in the competitive war with other firms. You continue to operate or you fail, depending on the effectiveness of your strategy.

- *Logistics has always been a critical issue.* In war, combat operations consume enormous amounts of weapons, ammunition, fuel, food, water and other supplies. Maintaining access to these supplies is absolutely essential. Similarly, in business, effective and efficient supply chains are essential for competitiveness, and the purchasing function plays a key role.

- In developing strategy, a wise *CEO consults with others*, both internally and externally. Internal consultation is with other executives, including those responsible for purchasing. External advice is obtained from consultants, and also from other executives in the CEO's personal network of acquaintances. The Board of Directors reviews and approves the proposed strategy.

- Strategy may be developed formally, through *a formal structured process of strategic planning*, or more informally, through an *intuitive feel* for what would work, often accompanied by some negotiation among top executives. There is no one way to do it!

- Strategic thinking *considers the organization as a whole* (i.e., as a complete system) and its overall relationship to its environment. This is often referred to as a **systems approach**.

- Business strategy has a *long-term focus*, although it can be adjusted in response to critical events. A firm that has a "strategy" that is always changing in fact has no strategy at all!

STRATEGIC ANALYSIS AND PLANNING

Strategy development and implementation are usually more likely to succeed if the firm has developed a formal strategic plan. Actually, a formal strategic planning process will generate a hierarchical set of plans that relate the functions, including purchasing, to the chosen corporate strategy. Specific plans for each of the firm's product lines are also part of this plan structure.

Figure 12.2 - Needed: A Set of Plans

In developing this set of plans, the overall strategic direction is set by top management, especially the CEO, as represented by the solid arrows in the figure above. However, top management draws on data and suggestions provided by business function management, including purchasing management, as represented by the dashed arrows in the figure above. Through its constant interaction with external suppliers, purchasing is often the first to notice trends in technology, competitor strategies, possible future price changes, potential supply shortages, etc. In effect, the purchasing process is also one of the firm's best intelligence collection processes. However, in order to maximize the flow of information, purchasing management must have access to top management and enjoy a good relationship with that management.

In analyzing the strategic situation and developing strategy for the future, the firm draws on *data about internal and external conditions.* **Internal data** describes the firm's structure, products and services, procurement of inputs, production processes, marketing and distribution methods, financing, and its financial results. Costs and profitability are key variables. **External data** describes economic and industry conditions, consumer characteristics (demographics), purchasing power and consumer confidence, stakeholder groups and their values, legal requirements and restrictions, relevant technology, etc.

Competitive data focuses on a combination of internal and external factors to describe the firm's position relative to its competitors. Included are the overall competitive strategies of the relevant players, their geographic and demographic market definitions, their chosen means of attracting customers, product pricing, distribution, and the resulting market shares. Market trend data, showing market size changes and market share shifts over a number of recent time periods (typically several years), is particularly important.

Some data is **hard data** because it is numerical; other data is **soft data** because it is descriptive but not easily quantifiable. For example, sales volume and inventory levels are usually stated as numbers (hard data), but employee morale is usually not quantifiable but can be described verbally (soft data). Sometimes there is a tendency to downplay soft data, but that is often a mistake. Again, continuing with the example of employee morale, we know that low morale can lead to less attention to product quality, more employee grievances, increased absenteeism, and poor employee retention. All of these increase costs and make the firm less competitive.

Some of this soft data describes ***expectations***. Expectations are what various internal and external stakeholders want to obtain *for themselves* from their relationships with the firm. For example, most workers expect a decent wage, fringe benefits, a safe working environment, employment security, and an adequate retirement package. Among other things, executives often expect much higher compensation; perks, such as a country club membership or access to the company plane; performance bonuses; and very attractive retirement packages. The owners or shareholders expect a return on their investment that at least matches the level of risk they undertook by investing in the firm. Customers expect quality products that are safe and suitable for meeting their needs or wants and that are reasonably priced.

Conflicts in expectations are commonplace and influence strategic choices. Expectations act as strategic filters. They eliminate some strategic opportunities from further consideration because these opportunities would make it difficult to meet certain stakeholder expectations, particularly the expectations of those in a position to shape strategy. For example, executives focused on short-term performance bonuses can attempt to reduce costs by outsourcing product components to the absolutely lowest bidders. This puts enormous pressure on purchasing to get very low prices from suppliers. Purchasing will naturally, in turn, put pressure on the suppliers to cut prices. However, this can have very negative consequences in two ways. First, lower supplier prices are often accompanied by a reduction in quality. This can endanger long-term product quality and the reputation of the firm. Second, if purchasing puts great pressure on suppliers, the quality of the relationships between purchasing and suppliers will deteriorate, leading to hostility rather than cooperation. In this kind of situation, purchasing is meeting top management expectations but possibly weakening the firm in the long run.

ENVIRONMENTAL SCANNING

At the beginning of this chapter, we stressed that business strategy focuses on the relationships between the specific business firm and forces in the environment outside the business. However, the external world is constantly changing! We need to monitor and analyze these external forces for changes that might signal new *strategic opportunities* or *strategic threats*; i.e., we need to engage in environmental scanning. **Environmental scanning** provides both inputs into strategic analysis and trigger points for rethinking strategy.

Very large businesses can afford to hire planning staff and formally organize to do this. Smaller businesses usually do not have the resources for organized formal scanning efforts and must rely on informal information collection and analysis. This means that these firms must use their networks of relationships, their sales force, their trade associations and trade shows, government publications, local and national media, the Internet, and customers as "sources of intelligence" for strategic information about environmental change. Any firm-to-external environment interaction is a potential intelligence source! *Purchasing, which is in contact with external vendors on a regular basis, can often be a source of insights*, particularly on such developments as changing technology, changes in competitor focus, looming shortages or surpluses of different inputs, and economic conditions.

It helps to organize your thinking about the external environment by identifying broad categories of scanning. One such model for organizing scanning is shown in the figure below. In this model, your firm is at the center of interactions with a number of environmental dimensions. Obviously your firm has very strong interactions with its industry or industries, but it is also affected by the characteristics of the physical & natural environments in which it operates, the relevant populations (demographics), the economic conditions, political and legal systems, social and cultural relationships and values, and technology.

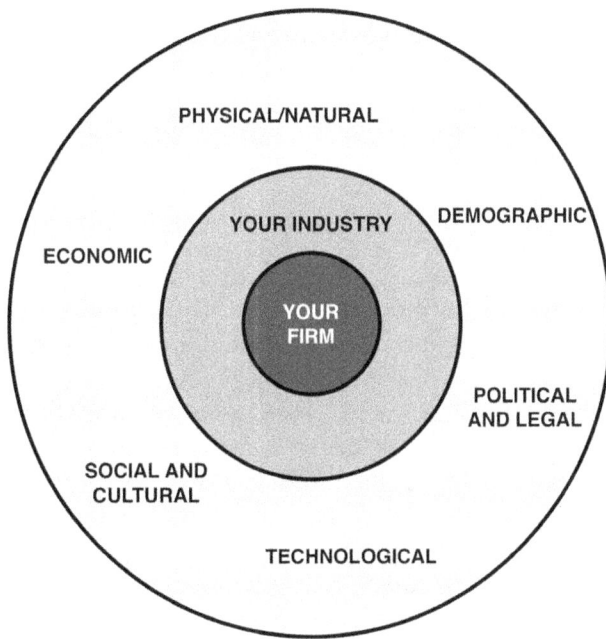

Figure 12.3 - Environmental Scanning Dimensions

The *physical/natural environmental dimension* consists of the conditions and restrictions a business faces as a consequence of its geographic location. We all live, work, produce, and buy and sell in specific geographic locations. All locations have natural features such as terrain, climate, lakes, rivers, coastlines, and deposits of natural resources. They also have various degrees of major infrastructure, such as roads, railroads, airports, ports, and utilities. These natural features and the presence or absence of appropriate physical infrastructure determine what can be efficiently sold, or be efficiently produced, in a specific location.

From a purchasing perspective, the characteristics of the natural/physical environment determine what natural resources are present, their relative costs of extraction and development, the costs of further infrastructure development, transportation costs, and risk exposure to natural disasters. A geographic area's natural/physical environment has, of course, shaped the local size and characteristics of the population, the economy, government, cultural and social values, and local costs.

In many parts of the world today, analysis of the physical/natural dimension would also include conditions and restrictions resulting from environmental quality laws, regulations, and forces. For example, purchasing rare tropical hardwood lumber from endangered rain forests might or might not be illegal, but would certainly raise questions about your company's environmental values.

> The basic issue of geographic scanning for purchasing can be reduced down to having a positive answer to the following question: **Is this a logical geographic region for meeting one or more of our specific sourcing needs?**

The **economic environmental dimension** consists of all the important characteristics of the economies in which you operate. The scale of the economic systems to be scanned varies all the way from purely local, such as your city or state, to regional, such as the Pacific Northwest, to national or international. Increasingly, for larger businesses, one end of the scale is global. As the financial and economic crisis of 2008-09 has demonstrated, we are living in a highly interconnected global economic web and even very local businesses are affected by global changes.

Descriptions of economies typically include a mix of standard measures of economic performance as well as measures very specific to a particular economy. Among the standard measures are the size and growth rate of the economy, the major components (key industries), interest rates, employment and unemployment, wage structures, and the direction and pattern of changes. We can classify economies as *highly developed*, *developing*, or *underdeveloped*. Very highly developed economies are heavily dependent on information technology, and often are called **knowledge economies**.

From a purchasing strategy perspective, a key strategic process is *outsourcing*, usually from firms in relatively developed economies to sources in underdeveloped or developing economies. The major reason for this outsourcing is cost reduction because of lower labor costs. Costs can also be lower because environmental and other regulations are weaker in less developed economies. However, as those economies develop further, their labor costs tend to rise and regulations increase. This forces many firms to constantly reevaluate where to go to for their outsourcing. Thus, continuous scanning of economic conditions and changes is very important for optimal outsourcing.

> The basic issue of economic scanning for purchasing can be reduced down to having a positive answer to the following question: **Does this economy offer sustainable cost or other advantages for sourcing?**

The **demographic environmental dimension** consists of all of the important characteristics of the populations where you operate. These populations provide your customers, your employees, and the employees of your suppliers. Fortunately, population data is collected by almost all levels of government and many other organizations, and much of this data is free and accessible on the Internet. The U.S. Census Bureau provides population data not just for the U.S., but also for many other countries.

> **A case example where demographics did not support a specific technology:**
>
> There is a story in consulting circles about the consultants who "computerized" production in a third-world steel plant by providing each foreman with a computer screen. Everything worked fine during the computerization process, but when the consultants left, production collapsed. A new consultant easily discovered the fundamental problem: most foremen were barely literate and simply could not handle the information on the computer screens by themselves!

Some examples of important demographic characteristics are age distribution, education, language, employment, economic status, personal income, nationality, race, religion, marital status, and household size. Literacy and work skills are particularly important. For example, in evaluating a third-world supplier's ability to provide high technology parts, we must evaluate the ability of the vendor's employees to develop an adequate understanding of the technology of the parts and the production technology.

> The basic issue of demographic scanning for purchasing can be reduced down to having a positive answer to the following question: **Does a potential sourcing location have an adequate supply of appropriately skilled labor to produce the materials, components, or finished products we want to purchase?**

The ***political/legal environmental dimension*** focuses on political forces and actions and their impact on business. In a sense, the political/legal environment defines who has power in a society, how it is acquired, and how it is used. It also describes whether a *rule of law* really exists in a society. A strong rule of law tends to lead to stable societies in which highly arbitrary government actions are uncommon, and a functioning court system will enforce business contracts. Thus, purchasing from businesses in stable societies with a rule of law is less risky.

In scanning and evaluating specific political/legal environments, we look at variables such as political philosophies, political systems, political power distribution, laws, regulations, treaties, trading block memberships, quotas and trade restrictions, tax policies, and government attitudes toward business and assistance to business.

> The basic issue of political/legal scanning for purchasing can be reduced down to having a positive answer to the following question: **Does a potential sourcing location have a sufficiently stable government and functioning legal system so that the risk of arbitrary government or legal actions is limited?**

The ***social/cultural environmental dimension*** consists of the values, preferences, and lifestyles of a society. Examples of these are attitudes toward work, roles of men and women, treatment of woman and minorities, significance of religion, ethical and moral values, and cross cultural awareness. The prevailing concept of the "good life," product/service expectations, and use of leisure time are also important. These values will influence the attitudes and productivity of the local work force, which will impact production costs and quality and political stability.

> The basic issue of social/cultural scanning for purchasing can be reduced down to having a positive answer to the following question: **Are the social and cultural norms and values prevailing in a potential sourcing location supportive of our kind of sourcing needs?**

The ***technological environmental dimension*** consists of the existing technologies, their relative importance, and the patterns and trends of technological change. A dominant characteristic of modern technology is that it is always changing. We want to forecast likely new technology developments and breakthroughs and how fast new technologies are being adopted by users. We are also interested in technology policy issues and government involvement in technology.

Among the technological questions and issues to be considered are:

- *What are the performance characteristics and costs of specific technologies?*
- *What is the most performance we could get from any specific technology?*
- *Which technologies are mature?*
- *Which technologies are ascending and will replace current technologies?*
- *Are there technology gaps? Where are they?*
- *What are the trends in research & development (R&D)?*

In order to purchase technological inputs we need to know where to shop for them. All advanced countries are high technology societies, but the relative strength of specific technologies varies significantly. For example, the U.S. is a world leader in computing chip technology, space technology, and agricultural technology. Japan is a world leader in optics and camera technology. It makes strategic sense to purchase technological inputs from firms that are part of strong technology clusters, which are often associated with specific countries or regions.

However, suppliers in these technology clusters might also be very expensive sources. An attractive alternative may be to obtain technological components at lower cost from producers in less developed societies. For example, many technological components are sourced from China and, increasingly, from India. There is a longer-term strategic threat here, however. Part of the outsourcing process may include teaching suppliers in these less developed countries how to make the technology. As they learn, at first they are suppliers for us, but with time, they can take that learning and become our competitors. The technical term for this is ***technology transfer***. For example, China, which has been a source of automotive components, is now developing strong competitive strategies for becoming a world-class automobile producer and global competitor.

Scanning the technological environment is not just important in order to decide *where to buy* technological inputs; it is also important for deciding *what to buy*. In a world with rapid technological change, technological products and their components can quickly become obsolete. Thus, *detecting early signals of technological change and breakthroughs is critical* for maintaining strategic advantage.

> The basic issue of technological scanning for purchasing can be reduced down to obtaining satisfactory answers to the following questions:
>
> **For materials or components that we want to purchase, what is the current technological state-of-the-art of such components and their associated production processes?**
>
> **In what direction(s) is that technology moving?**
>
> **Does our potential supplier have access to the appropriate level of technology today? In the future?**
>
> **Does our purchasing relationship transfer technological expertise to the supplier or to the supplier's location, which will enable that supplier to integrate forward and become our future competitor?**

We need to emphasize two additional points about environmental scanning. First, although our discussion of the environmental scanning process has been divided into six environmental dimensions, in reality, these dimensions often overlap. A change in one dimension very often leads to changes in one or more of the others. Second, to understand the business environment, we must have both a baseline description of the current situation, and we must be able to predict likely changes. It is the business environment of the future, and not that of the past, that will make a difference for business and purchasing strategy.

STRATEGIC INDUSTRY ANALYSIS

Every company operates in one or more industries. This makes industry analysis a critical part of strategy development. In this section, we look at several aspects of industry analysis that have strategic importance for purchasing. In doing so, we draw on some strategic concepts developed by Michael Porter of the Harvard Business School. Porter is widely acknowledged as a leading world expert on business strategy. We will also use Porter's ideas in the next section, which deals with fundamental strategic alternatives.

One of the strategic analysis tools that Porter introduced is the ***five forces model of industry attractiveness***. This model, represented by the gray boxes, is the central part of the diagram below. Over the years, other strategic thinkers have suggested that the model can be augmented by some additional forces, which are represented by the white boxes.

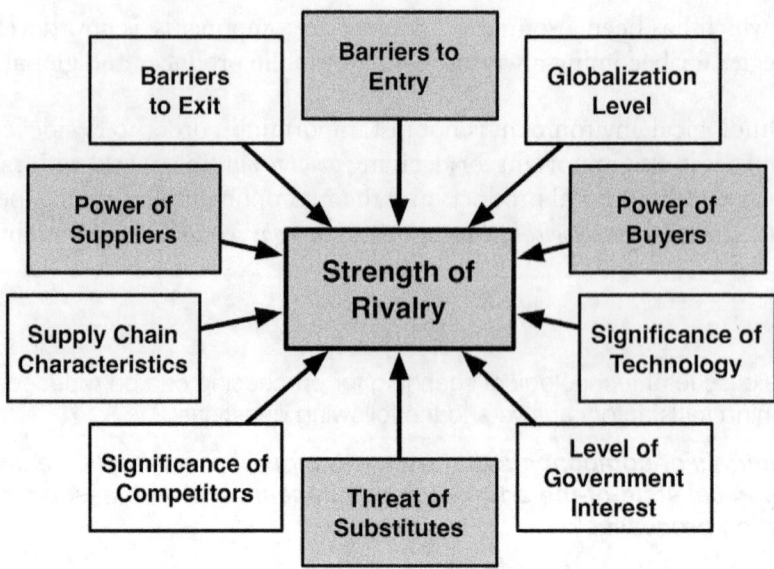

Figure 12.4 - Augmented Porter's Industry Forces Model

In the following discussion we will briefly explain each force, placing more emphasis on those forces with strong implications for purchasing. The personal computer (PC) industry provides a good example for our discussion. Firms in the PC industry design personal computers, assemble them from components that they generally buy from suppliers, and then sell them to customers. HP and Dell are among the well known firms in this industry. Examples of major supplier firms to the PC industry are Intel (computing chips) and Microsoft (software).

The PC industry has both individual and institutional customers. Most customers buy PCs in retail stores or on the web directly from the PC manufacturer. Buying directly allows the customer to get a PC assembled to meet the customer's preferred configuration and minimizes the PC firm's inventory costs. Therefore, buying directly usually gives the customer more computing power for less money.

Buying in the retail store allows the customer to compare the look and feel of several different computers. In recent years, an increasing customer preference for laptops has led to more customers actually wanting to see the physical computer before buying. Laptop customers are particularly interested in such critical aspects as screen size and quality, keyboard size and layout, and weight.

In looking at the model from a purchasing perspective, we start with the ***power of suppliers***. Strategically, firms in most industries would prefer to have relatively more power over suppliers rather than the other way around. Supplier firms generally gain power when what they supply is critically important and relatively scarce. They lose power when what they supply is available from many different suppliers and/or is of minor importance to the buying industry.

Supplier firms also gain power when they present a credible threat of forward integration; that is, they could start making the product for which they now supply only components. The reverse is also true. If the purchasing firms begin to make their own components, they weaken the position of suppliers.

In evaluating relative supplier power, we look at the number of suppliers, the importance of what they supply, the technological complexity of what is being supplied, the possibility of substituting a different component or input for what they supply, licensing and other restrictions limiting the number of supply sources, and our cost of switching suppliers. High supplier power makes being in our own industry less attractive and makes our industry-to-supplier relationships strategically much more significant. Low supplier power allows industry firms to squeeze suppliers for low prices and other concessions.

Many PC components are either high technology with many suppliers (memory, hard drives), relative low technology (keyboards, mice), or near commodity items (metal or plastic cases, power supplies). However, the initial availability of the latest versions of high technology components is often relatively limited and transfers power to suppliers. An example would be the latest versions of computing chips, the very heart of the PC, which have sometimes been rationed by chip makers to PC industry firms. For the customers who want the most powerful PCs, the latest technology matters. But overall, the PC industry suppliers generally have low power relative to the firms in the PC industry. This makes the PC industry attractive.

Raising supplier power by focusing on the ultimate consumer:

- ✦ Access to the latest technology is very attractive to some computer buyers. But as Intel has recognized, with time, high tech becomes ordinary tech and imitators come along. Part of Intel's solution is to emphasize its brand to the ultimate PC buyer through advertising and the "intel inside" sticker on the front of PC cases. This final consumer recognition of Intel puts pressure on firms in the PC industry to use Intel chips.
- ✦ Pharmaceutical firms do not sell directly to patients. Rather, the doctor prescribes the medication and the pharmacy sells it. But pharmaceutical firms now heavily advertise directly to patients, hoping patient pressure on the "doctor industry" will get doctors to prescribe their specific branded drugs, as opposed to other brands or generics.

Next, we look at the ***relative power of buyers***. Buyers are the ultimate consumers of PCs. Who has relatively more power in the relationship between PC industry firms and PC buyers? To answer this, we need to look at computer buyer characteristics.

We can categorize computer buyers into individuals or institutions. Individual buyers of course have very little power relative to firms such as HP or Dell, but individual buyers have many choices of computer open to them. When millions of individual buyers exercise these choices, the total impact of their decisions makes them very powerful as a group. Institutional buyers have the same choices and typically acquire more than one computer at a time. They are thus even more important to the PC industry firms than any individual buyers. Therefore, buyers in the aggregate are more powerful than PC industry firms. From this point of view, the PC industry is not very attractive.

PC industry firms deal with this by attempting to channel customer choice to their specific products by pursuing either a low price strategy, or by a differentiation strategy where their computers differ from the competition by offering more product features and computing power. Apple, Inc. is a classic example of a firm with a differentiation strategy. For the low price strategy to work, a PC firm's purchasing strategy must focus on *constantly lowering the cost of components*. For the differentiation strategy to work, purchasing strategy must focus on *obtaining the more advanced technology components at a reasonable cost*.

High **barriers to entry** make an industry attractive to firms already in the industry but discourage new firms from entering. Entry is difficult if a lot of capital is required, if volume plays a large role in cutting per-unit costs, if brand recognition is important to the ultimate consumers, if technological sophistication is required, and if access to critical components or inputs is limited. Often based on purchasing volume, the strong relationships that existing firms in the industry have with their suppliers create barriers for newcomers. Purchasing managers can ease entry if, at an early stage, they establish strong positive relationships with suppliers.

The PC industry is, for the most part, an assembler of parts. While the technology is sophisticated, the knowledge of how to do it is widespread. However, new entrants face two major hurdles. First, it takes time to build brand recognition. Second, high volume is required to keep costs low. This makes major entry feasible only for firms with established brand recognition and resources to bridge the low initial production volume stage. Again, initial positive supplier relationships are critical. These entry barriers make the PC industry attractive for existing players.

The **threat of substitutes** looks at whether a totally different solution to ultimate customer needs exists. In the Porter model, the threat of substitutes does not mean the threat of a different brand in the same industry. For example, coffee and tea are substitutes for each other but represent different industries. In a practical sense, there are limited substitutes for PCs, although there is increasing convergence with cell phones. This low potential for substitutes makes the PC industry attractive.

The threat of substitutes may increase with changing technology or changing social values. For example, buses and bicycles are, to some extent, substitutes for cars; there is now more social pressure to move toward increased use of these transportation substitutes. The concern for the physical environment and focus on sustainability (conserving resources, decreasing pollution, and slowing and reversing global warming) is increasingly becoming part of social value systems. In turn, political/legal systems are reacting by increasing financial and regulatory incentives for greener operations.

Purchasing must help seek out these alternatives. One example is the pressure in many locations to substitute paper or cardboard for plastic foam containers for fast food. Another example is the pressure to move toward alternative energy sources that are sustainable and have a low impact on greenhouse gas emissions. The pressure for more sustainable substitutes will require purchasing to modify existing supplier relationships and seek out new sources of supply.

The **strength of rivalry** describes the competitive intensity within the industry. Very high rivalry increases costs and reduces profits. Firms in the industry spend a lot of time and money fighting for market share. There is high pressure to be first with improved products, and product prices are likely to fall. Supplier relationships may be critical to ensure that the firm has access to the best input components at the best prices.

Rivalry in the PC industry is very strong. This is evidenced by the high level of advertising, the pressure for constantly improving PC performance, and the continuously dropping prices for ever more powerful PCs. Customers benefit greatly, but the industry attractiveness is decreased. Just as in warfare, in which superior logistics often determines who wins, superior purchasing effectiveness in industry makes a firm a much stronger rival.

We will only briefly identify the additional forces. **Barriers to exit** increase the pressure to succeed in the industry and increase rivalry as firms seek to survive. **Complementors** are those firms or industries that provide products or services that make your product usable. For the automobile industry, the gasoline industry is a major complementor; as gas prices rise, customers look for more fuel efficient vehicles. A major complementor for the PC industry is the software industry. Many industries, including the PC industry, bundle one or more complementor products with their own. This increases the scope of purchasing responsibility to evaluating and selecting the appropriate complementor products and supply firms.

The ***significance of technology*** varies between industries, but today, many historically low-tech industries have been transformed by technological advances, particularly information technology (IT). Technology is incorporated directly into many products, but it is also used to improve and manage the supply chain and other processes through innovations such as RFID. From a purchasing perspective, the firm must have knowledge of technological trends and sources of appropriate technology. Today, of course, the *globalization* level is very high, sourcing is global, and *supply chain characteristics* reflect these developments. The *level of government interest* may reflect different government roles relative to an industry. For example, government can be a booster for international trade, a creator of trade barriers, a sponsor of research and development, or a major customer.

The augmented Porter industry forces model is only one aspect of strategic industry analysis. Business strategists look at many other industry characteristics, such as industry history, size, growth trends, market shares, profitability, and traditional versus non-traditional methods of competition. Discussion of these, however, is beyond the scope of this chapter.

FUNDAMENTAL COMPETITIVE STRATEGY

Every business focuses on ***creating value*** for the customers. The customer looks at the product or service offered by the business and evaluates the value offered against the price the company wants the customer to pay. A product or service has value for a customer if it would satisfy the customer's ***needs*** or ***wants***. We will not make a big distinction between needs and wants except to suggest that, in some sense, needs are more fundamental than wants. For example, if you are very thirsty you *need* to drink something, but you may *want* to drink a brand-name cola. Much of advertising is focused on persuading us to want specific products, either to satisfy a basic need or to make us believe that the advertised product is itself a new need.

We can now provide a working definition of what an industry is: *An **industry** is a group of businesses focused on satisfying a related set of customer needs and/or wants by producing and selling a similar set of solutions.* For example, the automobile industry consists of firms trying to satisfy our needs and wants for individualized transportation by producing cars and light trucks.

It is very important to understand that what represents satisfaction (i.e., value) is in the mind of the customer. Customers vary greatly in how they identify and perceive relative value; that is, they have individual value "equations" that they apply to the purchasing decision. A rational customer would only buy if the product/service value were at least equal to, and preferably greater than, the asking price. Furthermore, if several competing businesses were offering similar products/services, the rational customer would either choose the least expensive value package (*cost leadership focused customer*) or choose a value package that offers features beyond the minimum to satisfy the need (*differentiation focused customer*).

This takes us to considering what Michael Porter has suggested are two generic competitive strategic approaches that firms should rationally choose between. The two alternatives are the *cost leaderships strategy* and the *differentiation strategy*.

With the **cost leadership strategy**, the firm attempts to be the least cost player in its marketplace. It does this by intensely seeking to minimize every possible cost. Cost minimization is pursued with a religious intensity in these firms. All costs are subject to minimization, whether it is linoleum rather than plush carpeting in the executive offices, shorter rather than longer operating hours, or just adequate rather than bright lighting.

Obviously, inventory costs will be a major target for minimization. Several points need to be made about inventory management in a cost leadership firm. Cost leadership does not mean that the firm seeks to minimize inventory costs by buying cheap junk. Rather, the firm buys inventory with a *quality focus* appropriate for the kind of customers it seeks to attract. The cost leadership firm may choose to reduce variety rather than quality of inventory; there will probably be fewer SKUs. The cost leadership firm will bargain extremely hard for quantity discounts, which suggests that a cost leadership strategy is more likely to work for larger firms that inherently have great bargaining power. The firm will be zealous in minimizing all inventory purchasing, holding, management and handling costs. Thus, purchasing effectiveness is of crucial importance for the success of cost leadership strategy.

The cost leadership firm wants everyone, including all insiders and outsiders, to know that cost leadership is its strategy. The cost leadership firm continuously sends messages to customers that it practices cost leadership and, therefore, can offer lower prices. These messages can take several forms, such as the appearance of the firm's physical premises, the lack of amenities commonly seen in competitors' premises, and even the business name. A cost leadership firm tries very hard to make sure that there is no customer confusion about the firm's strategy. Amazon provides an example of messages proclaiming cost leadership. When Jeff Bezos started Amazon, the media carried photos of his desk. The desk consisted of some kind of large piece of wood on top of two sawhorses proclaiming that, in Amazon, even the company founder minimizes his personal costs in the business.

The cost leadership firm also continuously emphasizes the cost leadership strategy to its own employees. In a cost leadership firm, every employee is aware of and focused on cost minimization; there should be absolutely no employee confusion. This awareness and focus is crucial, because additional costs can easily creep in.

One way to think of this cost increase pressure is to compare cost leadership to a castle protected by a moat, high walls, and strong gates, all designed to keep costs out. However, this castle is always under attack by unnecessary costs trying to creep in. Defending cost leadership is a constant process and some (perhaps many) inside the castle would actually welcome one or two cost increases that would make life more pleasant. These invading costs start to add up, however, ultimately ruining the cost leadership strategy. This makes cost leadership a very difficult strategy to implement, and very difficult to maintain. Only a very small fraction of firms are successful with this approach.

Done right, cost leadership strategy can be very profitable. The firm can use this profitability in a number of ways. It can use the cash to fund further expansion of the business, it can cut prices even more to attract additional customers, and it can increase its dividend payments. Cost leadership firms can also use the higher profitability for a very broadly based employee bonus program, thus creating a feedback loop to keep employees committed to cost minimization.

Porter's second strategic competitive approach is the ***differentiation strategy***, which is the broad and common alternative to cost leadership. A differentiation strategy is simply trying to be different from your competitors in some way that represents meaningful value for your customers. With a differentiation strategy, the firm offers its customers additional product features and/or more attractive buying experiences, believing that a significant number of customers will find additional value in this competitive approach and be willing to pay higher prices.

There are many ways in which a firm can combine additional product features and enhance the customer's buying experience. The trick is to find a combination that is both attractive and can be delivered at a reasonable price while increasing profitability. Differentiation almost always adds significant costs above those incurred by a firm pursuing a cost leadership strategy. These additional costs must be recovered by charging higher prices. However, customers do not know and seldom care what your costs really are. Customers only care that the value represented by your product or service is at least equal to and preferably greater than the price you are charging. There is a constant danger that your view of effective differentiation is not shared in practice by very many customers.

Why do companies choose differentiation as a basic strategy? First, the cost leadership alternative is very difficult to implement and hard to maintain. Logically, only one firm can be the real cost leader in a given market. In addition, not every customer is price driven, particularly in affluent societies. Finally, because of the many available implementation approaches, differentiation allows many more firms to compete in a given market.

We can illustrate the differences between a cost leadership strategy and a differentiation strategy by comparing some features of typical box discount stores with traditional full-scale supermarkets.

Cost Leadership Strategy: Box Discount Stores	Differentiation Strategy: Traditional Full-Scale Supermarkets
Low product variety: 4000 to 5000 SKUs	High product variety: 50,000+ SKUs
Inventory stored above sales level	Inventory stored in back of sales area
Customers forced to purchase large quantities of a product	Customers can choose between small, medium, and large quantities
Simple product displays	Eye catching product displays
Plain floors and shelves	More attractive floors and shelves
Open limited hours	Open long hours

Figure 12.5 - Cost Leadership Strategy and Differentiation Strategy in Big Box Stores and Supermarkets

The above comparison example suggests how purchasing would be focused differently for each kind of strategy. Each strategy will fail if purchasing is not aligned with the chosen strategic focus. For cost leadership, the purchasing focus is on low cost, low variety, high individual product volume, special packaging of large product quantities, and high inventory turnover. For differentiation, the purchasing focus is on higher product quality, high product variety, lower individual product volume, attractive packaging and displays, and the acceptance of slower inventory turnover.

In addition to the choice of basic competitive approaches, Porter further suggests that firms may choose how broad a scope of customer needs they will try to meet. The choices are either a *broad focus* or a *narrow focus* (**niche**) approach. A firm with a **broad focus** tries to meet all the specific needs within a product category. For example, a supermarket attempts to meet all common grocery needs. A firm with a **narrow focus** specializes on more intense coverage of a portion of a needs category. For example, a meat market focuses on meat rather than the full spectrum of groceries.

The choice of scope clearly results in corresponding degrees of scope in purchasing. A narrow focus approach reduces the number and variety of supplier relationships, but often requires purchasers to seek out specialized sources that are unique in their products or their product quality. A broad focus approach significantly increases the number and variety of supplier relationships.

When we combine the two competitive approaches with the two focus choices, we have a choice of four fundamental strategic positions. Porter argues that every firm should clearly choose one of these and act so that both employees and customers recognize the chosen strategic approach. When such clarity is not there, according to Porter, the firm is **stuck in the middle** and is strategically confused. Purchasing must operate within the clarity of the chosen strategy and provide essential support for implementing that choice.

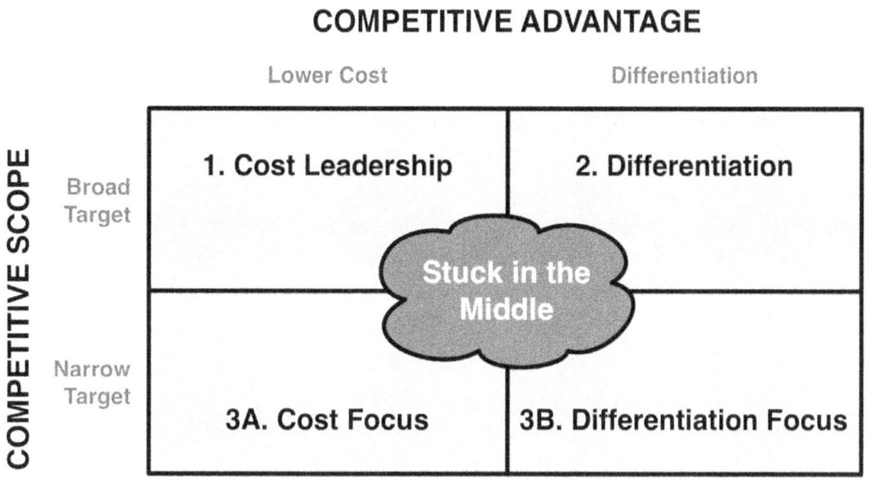

COMPETITIVE ADVANTAGE

	Lower Cost	Differentiation
Broad Target	1. Cost Leadership	2. Differentiation
Narrow Target	3A. Cost Focus	3B. Differentiation Focus

COMPETITIVE SCOPE

Stuck in the Middle

Figure 12.6 - Porter's Strategies and the Problem of *Stuck in the Middle*

STRATEGIC RELATIONSHIPS AND VALUES

Purchasing cannot maximize its contribution to corporate strategy if it operates in isolation or if its preferences are put above corporate strategic goals. The internal relationships purchasing managers have with others outside the purchasing function matter. Recognizing the importance of such relationships, building the relationships, and sharing common values can contribute greatly to strategic success.

Internally, two kinds of relationships matter for purchasing. The first is the ***vertical relationship*** between purchasing management and top corporate management. This relationship is successful if purchasing management becomes a contributing member of the strategy development team. It has already been pointed out that the purchasing function can provide valuable intelligence about the external environment. Being participants in strategy development also ensures that corporate strategy and purchasing strategy are tightly linked and that strategic expectations from purchasing are realistic. Being part of strategy and goal development strengthens purchasing management's commitment to the strategy.

The second kind of relationship that is important is the ***horizontal relationship*** between purchasing and other business functions. The business world is filled with examples of managers operating with a narrow focus on only their function and little concern for other functions in the firm. Two common terms for this attitude are having a "stovepipe" mentality or a "silo" mentality; each term describes a manager who has walled himself off from other functions but is strongly focused on relationships with executives above him. A common result is sub-optimization of the firm's performance because the functions are poorly integrated with each other. But paradoxically, stovepipe managers often think they are doing a great job because they are strong advocates for and defenders of their functional area.

In the comparatively slow moving business world of the past, the negative consequences of stovepipe thinking were somewhat mitigated by the greater response time firms had for dealing with change. Development of product lines was often sequential, with R&D designing the product, manufacturing then tooling up for production, purchasing identifying supply sources, and marketing developing sales programs. Today, instead of being sequential, these stages are often pursued in parallel. For example, manufacturing now starts developing the production process while R&D is still designing the product. This approach is necessary because rapid technological change and intense global competition has drastically shortened many product life cycles. Rapid response to competitive conditions is only possible if managers share information and goals horizontally as well as vertically. Only if purchasing has good internal functional relationships will it be able to anticipate supply needs and develop sources early.

In addition to the important vertical and horizontal internal relationships, purchasing must also optimize the relationships between the firm and its suppliers. These relationships can range from being highly adversarial to highly cooperative. In highly adversarial relationships, information is not shared, trust is minimal, and each side believes that the other is ready to take advantage of it. In highly cooperative relationships, information is shared (often including cost information), a feeling of trust develops, and the parties in effect become strategic allies. Confidence in the high quality of the relationship helps overcome the occasional stresses that are part of all relationships.

Positive vertical, horizontal, and external relationships all help optimize performance because now the whole firm and its external supply network are operating as a more integrated system. By building positive relationships, purchasing can make a significant contribution to the firm's strategic success.

STRATEGIC EVALUATION OF PURCHASING

Periodically, the firm needs to evaluate how its chosen strategy is working out in practice. This evaluation must consider the overall strategy as well as functional strategies, such as the purchasing strategy. Here we briefly identify several evaluation approaches, which are complementary rather than mutually exclusive.

Business performance is ultimately measured by numbers. Therefore, the first approach is to look at purchasing in terms of *the numbers*. For numbers to be meaningful indicators of performance, they must be compared in some fashion. For example, we can make internal comparisons of supply costs over time, supply costs as percentages of good sold, or our supply costs compared to known industry averages or compared to those of industry leading firms serving as benchmarks.

Second, we can perform a formal **logistics audit**, in which we answer a series of formal questions that attempt to measure how purchasing (and other logistics activities) are contributing to strategic objectives and set goals. The development of audit questions and the implementation of the audit should be done by a team with significant membership from outside logistics.

Third, we can use one of the most powerful yet least expensive strategic tools: the **SWOT analysis**. SWOT stands for strengths, weaknesses, opportunities and threats. The process consists of having four columns, each headed by one of the four SWOT category labels. A management group familiar with the current situation in purchasing identifies significant characteristics and lists them under the appropriate column heading. It then discusses the strategic implications of each entry, and what purchasing's strategic response should be.

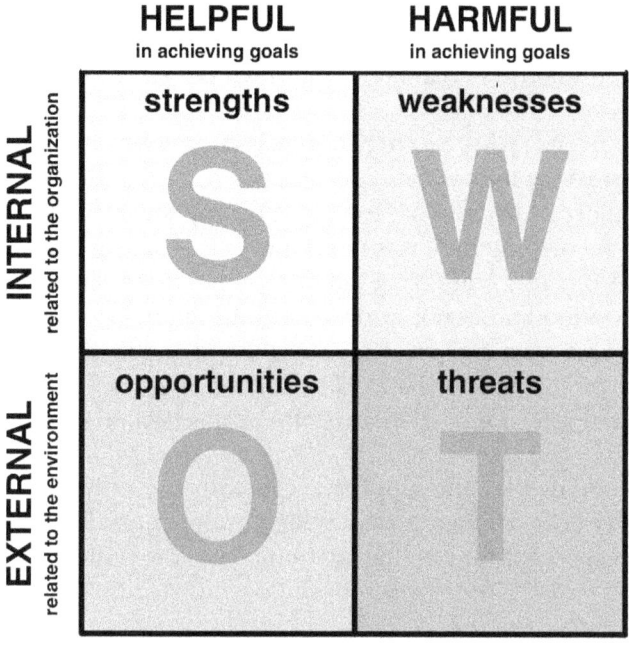

Figure 12.7 - Framework for a SWOT Analysis

No significant training is required to do SWOT, but it is important to know what is meant by each of the four column headings:

- A **strength** is something that is true now and confers some significant strategic purchasing advantage. Examples could be unique access to a scarce raw material or knowledge on how best to do business with suppliers in China. Another term for a *strength* is **differential advantage**.

- A **weakness** is also something that is true now, but it creates a problem for purchasing strategy. Examples could be a global shortage of an important component or a regulation limiting your access to some sources of supply without a corresponding limitation being imposed on most of your competitors. Another term for a *weakness* is **differential disadvantage**.

- An **opportunity** is something that is present now or will soon be present, which can improve the strategic performance of purchasing. Examples could be outsourcing to a lower cost region or substituting a cheaper raw material for the one currently being used.

- A **threat** is something that can be identified but has not yet occurred. If it does occur, it will have a negative strategic effect on purchasing performance. Examples could be a possible near-term bankruptcy of a key supplier or a possible political upheaval in country from which you obtain substantial outsourcing.

People who have never done a SWOT analysis are usually surprised at the ease and power of the process and the strategic insights it produces. SWOT, of course, is not limited to purchasing strategy analysis and can be applied to all levels of strategic evaluation. In fact, you, the purchasing student, can use SWOT to analyze your own personal strategy in life.

A fourth evaluative approach is ***purchasing contingency risk analysis***. Here the objective is to determine how robust your purchasing strategy is when something major goes wrong. We postulate a variety of failures and ask what the strategic impact and the recovery process of each failure would be. The goal of this analysis is not really one of minimizing the costs of recovery from a failure but rather one of immunizing against the possible failure in the first place. For example, assume we are a food processor and we are outsourcing to a region where costs are low but corruption is high. There is a danger of adulteration of the food either because of inadvertent carelessness or corruption. Two risk reduction responses could be either to move our outsourcing to a less corrupt region or to increase the inspection of the supplied goods.

For a second example, assume that one supplier is currently our only source of a critical component. If something goes wrong at that supplier, our own production could come to halt. One obvious strategic response is for purchasing to increase the number of sources for this component.

A "Riveting Tale" of Strategic Failure:

In April 1912, the passenger liner Titanic sank on its maiden voyage after hitting an iceberg in the Atlantic. Over 1500 people died. The Titanic was supposed to be "unsinkable." What happened?

Of course, the primary cause was hitting the iceberg, but the high extent of damage to the hull can be traced back to a purchasing problem. While building the Titanic, Harland & Wolff, the shipbuilder, was also building two other liners, the Britannic and the Gigantic, simultaneously. Not enough high quality rivets were available for all three ships, so some inferior ones were used. The ice sheared the weaker rivet heads off, creating a very large gash in the Titanic's hull, leading to rapid flooding and sinking.

We have covered only some aspects of strategy and the strategic role of purchasing. The strategic role of purchasing will be different in different industries and different firms. Strategy connects the firm with its external environment. By definition, purchasing acquires inputs from this external environment. Therefore purchasing is inherently potentially strategic. However, it does not automatically follow that the strategic nature and role of purchasing will be recognized in all firms and that purchasing will be managed for maximum strategic effectiveness. The purpose of this chapter has been to make you, the student, aware of the strategic potential of purchasing.

Chapter 12 Review Questions

1. Would a smart phone manufacturer engage in *strategically significant purchasing*? Why or why not?

2. Are a business' suppliers also its stakeholders? Why or why not?

3. If you were the owner of a small cafe, how would you engage in *environmental scanning*? List at least ten specific sources for *market intelligence*.

4. One of the elements of *Porter's five forces model of industry attractiveness* is the *power of suppliers*. This chapter provides examples of how computer and pharmaceutical firms increase their power as suppliers. Provide two additional examples of firms that have raised their power as suppliers by focusing on the ultimate customer. Please explain your answer.

5. What is the *threat of substitutes*? What are potential industry substitutes for each of the following: a.) apples, b.) wristwatches, c.) toilet paper, d.) dishwashers, and e.) printers?

6. What is a *cost leadership strategy*? Provide examples of at least three businesses you like and explain how they use this strategy.

7. What is a *differentiation strategy*? Give examples of at least three businesses you like and the differentiation strategies they use.

8. In the world of purchasing, what is the difference between a *vertical* and a *horizontal relationship*?

9. Complete a *SWOT analysis* for your workplace or school by listing at least three of each of its *strengths*, *weaknesses*, *opportunities*, and *threats*. Now complete a second SWOT analysis of yourself.

10. How was the Titanic an example of *strategic failure* in the world of purchasing?

Chapter 12 Case Exercise

Business Strategy, Purchasing, and Rogers Design Furniture

It was September 2014, and Bill Rogers, owner of Rogers Design Furniture (RDF) was facing a number of critical business decisions. RDF was a business that had grown out of a woodworking hobby that Bill Rogers had pursued for over twenty years. The most significant decisions dealt with the future expansion of the business. Up to this point, RDF had made custom pieces of very high quality furniture that had been specifically commissioned by individual interior designers. The expanded business would continue to accept individual commissions, but would also develop its own line of furniture that would be advertised in high-end publications such as *Architectural Digest*. As part of possible expansion Rogers needed to consider where he would purchase the much larger quantities of wood, hardware, glue, wood finishes such as shellacs and varnishes, tools, and other required supplies.

Rogers had studied mechanical engineering at a major university and upon graduation had gone to work for a company making woodworking equipment. The equipment was often innovative in its design and of very high quality. The most important measure of quality was the equipment's ability to repeatedly make extremely precise cuts in a variety of different types of hardwood and softwood lumber. As part of his job, Rogers had visited a large number of professional woodworking businesses, including makers of high quality furniture. As a result he became interested in trying to make furniture himself, both to better understand from direct experience what woodworkers expected from equipment and to give expression to his personal creativity. His employer encouraged him in this by allowing him to buy equipment at half the company's cost. Rogers initially set up a woodworking shop in his two-car garage, but kept his full-time engineering job.

As he became more proficient at furniture making, Rogers also began to study furniture styles ranging all the way from colonial American to very modern designs. Initially he replicated some classic style furniture, but with time he began to design his own furniture which usually looked very contemporary. At first, the pieces he made were for his own home and as gifts to some friends. Then he entered some design competitions, and to his surprise won twice. One of the pieces was even acquired by a museum for its modern design exhibit. This brought him to the attention of several interior designers who commissioned custom pieces for their wealthy clients' homes.

Over time requests from interior designers increased significantly, despite the fact that a typical piece of Rogers furniture usually sold for several thousand dollars. In 2006 Rogers realized that he had to make a choice between keeping his job or converting his hobby to a real business. He decided to become a full time furniture maker. His employer regretfully accepted Rogers' resignation, but persuaded him to agree to a consulting relationship where Rogers could test new equipment ideas in his shop in return for obtaining equipment at a fraction of the manufacturer's cost. Rogers bought a run down farm about 30 miles from Boston, and converted the barn to an efficient shop. Rogers continued to design the furniture himself and did much of the most intricate woodworking, but hired several students from a nearby community college to assist him with such tasks as rough cutting, sanding, and finishing.

By 2012, RDF sales had grown to over $800,000 per year, and Rogers employed up to six people to assist him in the shop. He used a part-time bookkeeping service to track his income and costs, and was pleased that the business had been consistently profitable. This was largely due to the fact that everything was made as a result of specific commissions from interior designers, and thus there was no unsold inventory of finished goods.

RDF furniture emphasized the natural beauty of wood, with the designs making maximum use of the natural grain characteristics of a variety of hardwoods. Typical products were executive desks (often with an inlaid leather top), chests, cabinets, dining room table and chair sets, and bookcases. RDF did not design or make heavily upholstered items such as sofas. A custom designed executive desk could sell for as much as $40,000. The styling was contemporary, although several times RDF had made very high quality reproductions of classic English or Colonial period furniture.

For the furniture RDF made, the main material was hardwood, in the form of boards, plywood, and veneer. Only the highest quality wood was used by RDF; quality was defined by the wood species (e.g., cherry, koa, maple, rosewood, walnut), the absence of defects such as knots or cracks, and especially by the grain pattern of the wood. The grain pattern was very important, because grain was what gave wood furniture much of its distinction and beauty. Grain was the result of a tree's growth cycle, and differed significantly between tree species. Because few trees were wide enough to allow a furniture surface to be made from just a single board, narrower boards were typically joined side by side to make surfaces; this required the adjoining grain patterns to be closely matched.

Before being made into furniture, the wood had to be seasoned—i.e., dried—to a specific moisture level. RDF bought most of its wood in small quantities to meet the needs of specific commissions, although occasionally Rogers would snap up a particularly attractive stock of wood for future commissions if the quality and price were attractive. The suppliers were usually specialty wood dealers within easy driving distance of his shop. Other inputs were cabinet hardware items such as knobs, drawer pulls, hinges, etc; varnishes and finishing oils; and leather or fabric for seats. Hardware was usually purchased from woodworker supplier catalogs. RDF outsourced upholstery, such as dining room chair seats, to a local upholstery shop but purchased the leather or fabric itself in order to insure quality. The total value of materials inventory not committed to a specific commission was usually less than $20,000.

The new business plan Rogers was contemplating would dramatically increase the scale of operations. Several interior designers had suggested to Rogers that while they were happy to continue to commission specific furniture for specific clients, they would also like to be able to choose Rogers pieces from a catalog of pre-designed furniture. The designers still expected the furniture to be of very high quality, but since the catalog pieces would be made in quantity the price should be somewhat lower and the delivery time much faster. Currently, a custom Rogers furniture item could take as much as four months to make and deliver.

In researching his options Rogers had concluded that while furniture manufacturing in the United States had declined dramatically due to foreign competition, very high end product lines could still be made here and be profitable. The market was basically the very affluent households that hired professional decorators. Rogers felt confident that his current decorator relationships would enable him to expand in this market. For initial planning purposes, he set a growth target of $5,000,000 sales for the year 2016. The catalog product lines would feature executive desks and office furniture, dining room sets, and bookcases and other furniture for home libraries. He would continue to do commission work in the converted barn, but would build a new manufacturing building next to it to make the catalog product lines. This would include substantial space for inventory storage.

For financing, Rogers contacted a Boston banker recommended by one of the interior decorators; the decorator had placed three Rogers furniture pieces in the banker's home. After reviewing Rogers' business plan and suggesting some changes, the bank agreed to provide the financing for the expansion. Rogers planned to hire more permanent production workers, particularly from the wood technology program at the community college where Rogers had been an adjunct instructor for several years. He realized that he would also have to professionalize management, and intended to hire an accountant as a first step. His former employer was willing to provide machinery for expansion at slightly above manufacturer's cost.

Rogers turned next to a consideration of sources of supply. He realized that wood for the catalog product lines would have to be purchased in much larger quantities. So would hardware and other materials. It was unlikely that he could depend only on local specialty wood suppliers. For one thing, they would not carry in their own inventories the quantities he would need. For another, he could probably purchase in large enough quantities so that he could deal directly with lumber mills or major regional distributors and thus not pay for the local distributors' profits. But up to now he had been able to personally look at each piece of wood before buying it from a distributor, thus making sure the wood met the required quality standards. He could probably insist in a contract with a mill that the wood be free of defects such as knots or cracks, but assuring that the grain patterns were attractive was another matter; the attractiveness of grain patterns was very subjective. Any potential supplier mill was hundreds of miles from Boston. On the other hand, buying wood from suppliers nationally would allow him to choose from a much larger variety of hardwoods. This could allow him to more effectively differentiate his product line.

Rogers decided to visit several mills. One mill had a very attractive wood inventory stock but Rogers was concerned about the mill's long term access to the right kind of lumber. The owner was willing to enter into a short-term supply contract, renewable by mutual consent, and with attractive prices. The owner pointed out that Rogers was not going to operate at full scale production for several years, and that as his needs grew the mill would itself develop its sources.

A second mill also had a good inventory, and clearly could replenish it over the long run. However, to get a good price Rogers had to commit to large quantity shipments; Rogers estimated that the first shipment would be almost enough to meet his first year needs. The third mill also had a good inventory and was willing to supply smaller shipments at a good price. It also had a stock of exotic wood that was very hard to find anywhere. This would enable RDF to produce some very unique commissioned pieces. However, Rogers got the impression that some of this lumber was illegally harvested in tropical forests that where increasingly being identified by environmentalists as endangered. Rogers was aware that there was a strong movement toward environmentally responsible wood harvesting, focused on sustainable forest yield management and the total environmental impact of the wood supply chain. He also knew from talking to designers that this was a significant issue for some high end clients.

When Rogers returned to the Boston area he talked about his expansion plans with one of the local hardwood distributors that he purchased from regularly. The distributor suggested that Rogers make him a permanent part of his hardwood supply chain. The distributor's logic was as follows: First, he knew Rogers and the quality RDF wanted, any piece not meeting that quality could be easily returned; second, he knew much more about the lumber mills and national distributors than Rogers did and also about where the mills got their lumber and about prices; third, combining RDF volume with the distributor's volume for other customers increased purchasing power; fourth, the distributors inventory for possible purchase by other customers would in effect also be a safety stock for RDF. The distributor said in conclusion "My business is buying lumber; yours is shaping it into furniture. We can grow together; therefore I am willing to cut my profit margin in return for a long term relationship." This distributor, one of three in the Boston area from which Rogers had bought hardwood, had been in business for five years. On reflecting on the relationship Rogers realized that the quality had always been good, the prices slightly higher than those of the other two distributors, and the business was well managed and growing. However, the other two local distributors appeared to have been in business much longer, and both were significantly larger operations.

Another supply issue was cabinet hardware. From a design point of view, hardware could be classified as either visible or hidden. Visible hardware could be seen on the outside of furniture, or easily seen as doors or drawers were opened. This hardware was therefore a part of the aesthetics of design, and also contributed strongly to the impression of quality. Visible hardware for furniture consisted primarily of knobs, drawer handles and pulls, hinges, and locks; there was also purely decorative hardware, such as rosettes (circular, rose patterned decorations). Visible hardware could be made of metal (brass, stainless steel, wrought iron, or silver-colored alloys), glass, ceramics, wood, or even plastics. Hardware designs ranged from modern reproductions of classic antique designs to very contemporary designs. Many catalog companies in the U.S. offered a wide variety of this hardware in many styles; some were also willing to manufacture custom designs although this was very expensive for small quantities. Hardware was also available from sources in other countries, such as certain traditional designs from English suppliers, or inexpensive hardware from China. One source listed over 30,000 available items.

Hidden hardware consisted of such items as drawer slides, a variety of bookcase shelf support systems, and interior hinges. Quality here was defined by very smooth operation of moving items such as slides and hinges, and by high precision which allowed very tight fitting of drawers and doors. Some hinge systems were clever designs protected by patents. But there were no quality purchasing issues here, as the required quality was easily obtainable from a number of sources. However, to make furniture assembly something that could be done by less skilled workers, Rogers would have to standardize on a very small number of slides, hinges, etc. Bolts and screws were also required, but these were standard items available everywhere.

Rogers had always thought that he could make his furniture more distinctive by designing custom visible hardware, to be cast from brass or sterling silver or sometimes even machined from stainless steel, with finishes ranging from matte to highly polished. Because of quality issues, he preferred to have it made locally, but price was also a consideration. At this point Rogers had not developed any specific hardware designs, and felt somewhat out of his depth in this area. Rogers thought that local sourcing might offer more flexibility in lot sizes, although per unit prices probably would be high. There was a silver smith tradition in the greater Boston area (Paul Revere had been a silver and copper smith), and a number of very knowledgeable craftsmen. Most local craftsmen tended to work in one or two types of metal, and were used to small lot sizes, often as small as one unit. Local sourcing would also allow Rogers to design the hardware in collaboration with the local designer craftsmen. Rogers felt that as far as wood went, he understood design and production, but he knew that that was not true for metal. One of the interior designers had recommended a designer/craftsman working mostly in silver, but another interior designer said that in her experience this craftsman was very temperamental and seldom met promised deadlines.

Several of the catalog companies could provide custom hardware in a large variety of pure and alloyed metals. However, the catalog companies' prices and delivery schedules for custom designs generally required relatively large quantity purchases; Rogers estimated that in order for the prices to be reasonable, he would have to commit to lot sizes that could take several years of his production to absorb. And of course there was a risk that what he thought was an attractive design would not be seen that way by the decorators and their clients. In fact, he really did not know how much difference custom designed hardware would make from a decorator and final client viewpoint.

Another purchasing issue was leather or fabric upholstery. For his custom furniture business Rogers had outsourced all upholstery work, such as dining room chair seats, to a local upholstery shop. The volume of outsourced work had been small and easily fitted within the upholsterer's work schedule. Rogers himself had learned how to inlay leather into furniture (a highly precise task where it was easy to make a mistake), such as desk tops. Again, the volume of this work had been small. But volume for both kinds of work would increase very significantly with the new catalog furniture lines. Rogers knew he could no longer do the inlay work himself, but would it be better to outsource it? Continue to outsource the upholstery? While he would not have enough of either kind of work to keep an employee fully focused on this work initially, if his business plan projections were correct, within a year there would be enough work to almost keep a full time employee occupied, particularly if the employee did both upholstery and leather inlays.

There were of course other purchasing areas, such as machinery, small power tools, hand tools, consumables such as sandpaper, and oils and other wood finishing materials. Rogers understood all of these areas very well. His old employer would be the source of most of the large woodworking machinery, and other high-quality tools very readily available from a number of sources. Besides, once his facility was equipped, tool purchases would be relatively infrequent. Consumables, such as sandpaper were also standard items, although Rogers thought he should now seek out significant quantity discounts. The same was true for wood finishing materials (e.g., shellac, varnishes, oils, waxes, dyes), and Rogers, like most experienced woodworkers, had developed his own wood finishing recipes. But again, he should now get quantity discounts.

It was Saturday morning, and Rogers was on his third cup of coffee, with his business plan in front of him. The banker had stressed the importance of a clear strategic focus for his business, and that all of his business activities must fit and ideally support the chosen strategy. He had also emphasized that Rogers own role in the business will change in a number of major ways. He had said, "Bill, you are no longer going to be the craftsman selling a few products you made mostly with your own hands; you are now going to be mostly a manager who may only occasional find time to shape a piece of wood." As he reviewed future purchasing issues, Rogers realized with some sense of shock that his investigation of possible wood sources alone had consumed more than a week of his time.

INSTRUCTIONS:

You have been hired as a purchasing consultant to advise Rogers Design Furniture. Drawing on everything you have read in this book, how would you advise RDF on its future purchasing needs?

Index

3PLPs	87
3PLs	87
accommodating approach	137
acquisition	14
acts of God	155
agreement	100
air	89
anchor	141
annual holding cost	46
annual ordering cost	46
anticipatory breach	167
anticipatory statements	207
ASEA	187
assignable variations	68
Association of Southeast Asian Nations	187
attractiveness	143
attributes	69
automatic inventory replacement	19
avoidance approach	136
B/L	189
Balfour v Balfour	165
banking documents	190
bargaining zone	139
barriers to entry	226
barriers to exit	227
BATNA	139
battle of the forms	162
best alternative to a negotiated agreement	139
bid	102
bilateral	185
bill of lading	189
bill of materials	79
binding	159
blanket purchase order	28, 97
bluffing	146
boiler plate	154
BOL	189
BOM	79
boulwarism	142
BPO	28, 97
brainstem	200
breach	154
breach of contract	167
broad focus	230
buffer stock	51
bulk discounts	85
buyer's aspiration point	138
buyer's reservation price	138
buying agencies	182
capacity	167
capital goods	17
carrier	87
carrier documents	189
cash discounts	104
central limiting theorem	68
centralized purchasing	18
certificate of origin	189
collaborative approach	137
COMESA	187
commodity item	96, 116
common law	158
Common Market of Eastern and Southern Africa	187
compensatory damages	169
competitive approach	136

competitive bid process	100	economic order quantity model	37
competitive bidding	26	effective negotiation behaviors	147
competitive data	217	electronic point of sale	40
competitive strategy	214	embargo	188
complementors	227	emotional intelligence	200, 201
compromise approach	136	enforceable	156
concessions	142	environmental scanning	218
confirmed irrevocable letter of credit	190	environmental stakeholders	214
conflicts in expectations	218	EOQ	43, 47
consequential damages	169	EOQ model	37
consideration	163, 164	EPOS	40
consumption rate	38	EPZ	187
contract	154, 156	EQ	201
control chart	69	EU	186
cost leadership strategy	228	European Union	186
cost-based pricing	102	exemptions	188
counteroffer	162	expectations	218
creating value	227	expedite	29
cultural stakeholders	214	export documents	189
currency management	187	export processing zone	187
decentralized purchasing	18	express warranty	170
decoupling	38	external data	217
Defense Federal Acquisition Regulations	30	external relationships	199
demand	38	extraversion (MBTI)	203
demand-based pricing	103	fair price	96, 99
demographic environmental dimension	220	FAR	30
DFAR	30	Federal Acquisition Regulations	30
differential advantage	233	feeling (MBTI)	204
differential disadvantage	233	finished goods	16
differentiate	214	finished goods inventory	39
differentiation strategy	229	five forces model of industry attractiveness	223
dilemma of trust	145	fixed price contract	28
direct exporting	177	force majeure	155
distributive negotiation	135, 136, 141	forward buying	19
distributor	119, 183	fraud	168
duress	168	free trade area	185
e-procurement	121	free trade zone	187
economic environmental dimension	220	freight forwarder	183
economic factors	184	friendliness	143
economic order quantity	43, 47	frontal lobes	200

FTA	185	introversion (MBTI)	203
FTZ	187	intuition (MBTI)	203
geographic location discount	106	inventory	3
global purchasing	178	inventory holding cost	41, 105
global sourcing	178	inventory management	38
globalization	176	inventory records file	79
good will	125	invitation to treat	160
goods	16	ISO	67
goods-specific documents	190	JIC	83
green products	215	JIT	83
hard data	217	joint venture	177
hardball tactics	141	judging (MBTI)	204
hedging	188	just in case	83
high volume	100	just in time	40, 83
holding cost curve	45	key performance indicators	127
horizontal relationships	198, 231	knowledge economies	220
I statements	207	KPI	127
ICC	110	lack of consideration	164
illegality	168	landed price	28
implied warranty	170	law	153
import broker	183	law of supply and demand	99
import documents	189	LCL	69
import duties	188	lead time	51, 80
inbound logistics	6	legal detriment	163
INCOTERMS	191	legitimate power	143
indirect exporting	177	limbic system	200
industry	228	listening	207
inputs	37	lock in	160
insourcing	23, 31	logistics	4
integrative negotiation	135, 137, 140	logistics audit	232
integrative solutions	141	logrolling	142
integrity	143	long-term relationships	125
internal data	217	lose-lose negotiation	136
internal relationships	199	lose-win negotiation	137
International Commercial Terms	191	lost opportunity costs	41
international purchasing	178	lower control limit	69
International Standards Organization	67	mailbox rule	161
international trade documentation	189	make or buy decision	23
interpersonal relationships	199, 202	maquiladora	187
Interstate Commerce Commission	110	marginal costs	97

marginal revenues	97	NVOCC	183
market entry strategy	177	off-the shelf	24
market operating strategy	177	offeree	160
market strategy	214	offeror	160
market-based pricing	103	oligopoly	98
master production schedule	79	one-off purchase	18
material (in the law)	167	order cost curve	45
materials management	6	order qualifiers	62
materials requirement plan	81	order quantity	38
materials requirement planning	79	order winner	62
MBTI	203	ordering costs	41
mean charts	69	overstocking	40
mean value	69	P-charts	71
MERCOSUR	186	paradigm	202
minor	158	paraphrasing	207
mode of transportation	88	partnership	125
modified purchase	25	Peppercorn Theory of Consideration	163
modified reorder point formula	51	perceiving (MBTI)	204
monopoly	98	perfect competition	97
MPS	79	personality type	202
MRO supplies	16	physical/natural environmental dimension	219
MRP	79, 81	pipeline	90
multilateral	185	policy	30
multiple sourcing	124	policy stock	51
Myers Briggs Type Indicator	203	political/legal environmental dimension	221
NAFTA	186, 187	political/legal factors	184
narrow focus	230	positive bargaining zone	139
natural variation	68	power	143
necessaries	159	power of suppliers	224
needs	227	precedents	159
negative bargaining zone	139	preferred suppliers	23, 29, 100
negotiated discount	100	price range	103
negotiation	26, 134	process average value	69
net requirement	81	procurement	14
new competitive purchase	25	product liability	63, 170
niche	230	promissory estoppel	165
no zone of potential agreement	139	promotional discounts	106
non-tariff barriers	188	pull system	40
non-vessel operating common carrier	183	purchase agreement	27
North American Free Trade Agreement	186, 187	purchase order	27

purchase requisition	22	RFP	24, 101, 181
purchasing	3, 6, 14	RFQ	24, 101, 181
purchasing contingency risk analysis	234	right supplier	115
purchasing department	14	RMR	79
purchasing information database	120	road	88
purchasing procedures	31	Robinson-Patman antitrust law	111
purchasing process	21	ROP	50
push system	40	RTA	186
QC	63	safety stock	51
qualitative metric	65	safety stock lead time	52
quality	64	safety stock policies	51
quality circles	64	sanction	188
quality control	63	seasonal discount	106
quantitative metric	65	seller's aspiration point	138
quantity discounts	105	seller's reservation price	138
quasi contract	165	semi-finished goods	16
quotas	188	sensing (MBTI)	203
R-charts	71	sensitivity analysis	44
rail	88	service contract	158
range charts	71	services	17
raw material inventory	39	Sherman antitrust law	110
raw materials	16	short-term relationships	125
reciprocity	23	shrinkage	42
recurring purchase	97	significance of technology	227
regional trade agreement	186	single source	123
rejection	162	single source purchasing	84
relative power of buyers	225	single transaction	125
reorder point	50	social/cultural environmental dimension	222
repetitive delivery contracts	125	social/cultural factors	185
report of materials requirements	79	soft data	217
representative	183	sole source	123
request for information	24	Southern Common Market	186
request for proposal	24	SPC	68
request for quotation	24	special item	97
rescinded	159	specialized cross-functional team	118
resources	143	specialty item	116
revenue stream	96	specific performance	170
reverse auction	27, 102	specifications	22
revocation	162	split-the-difference negotiation	136
RFI	24, 101, 181	stakeholder	214

stare decisis	158
statement of work (SOW)	22
statistical process control	68
straight purchase	25
straight repurchase	25
strategic alliance	125
strategically significant purchasing	213
strategy	213
strength of rivalry	226
stuck in the middle	230
supplier	115
supply chain	5
supply chain management	4
supply management	7
Surface Transportation Board	110
SWOT analysis	232
systems approach	216
tactics	140
TCO	108
technological environmental dimension	222
technology transfer	222
tendering process	161
the five Rs	182
thinking (MBTI)	204
third party logistics service providers	87
threat of substitutes	226
total cost curve	45
total cost of ownership	108
trade agreement	185
trade bloc	186
trade boycott	188
trade-off principle	90
trading companies	182
transaction documents	189
transportation	86
UCC	157
UCL	69
UETA	161
unconscionable	168
undue influence	168
unenforceable contract	166
Uniform Commerce Code	157
Uniform Electronic Transactions Act	161
unique need	97
upper control limit	69
value-based pricing	103
variable	28
variables	69
vendor	115
vendor rating	182
vertical relationship	198, 231
void	166
void contract	166
voidable contract	166
wants	227
warranty	170
warranty of fitness	171
water	89
weighted evaluations	127
wholly owned subsidiary	177
win-lose negotiation	136
win-win negotiation	137
work-in-process	16
work-in-process inventory	39
World Trade Organization	186
WTO	186
x-bar charts	69
zone of potential agreement	139

About the Authors

Dr. Philip Price is a professor of logistics and chair of the department of logistics at the College of Business and Public Policy at the University of Alaska Anchorage. He is an expert in supply chain management and international business. He is the author of *Looking at Logistics: A Practical Introduction to Logistics, Customer Service, and Supply Chain Management*; *Warehouse Management and Inventory Control*; *Stores and Distribution Management*; and *Integrated Materials Management*.

Natalie Harrison, M.Ed., is a business education specialist and corporate communications and training consultant. She is an expert in communications, training, and applications of the MBTI personality type theory. Along with Dr. Price, she is the author of *Looking at Logistics: A Practical Introduction to Logistics, Customer Service, and Supply Chain Management* and *Warehouse Management and Inventory Control*.

Dr. Morgan Henrie is the president of MH Consulting, Inc. and is a certified Project Management Professional. He is an expert in project management, telecommunications, and the oil and gas industry. He is the author of *Multi-National Project Team Communications: International Cultural Influences* and *Cultural Influences in Engineering Projects*.

Dr. Francis Jeffries is a professor of management at the College of Business and Public Policy at the University of Alaska Anchorage and is an expert in organizational behavior, organization development, emotional intelligence, and negotiations. He is the author of extensive research in the fields of organizational behavior and emotional intelligence.

Dr. George Geistauts is a professor of business administration at the College of Business and Public Policy at the University of Alaska Anchorage and is an expert in strategic management. He is the author of *Alaska's Future: Commentary on a Delphi Perspective*, *The Alaska Small Business Planning Guide: A Manual to Help Entrepreneurs Formulate and Use a Business Plan and Financing Proposal*, and *Toward an Effective Board: A Manual for Public Broadcasting Station Board Members*.

www.ingramcontent.com/pod-product-compliance
Lightning Source LLC
Chambersburg PA
CBHW080732300426
44114CB00019B/2557